First World War
and Army of Occupation
War Diary
France, Belgium and Germany

I0311140

20 DIVISION
Divisional Troops
Durham Light Infantry
11th Battalion Pioneers
21 July 1915 - 24 June 1919

WO95/2108/2

The Naval & Military Press Ltd
www.nmarchive.com
Published in association with The National Archives

Published by

The Naval & Military Press Ltd

Unit 10 Ridgewood Industrial Park,

Uckfield, East Sussex,

TN22 5QE England

Tel: +44 (0) 1825 749494

www.naval-military-press.com

www.nmarchive.com

This diary has been reprinted in facsimile from the original. Any imperfections are inevitably reproduced and the quality may fall short of modern type and cartographic standards.

Contents

Document type	Place/Title	Date From	Date To
Miscellaneous	2108/2		
Heading	20th Division 11th Bn Durham Light Infy. (Pioneers) Jly 1915-Jun 1919		
Heading	20th Division 11th Durham L.I. (Pioneers) Vol I July To Aug 15		
Heading	War Diary of 11th Bn. Durham L.I. Pioneers From July 20th To August 31st 1915 (Volume I)		
War Diary	Havre	21/07/1915	23/07/1915
War Diary	Esquerdes	24/07/1915	27/07/1915
War Diary	Lynde	28/07/1915	29/07/1915
War Diary	Merris	30/07/1915	05/08/1915
War Diary	La Rue Du Bois	06/08/1915	31/08/1915
Heading	20th Division 11th D.L.I. Vol II Sept 15		
War Diary	La Motte Au Bois	01/09/1915	20/09/1915
War Diary	Estaires	21/09/1915	28/09/1915
War Diary	In The Trenches	29/09/1915	30/09/1915
Heading	20th Division 11th D.L.I. Vol 3 Oct 15		
Heading	War Diary of XIth Bn. Durham L.I (Pioneers) From Oct 1st To Oct 31st 1915 Volume III		
War Diary	Trenches 60th Bde	01/10/1915	30/10/1915
Heading	20th Division 11th D.L.I. Vol 4 Nov 15		
Heading	War Diary of XIth. Durham L.I. (Pioneers) From Nov 1st To Nov 30th 1915 Volume 4		
War Diary	Billets Rue De Paradis M.3.d.5.0 Sheet 36	01/11/1915	01/11/1915
War Diary	Trenches	02/11/1915	05/11/1915
War Diary	Billets At Epinette & La Flin Rue Farm M.16.b. Sheet 36	06/11/1915	09/11/1915
War Diary	Trenches	10/11/1915	14/11/1915
War Diary	Billets Laventie. E. M. 5. A	14/11/1915	23/11/1915
War Diary	Billets Rue De Bruges G.24.a. Sheet 36	24/11/1915	30/11/1915
Heading	20th Div 11th D.L.I. Vol 5		
Heading	War Diary of XIth Bn. Durham L.I. (Pioneers) From Dec 1st To Dec 31st 1915 Volume 6		
War Diary	Hdqrs. Rue De Bruges G.24.a	01/12/1915	31/12/1915
Heading	20. 11th D.L.I. Vol 6 Jan 16		
Heading	War Diary of XIth Durham L.I. (Pioneers) From Jan 1st To Jan 31st 1916 Volume 7		
War Diary	Rue De Bruges	01/01/1916	01/01/1916
War Diary	G.24.a. Sheet 3b Bn Hdqts	01/01/1916	31/01/1916
Heading	War Diary of XIth (S) Bn. Durham L.I. (Pioneers) From Feb 1st To Feb 29th 1916 Volume 8		
War Diary	Zermezeele Sheet 27	01/02/1916	29/02/1916
Heading	War Diary of XIth Bn. Durham L.I. (Pioneers) For March 1916 Volume IX		
War Diary	Elverdinghe B. 14 Central Sheet 28	01/03/1916	31/03/1916
Heading	War Diary of XIth Bn. Durham L.I. (Pioneers) From April 1st To 30th 1916 Volume 10		
War Diary	Elverdinghe Chateau B.14 Central Sheet 28	01/04/1916	17/04/1916
War Diary	Oudezeele J.14.a.Sheet 27	18/04/1916	30/04/1916

Heading	War Diary of XIth (S) Bn. Durham L.I. (Pioneers) From May 1st To 31st 1916 Volume XI		
War Diary	Oudezeele J.14 A Sheet 27	01/05/1916	31/05/1916
Heading	War Diary of XIth (S) Bn. Durham. L.I. (Pioneers) From June 1st-30th Volume XII		
War Diary	Brandhoek Sheet 28 G.12.b	01/06/1916	30/06/1916
Heading	Pioneers 20th Div. War Diary 11th Battn. The Durham Light Infantry July 1916		
War Diary	Brandhoek G.12.b. Sheet 28	01/07/1916	31/07/1916
Heading	20th Divisional Troops. Pioneers 11th Battalion Durham Light Infantry August 1916		
War Diary	The Dell	01/08/1916	16/08/1916
War Diary	Orville	17/08/1916	18/08/1916
War Diary	Berneuil	19/08/1916	20/08/1916
War Diary	Morlancourt	21/08/1916	21/08/1916
War Diary	Citadel	22/08/1916	22/08/1916
War Diary	Trenches	23/08/1916	31/08/1916
Heading	H.Q. 20th Division I forwards herewith War Diary for Month of August 1916.		
Heading	20th Divisional Troops 11th Battalion Durham Light Infantry (Pioneers) September 1916		
Miscellaneous	Headquarters 20th Division	02/10/1916	02/10/1916
War Diary	In Trenches	31/08/1916	04/09/1916
War Diary	Craters	05/09/1916	06/09/1916
War Diary	Bois-De-Tailles	07/09/1916	08/09/1916
War Diary	Mericourt	09/09/1916	12/09/1916
War Diary	Sand Pits	13/09/1916	14/09/1916
War Diary	Citadel	15/09/1916	15/09/1916
War Diary	Talus Bois	16/09/1916	17/09/1916
War Diary	Bernafay Wood	18/09/1916	20/09/1916
War Diary	Sand Pits	21/09/1916	22/09/1916
War Diary	Meaulte	22/09/1916	25/09/1916
War Diary	Citadel Maltz Horn Vally	26/09/1916	27/09/1916
War Diary	Talus Boise	28/09/1916	29/09/1916
War Diary	Trones Wood	30/09/1916	30/09/1916
Heading	20th Divisional Troops 11th Battalion Durham Light Infantry (Pioneers) October 1916		
Heading	Vol 15 11th D L I		
War Diary	Tatler Trench	01/10/1916	08/10/1916
War Diary	Waterlot Farm	09/10/1916	09/10/1916
War Diary	Meaulte	10/10/1916	15/10/1916
War Diary	Treux	16/10/1916	16/10/1916
War Diary	Ville	17/10/1916	18/10/1916
War Diary	Citadel	19/10/1916	25/10/1916
War Diary	Citidal	26/10/1916	31/10/1916
Miscellaneous	Headquarters 20th Division	31/10/1916	31/10/1916
Heading	20th Divisional Troops Pioneers 11th Battalion Durham Light Infantry November 1916		
War Diary	Citidal	31/10/1916	01/11/1916
War Diary	Salieux	02/11/1916	02/11/1916
War Diary	Bourdon	03/11/1916	08/11/1916
War Diary	Picquigny	09/11/1916	16/11/1916
War Diary	Corbie	17/11/1916	24/11/1916
War Diary	Citadel	25/11/1916	26/11/1916
War Diary	Montauban	27/11/1916	29/11/1916

Heading	H.Q. 20th Division. Herewith War Diary for Month of November 1916		
Heading	20th Divisional Troops. 11th Battalion Durham Light Infantry (Pioneers) December 1916		
War Diary	Montauban	01/12/1916	31/12/1916
Heading	Head Quarters 20th Division Enclosed Herewith War Diary for December 1916		
Heading	War Diary of The Vol 18 11th. Bn. Durham. L.I. (Pioneers) January 1917		
War Diary	Ville	01/01/1917	31/01/1917
Heading	War Diary of XIth Bn. The Durham L.I. (Pioneers) From Feb. 1st To Feb. 28th 1917 Volume 20		
War Diary	Meaulte	01/02/1917	28/02/1917
Operation(al) Order(s)	XIth Durham L. Inf. (Pioneers) Operation Order No. 35	25/01/1917	25/01/1917
Operation(al) Order(s)	Operation Order No. 36	06/02/1917	06/02/1917
Operation(al) Order(s)	XIth Bn. Durham L.I. (Pioneers) Operation Order No. 37	15/02/1917	15/02/1917
Operation(al) Order(s)	XIth Bn. Durham L. Infantry (Pioneers) Operation Order No. 38	24/02/1917	24/02/1917
Operation(al) Order(s)	XIth Durham L.I. (Pioneers) Operation Order No. 39	26/02/1917	26/02/1917
Operation(al) Order(s)	XIth Durham L.I. (Prs.) Operation Order No. 40	27/02/1917	27/02/1917
Operation(al) Order(s)	XIth D.L.I. (Pioneers) Supplement To O.O. 40	27/02/1917	27/02/1917
Heading	War Diary of XIth Durham L.I. (Pioneers) From March 1st To 31st 1917 Volume XXI		
War Diary	Montauban	01/03/1917	31/03/1917
Miscellaneous	To C.R.E. 20th Division	14/03/1917	14/03/1917
Miscellaneous	To C.R.E. 20th Division	27/03/1917	27/03/1917
Miscellaneous	To C.R.E. 20th Division	30/03/1917	30/03/1917
Operation(al) Order(s)	XIth D.L.I. (Pioneers) Operation Order No. 41	04/03/1917	04/03/1917
Operation(al) Order(s)	XIth Durham Light Infantry (Pioneers) Operation Order No. 42	12/03/1917	12/03/1917
Operation(al) Order(s)	XIth Durham Light Infantry (Pioneers) Operation Order No. 43	19/03/1917	19/03/1917
Operation(al) Order(s)	XIth Durham Light Infantry Pioneers Operation Order No. 44		
Operation(al) Order(s)	Operation Order No. 45		
Operation(al) Order(s)	XIth Bn Durham L.I. Pioneers Operation Order No 46	28/03/1917	28/03/1917
Miscellaneous	Battalion O.O 41-46 (Inclusive)		
Heading	War Diary of XIth Durham L.I. (Pioneers) From April 1st To April 30th 1917 Volume XXII		
War Diary		01/04/1917	30/04/1917
Heading	War Diary of XI Bn. Durham L.I. (Pioneers) From May 1st To May 31st 1917 (Volume 23)		
War Diary	Ytres	01/05/1917	31/05/1917
Operation(al) Order(s)	XIth Durham L. Inf. (Pioneers) Operation Order No. 47	01/05/1917	01/05/1917
Operation(al) Order(s)	XIth Bn. Durham L. Infantry Operation Order No. 48	03/05/1917	03/05/1917
Miscellaneous	Reference Operation Order No. 48	04/05/1917	04/05/1917
Operation(al) Order(s)	XIth Durham L.I. (Pioneers) Operation Order No. 49	06/05/1917	06/05/1917
Miscellaneous	XIth Durham L. Infantry (Pioneers) Move Order Reference Sheet 57c.	23/05/1917	23/05/1917
Operation(al) Order(s)	XIth Durham L. Inf. (Pioneers) Operation Order No. 51	08/05/1917	08/05/1917
Miscellaneous	Diary		
Operation(al) Order(s)	XIth Durham L.I. (Pioneers) Operation Order No. 52	20/05/1917	20/05/1917
Operation(al) Order(s)	XIth Durham L.I. (Prs) Operation Order No. 53	21/05/1917	21/05/1917
Heading	War Diary-June 1917 11th Bn Durham L.I. (Pioneers) Vol 23		

War Diary	Vaulx	01/06/1917	30/06/1917
Heading	War Diary 11th (P) Bn Durham L.I. July 1917 Vol 24		
War Diary	Domart	01/07/1917	19/07/1917
War Diary	Doullens	20/07/1917	20/07/1917
War Diary	Proven	21/07/1917	30/07/1917
War Diary	Camp A 16. b.2.4	31/07/1917	31/07/1917
War Diary	G Camp A 16. b.2.4 Sheet 28	31/07/1917	31/07/1917
Operation(al) Order(s)	XI Durham L.I. (Pioneers) Operation Order 58. Appex 3	30/07/1917	30/07/1917
Miscellaneous	War Diary		
Operation(al) Order(s)	XI Durham L.I. (Pioneers) Move Order No. 56 Appen I	19/07/1917	19/07/1917
Operation(al) Order(s)	XI Durham L.I. (Pioneers) Movement Order No. 57 Appen 2	19/07/1917	19/07/1917
Heading	War Diary-Aug 1917 11th Durham Light Infantry Vol 25		
War Diary	G Camp A 16. b. 2.4 Sheet 28	31/07/1917	31/07/1917
War Diary	A 16 b. 2.4 Sheet 28	01/08/1917	06/08/1917
War Diary	C 19.a.0.3 Sheet 28	07/08/1917	07/08/1917
War Diary	Canal Bank C.19.a.0.3	08/08/1917	09/08/1917
War Diary	Canal Bank C 19.a.0.3 Sheet 28	10/08/1917	16/08/1917
War Diary	Canal Bank	17/08/1917	17/08/1917
War Diary	Malakof Farm Arear B 23. C, Central Sheet 28	18/08/1917	19/08/1917
War Diary	Seaton Camp F5. C.4.6 Sheet 27	20/08/1917	24/08/1917
War Diary	Seaton Camp F 5. C.4.6	25/08/1917	31/08/1917
Operation(al) Order(s)	XI Durham L.I. (Pioneers) Operation Order No. 59	05/08/1917	05/08/1917
War Diary	Seaton Camp F.5.c.4.6	01/09/1917	07/09/1917
War Diary	Seaton Camp F.5.c.4.6 S 27	08/09/1917	08/09/1917
War Diary	C.19.a.0.2 Sheet 28 Canal Bank	09/09/1917	09/09/1917
War Diary	C.19.a.0.2 Sheet 28	10/09/1917	27/09/1917
War Diary	Seaton Camp F.5. C.4.6	28/09/1917	02/10/1917
War Diary	Bapaume H.33.b.	03/10/1917	03/10/1917
War Diary	Barastre	04/10/1917	05/10/1917
War Diary	Ytres P.20.d.0	06/10/1917	06/10/1917
War Diary	Camp W 3. C.5.7	07/10/1917	21/10/1917
War Diary	W.3.C.5.7.	22/10/1917	25/10/1917
War Diary	F.5.C.4.6	26/10/1917	31/10/1917
War Diary	W.3.C.5.7	01/11/1917	16/11/1917
War Diary	W.5.b.	17/11/1917	19/11/1917
War Diary	Q.36.a.8.2	20/11/1917	30/11/1917
Heading	20th Division 11th D.L.I. Pioneers		
Miscellaneous	No. 7 11th D.L.I (Pioneers)		
Miscellaneous	VIII	30/11/1917	30/11/1917
Miscellaneous	Commends Etc Aug 1914 To Date		
Miscellaneous	Major J.G. Jaylor Awarded MC (L.G. 1.1.17)		
Miscellaneous	Miscellaneous Draft Joined Battalion-16 Durham L.I. An August 3rd 1915	03/08/1915	03/08/1915
Miscellaneous	Honours And Rewards		
War Diary	Border Ridge	01/12/1917	01/12/1917
War Diary	La Vacquerie	02/12/1917	03/12/1917
War Diary	Q 34. C. 8.5	03/12/1917	03/12/1917
War Diary	Fins	04/12/1917	04/12/1917
War Diary	Sorel	05/12/1917	08/12/1917
War Diary	Hesden	09/12/1917	09/12/1917
War Diary	Ecpuemicourt	10/12/1917	11/12/1917
War Diary	Wardrecques	12/12/1917	16/12/1917
War Diary	Dickebush	16/12/1917	05/01/1918

War Diary	I.15.d.1.3	06/01/1918	31/01/1918
War Diary	Zillebeke Bund	01/02/1918	17/02/1918
War Diary	Racquinghem	18/02/1918	21/02/1918
War Diary	Nesle	22/02/1918	22/02/1918
War Diary	Golancourt	23/02/1918	28/02/1918
Heading	20th Divisional Pioneers 11th Battalion Durham Light Infantry March 1918		
War Diary	Golancourt	01/03/1918	31/03/1918
Miscellaneous	B Coy		
War Diary		24/03/1918	26/03/1918
Miscellaneous	D Coy		
War Diary		21/03/1918	01/04/1918
War Diary	Quevauvillers	02/04/1918	06/04/1918
War Diary	Lincheux	07/04/1918	10/04/1918
War Diary	Huppy	11/04/1918	11/04/1918
War Diary	Rieux	12/04/1918	18/04/1918
War Diary	Frevillers	19/04/1918	30/04/1918
War Diary	Strength	01/04/1918	01/05/1918
War Diary	Frevillers	01/05/1918	02/05/1918
War Diary	Chateau De La Haie	03/05/1918	04/05/1918
War Diary	Ratata Camp Carency	05/05/1918	12/05/1918
War Diary	Carency	13/05/1918	21/05/1918
War Diary	Ratata Camp Carency	22/05/1918	29/05/1918
War Diary	Carency Ratata Camp	30/05/1918	31/05/1918
War Diary	Strength	01/05/1918	01/06/1918
War Diary	Carency	01/06/1918	31/07/1918
War Diary	Carency (Ratata Camp) X.16.d.1.4.	01/08/1918	11/08/1918
War Diary	Carency X.16.d.1.4	12/08/1918	30/09/1918
War Diary	Carency Ratata Camp X.16.d.1.4	01/10/1918	05/10/1918
War Diary	Estree Cauchie	06/10/1918	30/10/1918
War Diary	Tincques	31/10/1918	31/10/1918
War Diary	Cambrai	01/11/1918	02/11/1918
War Diary	Rieux	03/11/1918	03/11/1918
War Diary	Montrecourt	04/11/1918	07/11/1918
War Diary	Sepmeries	08/11/1918	09/11/1918
War Diary	St. Waast-La-Vallee	10/11/1918	11/11/1918
War Diary	Feignies	12/11/1918	23/11/1918
War Diary	Le Pissotiau	24/11/1918	24/11/1918
War Diary	Maresches	25/11/1918	25/11/1918
War Diary	St. Aubert	26/11/1918	27/11/1918
War Diary	Cambrai	28/11/1918	02/12/1918
War Diary	Thievres	03/12/1918	08/12/1918
War Diary	Grenas	09/12/1918	09/05/1919
War Diary	Pas En Artois	10/05/1919	31/05/1919
Heading	H.Q. 20th Division herewith War Diary for Month of June 1918	30/06/1919	30/06/1919
War Diary	Pas En Artois	01/06/1919	15/06/1919
War Diary	Mondicourt	16/06/1919	18/06/1919
War Diary	Havre	19/06/1919	19/06/1919
War Diary	Harfleur	20/06/1919	22/06/1919
War Diary	Havre	23/06/1919	23/06/1919
War Diary	Southampton	24/06/1919	24/06/1919
Miscellaneous	14.8.17		

2108/2

20TH DIVISION

11TH BN DURHAM LIGHT INFY.
(PIONEERS)
JLY 1915 - JUN 1919

20th Division

121/6787

11th Durham L. I. (Pioneers)

Vol I

July & Aug 15

2

July 15 – June 19

Confidential.

WAR DIARY.

of

11th Bn. DURHAM L. I. PIONEERS

from July 20th to August 31st 1915

(Volume 1)

Army Form C. 2118.

Instructions regarding War Diaries and Intelligence Summaries are contained in F. S. Regs., Part II. and the Staff Manual respectively. Title pages will be prepared in manuscript.

WAR DIARY
or
~~INTELLIGENCE SUMMARY.~~
(Erase heading not required.)

Place	Date	Hour	Summary of Events and Information	Remarks and references to Appendices
HAVRE	July 21st.	12 noon.	Left SALISBURY PLAIN. Arrived SOUTHAMPTON WATERS: remained till 8 p.m. 6 hours voyage arrived HAVRE 2 a.m. July 21st. Marching out strength 30 officers + 922 other ranks. Capt. R.F. HIGGENS left behind sick: struck off strength July 20th. + attached to 16th. Reserve Bn. Durham Light Inf.	
			Marching out strength confirmed at HAVRE. Left boat 7 a.m. marched to REST CAMP. accident on bridge near docks: 2 horses + heavy wagon dashed into troops: one rifle lost in river. Court of Inquiry held. Finding:- Cost of replacing the rifle to be borne by public.	
"	22nd.			
	23rd.		Left Rest Camp at 8.30 a.m. entrained at 1 p.m. Arrived ST. OMER 9 a.m. July 23rd. Marched to ESQUERDES: arrived 2 p.m. Billeted in cottages. Q.M.S. PAYNTER left for Base H.Q.	
Esquerdes	24th		Nothing to report	
"	25th		—do—	
"	26th		10 mile route march	
"	27th		Nothing to report	
LYNDE	28th		Marched to LYNDE	
"	29th		Reveille 3.30 am. Marched to MERRIS	
MERRIS	30th		A and B coys marched to LA RUE DU BOIS for Pioneer work on roads and clearing ditches. Purpose to allow water to run freely from canal for use of artillery en route for the front.	
"	31st		'C' coy joined A + B coys during afternoon	
"	August 1st		A, B, C coys working, balance Church Parade	
"	2nd		Nothing to report	
"	3rd		'C' coy left for FLEURBAIX for Pioneer work (constructing forts) attached 25th Bge, 8th Div. 3rd Corps, 1st Army.	
"	4th		~~Nothing to report~~ No 17199 Pte J A BOWLT accidently killed 'C' coy	
"	5th		'D' coy and Head Quarters marched to LA RUE DU BOIS	
LA RUE DU BOIS	6th		A, 'B' coys marched to FLEURBAIX. 'D' coy making hurdles in wood at LA MOTTE.	
"	7th		} Nothing to report	
"	8th			
"	9th			
"	10th		No 16006 Pte T. STOBBART 'D' coy accidentally shot through thigh	

1577 Wt. W10791/1773 500,000 1/15 D. D. & L. A.D.S.S./Forms/C. 2118.

Instructions regarding War Diaries and Intelligence Summaries are contained in F. S. Regs., Part II. and the Staff Manual respectively. Title pages will be prepared in manuscript.

WAR DIARY

or

~~INTELLIGENCE SUMMARY.~~

(Erase heading not required.)

Army Form C. 2118.

Place	Date	Hour	Summary of Events and Information	Remarks and references to Appendices
LA RUE DU BOIS	August 11th		Nothing to report	
"	12th		Battalion bombing school commenced under 2/Lt R. S. Rigby. 12 men & 1 N.C.O. per company also 4 officers under instruction. Draft of 50 men from 16th Bn D. L. I. arrived. Attached D Coy for instruction in hurdle making	
"	13th 14th		Nothing to report	
"	15th		Church parade morning. Hurdle making by D Coy from 2 to 6 p.m.	
"	16th 17th 18th 19th 20th 21st		Work as usual. Nothing to report	
"	22nd		Church parade 10.30 am followed by drill in fixing respirators and helmets. Draft of 50 men from 17th Bn D. L. I. arrived. Lt GAINE & 2nd/Lt MACLAREN, TAIT & DOUGLAS finished course at Grenade School & returned to duty.	
"	23rd		Lt PEMBERTON & 2nd Lt WARD & FLOYD attached Grenade School for course. New draft attached D Coy for instruction	
"	25th		Lt GAINE ordered by Head Quarters to proceed to Hd Qrs III Corps for interview with G. S. O. I(c) map section	
"	24th		Nothing to report	
"	26th		9 men (1 B. & ...) signallers proceeded to Estaires to work in Starch Factory laying pipes, attending machinery and preparing portion of Building for Baths.	
"	27th 28th		Nothing to report	
"	29th		Lieut. Pemberton, 2nd/Lt WARD, batmen, 39 men A B & C Coys & 7 men of A B C Coys left behind sick marched to Fleurbaix to rejoin their Coys. 2nd/Lt WOOD, batman, 4 machine gunners & 3 drivers with 2 Lewis Machine Guns proceeded to ESTAIRES to join Lieut. PALMER, O/C Machine Gun section who with his men and two guns reported Saturday 29th to 6 C. D.M.T. at ESTAIRES	
"	30th		The draft of 50 from 16th D. L. I. commenced bombing course at Bn Grenade School.	
"	31st		Corpl. McLean & Pte McLean "C" Coy granted leave for one week to visit father reported dying	

[signature] Col.
Comdg XI (Ser) Bn Durham L.I.

20th Division

P/20.

121/6971

11th D.L.I.

Vol: II

Sept. 15.

Instructions regarding War Diaries and Intelligence Summaries are contained in F. S. Regs., Part II. and the Staff Manual respectively. Title pages will be prepared in manuscript.

WAR DIARY
or
~~INTELLIGENCE SUMMARY.~~
(Erase heading not required.)

Army Form C. 2118.

Place	Date	Hour	Summary of Events and Information	Remarks and references to Appendices
LA MOTTE AU BOIS	1-9-15		'C' Coy left Fr FLEURBAIX at 9 a.m. and arrived at La RUE DU BOIS at 5 p.m. Billetted on the VIEUX BERQUIN – LA MOTTE road at E22 a Map 36 A.	
"	2-9-15		'C' Coy joined 'D' Coy in making hurdles. Draft of 50 N.C.O.s and men arrived from 16th Bn. D.L.I. Not suitable men for a Pioneer Batt. Attached to C & D Coys for instruction.	
.	3-9-15 4-9-15 5-9-15		Nothing to report	
.	6-9-15		2nd Lieut WARD rejoined his own Coy (A) at Fr FLEURBAIX. Course at Grenade School commenced. Capt SCOTT Lieut CUNNINGHAM, Lieut FISHER and 50 men of new draft attended. 'B' Coy under 3rd Corps orders left Fr FLEURBAIX and reported to 20th DIVISION at ESTAIRES. They then marched to LE NOUVEAU MONDE for pioneer work, later to LAVENTIE to work by night in front of trenches. 'B' type ammunition found unsuitable rapid fire; withdrawn and sent to Machine Gun section	
.	7-9-15		Major COLLINS with 'A' Coy arrived at ESTAIRES. Working under orders of C.R.E 20th Division	
.	8-9-15 9-9-15 10-9-15		Nothing to report	
.	11-9-15		Lieut. PALMER and Machine Gun Section returned from trenches to ESTAIRES. 2nd Lieut. WOOD and reserve Machine Gun section leave for trenches. Attached 59th Brigade	
	12-9-15		Grenade Course finished. Draft rejoin respective Coys. 'B' Coy casualty 24113 Pte J. Owen wounded	
	13-9-15		Draft from 17th commence Course at Grenade School with dummy bombs only as live bombs returned to Division	
	14-9-15 15-9-15		Nothing to report	
	16-9-15		17439 Pte D Lister 'C' Coy (M.G) killed	
	17-9-15		Nothing to report	
	18-9-15		'D' Coy moved to ESTAIRES to be attached to 61st Brigade.	
	19-9-15		Nothing to report	
	20-9-15		Head Quarters marched to ESTAIRES	
ESTAIRES . .	21-9-15 22-9-15 23-9-15		Standing to. Reserve Divisional troops. Interpreter left.	
	24-9-15		B & D Coys returned from 60th & 61st Bge. to ESTAIRES. 1 Platoon under Lieut PEMBERTON mining with 181st Mining Coy rejoined Battalion.	

Instructions regarding War Diaries and Intelligence Summaries are contained in F. S. Regs., Part II. and the Staff Manual respectively. Title pages will be prepared in manuscript.

WAR DIARY
or
~~INTELLIGENCE SUMMARY.~~
(Erase heading not required.)

Army Form C. 2118.

Place	Date	Hour	Summary of Events and Information	Remarks and references to Appendices
ESTAIRES	25-9-15		Standing to. Lieut MARPLES, 4 Sergts and 40 men detailed as escort for prisoners but were not required. 2nd Lieut WIND + WRIGHT 7th K.O.Y.L.I. could not join their unit as it was in firing line. Attached 11th D.L.I.	
	26-9-15		Standing to. 'D' Coy attached 60th Brigade. 2 Platoons at R.E. Stores, 83rd Field Coy, 2 platoons at LA FLINQUE POST	
	27-9-15		Machine Gun Section arrived from 60th Bge (in trenches) and billetted in Estaires	
	28-9-15		Working parties sent at 8.30 am + 12.30 p.m to unload barge at R.E. Park Nouveau Monde. 2 Officers of 7th K.O.Y.L.I. joined their Battalion. 2 Platoons 'B' Coy marched out at 1.30 p.m. under Lieut. FISHER for mining at FORQUISSART M24. C. 0. 4 Map 36. 18091 Pte Charles WILSON 'D' Coy accidently wounded. Letter of appreciation received from C.E. 3rd Corps and Lieut. General Sir W. PULTENEY, on the pioneer work done by the Battalion. Order received from the Division at 1.30 p.m. that the Battalion less 'C' Coy at LA MOTTE would take over section of the line that evening. Orders to be received from G.O.C. 60th Brigade to whom Batt. would be attached. C.O and Adjutant left ESTAIRES at 3 p.m. for 60th Brigade HQ Qrts. A, B Coys, Machine Gun Section and Head Quarters marched out at 4 p.m under Major A. E. Collins, halting at the X roads at M.9.D for orders. Under orders from G.O.C. 60th Brigade A+B Coys and M.G. section marched down to No2 Battalion position and relieved the 9th Ghurkas about 9 p.m. Head Quarters took over Cuthbert House about 600 yards in rear.	
IN THE Trenches	29-9-15		2 Platoons to report to 173rd Tunnelling Coy to commence work on 1st prox. Mr TAIT, another officer and 2 platoons of "D" Coy detailed. 'C' Coy left LA MOTTE for the trenches leaving a guard of 5 N.C.O's and 35 men at 3rd Corps HQ Qrts. 1 Platoon went into fire trench in conjunction with 'B' Coy. 3 Platoons in reserve trench. Quiet day in the trenches. Work hindered by weather conditions. Casualties. H. McDONALD 'D' Coy killed. 2 Platoons of 'D' Coy in fire trench.	
	30-9-15		Enemy quiet. Work progressing. Cleaning, draining fire + communicating trench, repairing parapet + wire in front of parapet. Casualties, 20997 Pte W. JARDINE 'A' + 22536 Pte A. TURNER 'C' wounded. C.O. left about 8.30 p.m. to report to 60th Brigade HQ Qrts. Major A.E. COLLINS took command	

1577 Wt. W10791/1773 500,000 1/15 D. D. & L. A.D.S.S./Forms/C. 2118.

20th Division

Mot

11th D.L.I.
Vol: 3

121
7761

Oct 15

Confidential.

War Diary

of

XIth Bn. Durham L. I. (Pioneers)

from Oct. 1st to Oct. 31st. 1915.

Volume III

Army Form C. 2118.

Instructions regarding War Diaries and Intelligence Summaries are contained in F. S. Regs., Part II. and the Staff Manual respectively. Title pages will be prepared in manuscript.

WAR DIARY
or
INTELLIGENCE SUMMARY.
(Erase heading not required.)

XIth Bn Durham L. I. (Pioneers).

Place	Date	Hour	Summary of Events and Information	Remarks and references to Appendices
			Bt. Col. G M Davidson relinquished command of the Batt. Maj. A. E. Collins DSO is in command.	
Trenches 60th BDE	Oct 1st	2nd, 3rd	Garrison duties. Repairs to trenches, parapets etc. wiring repaired. Fire & communication trenches drained.	
			Relieved at 7pm by 12 KRR. Headqrs removed to RUE PARADIS. 4 carpenters despatched to 83rd FIELD, SE and	
	4th		Coy. This continual drain of best skilled workers seriously affects efficiency of Pioneer Battalion.	
			7 Men (carpenters) blacksmiths etc. sent to 20th Div Supply Column. Supply usual working parties	
	5th		for Engineers whilst we are in billets. 3 posts MIN. RUGBY and N. TILLELOY held by this	
			battalion. Men engaged on salvage work. Wind northerly.	
	6th		Brigadier inspected troops in billets. 3 carpenters sent to 83rd F Coy RE. 2nd Lt TAIT &	
			2 platoons D Coy have rejoined Bn from 173rd Tunnelling Coy. Wind at 7.30 AM N. Westerly.	
	7th		Usual working parties.	
	8th		Returned to trenches, less 3 platoons engaged on tunnelling work.	
	9th		Ammunition expended 1400 rounds. Enemy shells over parapet 15. Usual work carried on. Wind at 7.30 AM NE	
	10th		Shells over parapet 23. Ammunition expended 1670 rounds. Wind East, light.	
	11th		Dangerous localities in front line noted & steps taken to guard agst enfilading or reverse fire. Wind SE	
	12th		S.S.E wind 7.30 AM. Shells over parapet 85. Ammunition expended 2140 rounds. Distribution of reserve ammunition carried out.	
	13th		Demonstration by 60th BDE. Heavy bombardment of German lines. Enemy replied from noon for about 1½ hrs, chiefly firing on Reserve trenches. Smoke barrage. Dummies worked on parapet to make enemy believe that it was thickly manned & that attack was about to be made.	
			Casualties 3 killed 14 wounded. Ammunition expended 31.000 rounds.	
	14th		Relieved by 12th KRR this evening. GRANT, WINCHESTER, & DREADNOUGHT posts held by the Bn.	
	15th 16th 17th		Whilst in billets, 25 Men attend BDE bombing school. Usual working parties.	
		18th	Brigadier inspected Men in billets. 2nd Lt TAIT & 2nd Lt DOUGLAS left Bn to join tunnelling Coys.	

Instructions regarding War Diaries and Intelligence Summaries are contained in F. S. Regs., Part II. and the Staff Manual respectively. Title pages will be prepared in manuscript.

~~WAR DIARY~~
or
INTELLIGENCE SUMMARY.
(Erase heading not required.)

XIth Durham L.I. (Pioneers)

Army Form C. 2118.

Place	Date	Hour	Summary of Events and Information	Remarks and references to Appendices
	Oct 19th		Major HAYES Capt LLOYD proceeded to England on leave. Usual working parties	
	20th		Return to trenches	
	21st		Shells over parapet 19. Ammunition expended 1500 rounds	
	22nd		RQMS SPALDING & SERGT PAYNTER selected as candidates for Commissions	
			Draught of 67 Men (including 15 of this Bn returned from hospital) arrived from Base from 16th & 17th Bn	
	23rd		Shells over parapet 29 ammunition expended 2450 rounds	
			14 Men went to England on leave. CSM Bonsfield placed under arrest - drunk on duty	
	24th		Shells 60, ammunition 2000. 1 more platoon sent to 59th BDE.	
	25th		Ammunition expended 1350 rounds 2 Men sent to 60th BDE for instruction in working STOKES gun	
	26th		Ammunition expended 1200 rounds Shells over parapet over 100.	
	27th & 28th		Wind NNE Bn relieved	
	29th & 30th		Usual working parties	
	30th		Night work in front of firing line. 320 men engaged on digging parties 20 men covering parties. 60th BDE engaged on straightening line at DUCKS Bill	
			3 Officers & 14 Men went to England on leave	

[illegible signature]

20th Division

11th D.L.I.
Vol: 4

L.

121
7693.

Nov. 15

nil
Ans.

Confidential.

WAR DIARY
of
XIth Bn. DURHAM L. I.
(PIONEERS)

from Nov. 1st to Nov. 30th 1915

Volume 4.

Angus E Collins Lt. Col.
Commanding XIth D. L. I.
(Pioneers).

Instructions regarding War Diaries and Intelligence Summaries are contained in F. S. Regs., Part II. and the Staff Manual respectively. Title pages will be prepared in manuscript.

~~WAR DIARY~~
or
INTELLIGENCE SUMMARY.
(Erase heading not required.)

Army Form C. 2118.

Place	Date Nov	Hour	Summary of Events and Information	Remarks and references to Appendices
Billets RUE du PARADIS M.3.d.5.0 sheet 36	1.		Provided working parties for 83rd Fd Coy. R.E. Direction of wind at 7.30 a.m. due E.	AWD
Trenches.	2.		Relieved 12th K.R.R. Relief completed at 6.30 p.m. Section of line: North TILLELOY ST. to WINCHESTER RD. exclusive. Map 36 S.W.1. Direction of wind at 7.30 a.m. due S.	AWD
	3.		Shells over parapet 57. Ammunition expended 1191 rounds. Quiet all along front line. Bad weather conditions	
	4.		Shells over parapet 23 light field gun. Am. expended 1580 rounds. Work on parapet, parados + communication trenches. Enemy snipers very active all night. Direction of wind at 7.30 a.m. W.N.W.	AWD
	5.		Shells over parapet 18. Am. expended 1430 rounds. Work: repairing parapet, parados, + fire trenches: bailing out traffic trenches + reconstructing dug-outs. Wind due N	
Billets at EPINETTE + LA FLINQUE FARM M.16.b sheet 36.	6.		12th K.R.R. relieved this battalion at 8.40 p.m. Am. expended 1490 rounds. GRANT, DREADNOUGHT + WINCHESTER Posts held by the battalion. Work as yesterday. Sergeant FREDERICK WILLIAMS 'B' Coy presented with "Medaille Militaire" for general good work in trench + in front of parapet. Direction of wind N.N.E.	AWD
	7.		Usual working parties for R.E.	
	8		" " " " Lt G. S. RIGBY wounded.	AWD
	9.		1 platoon making winter stables for Transport rejoined Coy. now working under 59th BDE. Direction of wind S.S.W. Capt G. R. SCOTT + Capt A. W. DAWSON + 14 O.R. went on leave to England	
Trenches.	10.		1 Coy + HDQTT. relieved 12 K.R.R. Section of trench BIRDCAGE to WINCHESTER (exclusive). Before going to trenches, billets at EPINETTE shelled: 3 men killed: 7 wounded. 2 later died in hospital. MAJOR A.E. COLLINS D.S.O., CAPT POLLOCK; CAPT VICK returned from leave	
	11.		Repairing work as usual. Irish Guards visited HDQTT in trenches + arranged about reliefs.	AWD

Instructions regarding War Diaries and Intelligence Summaries are contained in F. S. Regs., Part II. and the Staff Manual respectively. Title pages will be prepared in manuscript.

WAR DIARY
or
INTELLIGENCE SUMMARY.
(Erase heading not required.)

Army Form C. 2118.

Place	Date Nov.	Hour	Summary of Events and Information	Remarks and references to Appendices
	12		Shells over parapet 15. Usual repairing work. Am. expended 450 rounds. Very wet. Trenches in very awful condition.	AWA
	13.		Direction of wind: N.W. no. of shells over parapet 19. Work continued on parapet which has again fallen, in several places. Trench bottoms placed in fire bays.	AWA
	14.		Am. expended 250 rounds. Shells over parapet 19. artillery active all day. Weather fine. Irish Guards relieved at 4.30 p.m. Relief complete 9.30 p.m. Moved into billet at LAVENTIE EAST.	AWA
BILLETS. LAVENTIE. E. M.5.a.			Position of Coys. 'A' Coy. with Tunnelling Coy. 59th BDE. 'B' Coy. 2 platoons mining; 2 platoons at HDQTS. 'C' Coy. with HDQTS. 'D' Coy. 2 platoons draining: with 59th BDE. 2 platoons with HDQTS. less 25 men engaged making horse-standings at Transport Lines.	
	15		Platoons at HDQTS. cleaning equipment + arms etc. Other platoons: work as usual.	AWA
	16.		Platoons at Bn. HDQTS. commence work under C.R.E. 20th Div. on 2 roads to Canal. LA LYS at Le NOUVEAU MONDE. G.27.C.5.1. Sheet 36. One road corduroy, the other simply formed. Party of men working saw bench on 6 hour shifts, night + day work.	AWA
	17.		Lt. FISHER + Lt. WARD, R.A.M.C. went on leave to England. Capt SCOTT + Capt. DAWSON returned from leave. Boulogne harbour closed: landed at CALAIS.	AWA
	18		Weather fine + frosty. 2 platoons went out to mine working under orders of 183rd Tunnelling Coy.	AWA
	19.		Weather frosty. working parties continue as above. Capt. LEESON + 14 O.R. went on leave.	
	20.		Work as above.	AWA

1577 Wt. W10791/1773 500,000 1/15 D. D. & L. A.D.S.S./Forms/C. 2118.

Instructions regarding War Diaries and Intelligence Summaries are contained in F. S. Regs., Part II. and the Staff Manual respectively. Title pages will be prepared in manuscript.

WAR DIARY
or
INTELLIGENCE SUMMARY.
(Erase heading not required.)

Army Form C. 2118.

Place	Date Nov.	Hour	Summary of Events and Information	Remarks and references to Appendices
	21		Work suspended. Church parade at ESTAIRES. AWA	
	22.		Weather fine + frosty. Work as before.	
	23.		" " " " " ". Draft of 32 N.C.O's + men arrived from base from 16th Bn. Durham L. I. Strong, well-set-up, healthy looking men. AWA	
Billets RUE de BRUGES G.24.a sheet 36	24.		moved from LAVENTIE E. to RUE de BRUGES. moved by platoons at ¼ hr. intervals. AWA 'C' Coy. to work 50 men on drainage under CAPT PERROT. R.E. 'A' Coy. + balance 'C' Coy continue road making	
	25.		Work as above. 2nd Lt. R GRIMSHAW. 2nd Lt. M. COOPER joined this battn. from 16th D.L.I. AWA MAJOR. A.E. COLLINS, D.S.O gazetted to command this Battalion. AWA	
	26.		'C' Coy. moved to FLEURBAIX + work on drainage behind line BOIS GRENIER. H.30.b sheet 36	
	27.		Lt. FISHER + Lt. WARD. R.A.M.C. returned from leave. 1 platoon to go to CROIX MARECHAL to repair post. AWA	
	28.		Rest day	
	29.		Capt LEESON + 12 O.R returned from leave. 2 men absent, reported to A.P.M. AWA Situation of troops with regard to work. A Coy. 3 platoons on communication trenches under 83rd Fd Coy. 1 platoon mining 181st Tunnelling Coy. B Coy 1 platoon repairing CROIX MARECHAL Post. 3 platoons road-making. C Coy. engaged on drainage scheme at BOIS GRENIER. AWA D Coy with 61st BDE 2 platoons drainage. 2 platoons 181st mining Coy.	
	30.		Lt. J. ROBERTSON. Lt. MARPLES + 14 O.R were to go on leave. leave train cancelled. AWA	

Vol: 5

121/7824

Confidential.

War Diary

of

XIth Bn. Durham L. I. (Pioneers)

from Dec 1st to Dec. 31st 1915

Volume 6

Instructions regarding War Diaries and Intelligence Summaries are contained in F. S. Regs., Part II. and the Staff Manual respectively. Title pages will be prepared in manuscript.

WAR DIARY
or
~~INTELLIGENCE SUMMARY.~~
(Erase heading not required.)

XIth Durham L. I. (Pioneers)
December. Vol. VI.

Army Form C. 2118.

Place	Date Dec.	Hour	Summary of Events and Information	Remarks and references to Appendices
HDQRTS. RUE de BRUGES G. 24. a.	1st		Engaged on Pioneering work for the whole month. 2 platoons road making at NOUVEAU MONDE, G. 27. C.	
	2nd.		2 platoons engaged on drainage at CROIX MARECHAL H. 34. a. One Coy. attached 61st. BDE. on drainage + mining. 3 platoons working on communication trenches under 83rd. Field Coy. 1 platoon mining. One Coy. drainage under R.E.	Reference Maps 36 + 36 a.
			Test Gas N/9/1 sent. Various detachments warned in 10 minutes.	
	3rd.		C Coy. drainage on roads + LAIES RIVER N. 9. b. A + D Coys. attached 60th + 61st. BDES. Ditch from BOUTILLERIE CROSS ROADS N. 5 d. to front line cleaned out, deepened + widened. Work continued on RIVER LAIES between RUE DAVID (N. 5. b.) + RUE GUNNERIE (H. 36. c.)	
	4th		59th BDE. relieved 61st. BDE. Ditch which enters river LAIES at H. 36. a. 10. 6 (sheet 36) deepened for 100 yds. behind support line. Widening Laies continued between RUE DAVID + RUE GUNNERIE. D Coy. took charge of centrifugal pump at V. C. Corner. N. 2. c. 8. 1. 3 platoons at CROIX MARECHAL. Roads all under water.	
	5th		Work suspended. Church parade + baths.	
	6th		Work as before.	
	7th		1 platoon at TROU FARM N. 9. a. RUE PETILLON. 1 platoon Cellar Farm Avenue N. 3. b. work on communication trenches. Other platoons as above.	
	8th		No work last night at LAIES + CORDONNERIE (as arranged) as R.E. failed to provide tools. Very heavy artillery fire on V.C. Corner + Two Tree Farm N. 2. c. 3. 8. Lts. Cunningham + PUNTIN went on leave to England. One Coy. continued work on ditch entering Laies at H. 36. a. 5. 4. + Started revetting east bank of R. Laies near City Rd.	
	9th		Work as above continued. Lts. Robertson + Maples returned from leave, having been detained 1 day at Boulogne. 20th Div. telegram reads:- "In case of attack you will assemble in immediate vicinity of billets + await orders."	
	10th		Work as above,	
	11th		" " "	

1577 Wt. W10791/1773 500,000 1/15 D. D. & L. A.D.S.S./Forms/C. 2118.

Instructions regarding War Diaries and Intelligence Summaries are contained in F. S. Regs., Part II. and the Staff Manual respectively. Title pages will be prepared in manuscript.

WAR DIARY
or
INTELLIGENCE SUMMARY.
(Erase heading not required.)

Army Form C. 2118.

Place	Date	Hour	Summary of Events and Information	Remarks and references to Appendices
	12th		Church parade for HDQTS. Machine Gun Section & part of B Coy. Balance of B working at Laies River Post by night. Other Coys. resting.	
	13th		2nd Lt. A. FLOYD commenced 12 days' course at Divisional School for Infantry Officers. 2nd Lt. G. S. Wood " 5 days' " " Machine Gun School. Work as before.	
	14th		A & D Coys. work under Brigades. B. Coy 2 platoons Laies post night work. 2 platoons at Croix Marechal. C Coy. 3 platoons night work: 1 platoon day work at CORDONNERIE.	
	15th		B Coy. 60 men Cellar Farm Avenue under direction of R.E. Officer. Balance at Laies Post by night. C Coy. as before. A & D Coy. with Right & Left BDES.	
	16th		Lts. Pemberton & Rigby went on leave to England. Work as before. Lt. Puntin returned from leave. 25200 L/Corp. Stonebank selected for Transport course at Aberville (3 weeks).	
	17th		A & D Coys. attached Right & Left BDES. revetting & draining, making BDE. HDQTS. dugouts & mining. B & C Coys. work as above. Lt. Cunningham returned from leave.	
	18th		A Coy. raising trench boards & general repairs, rebuilding dugouts; putting up head-cover on Boutillerie Avenue. (all under 61st. BDE. orders). B Coy. work as above. D Coy. work under 59th BDE. C Coy. 1 platoon on Gas Cylinders front line at 4 a.m. Remainder work on CORDONNERIE (day & night).	
	19th		C & D Coys. work as above. A & B Coys. resting. Baths & Church Parade.	
	20th 21st 22nd, 23rd		Work as above. B Coy. 11 men repairing Trench lines. 5 men hurdle making. 5 men hut building. 1 platoon night work at MILL RD. POST. N.4. d. 3. 5.	
	24th		Work as above. Lts. Pemberton & Rigby returned from leave. Lts. C. Palmer & 2nd Lt. A. Floyd went on leave.	
	25th		Xmas day. Work suspended.	

Instructions regarding War Diaries and Intelligence Summaries are contained in F. S. Regs., Part II. and the Staff Manual respectively. Title pages will be prepared in manuscript.

WAR DIARY
or
INTELLIGENCE SUMMARY.
(Erase heading not required.)

Army Form C. 2118.

Place	Date	Hour	Summary of Events and Information	Remarks and references to Appendices
	26th		A Coy. making traverses + repairing parapet Section A Well Close Chord. BDE. dugouts. Work on BOOTILLERIE Post. B + C Coys. as before. D Coy. with right + left Bns. under 59th BDE	
	27th		Same work.	
	28th		" "	
	29th		" "	
	30th		" "	
	31st		" "	

[illegible]

1577 Wt. W10791/1773 500,000 1/15 D. D. & L. A.D.S.S./Forms/C. 2118.

20

11th D.L.I.
Vol 6

Jan '16

Confidential

War Diary

of

XIth Durham L. I. (Pioneers)

from Jan. 1st to Jan. 31st 1916

Volume. 7.

Instructions regarding War Diaries and Intelligence Summaries are contained in F. S. Regs., Part II. and the Staff Manual respectively. Title pages will be prepared in manuscript.

~~WAR DIARY~~
or
INTELLIGENCE SUMMARY.
(Erase heading not required.)

Vol. 7.

Army Form C. 2118.

Place	Date	Hour	Summary of Events and Information	Remarks and references to Appendices
RUE de BRUGES G. 24 a sheet 36. Bn HDQTS.	Jan 1916 1		A Coy. working under 61st. BDE. Well Farm Chord; BOUTILLERIE Avenue, City Rd. Trench; Advanced Brigade HDQTS. dugouts. 'B' Coy. working under C.R.E. 20th Division at MILL Rd. Post + at WATLING ST. laying Trench boards etc. 'C' Coy. under C.R.E. 20th Div. working at CORDONNERIE. 'D' Coy. working under 60th BDE. orders at Cellar Farm Avenue; avenue pumps; Tramways; V.C. Corner (pump). Lts. Ward + Maclaren went on leave Jan. 1st. 1916.	Sheet 36. N. 2. d. and 3. c. N. 10. a. N. 2. c. 8. 1
	2.		'A' Coy. work as above. B. C. D. resting. Baths and church parade.	
	3.		Same work as for 1st.	
	4.		Same work: Lts. Palmer + Floyd returned from leave.	
	5.		Same work by day + night. 2nd Lt. R. H. STUBBS transferred from 13th Bn. Durham L. I. to this battalion in exchange for 2nd Lt. BAGGULEY, who originally belonged to the 13th. Mr Stubbs formerly belonged to this battalion. 2 machine guns in ~~emplac~~ ruined farm at V.C. Corner (N. 2. c. 8. 1) were shelled by enemy + destroyed. 1700 rounds S.A.A. also destroyed. Guard endeavoured to save guns but without avail. Gun emplacements (150 yds. nearer German line) were not damaged.	
	6. + 7th		Work as above.	
	8th		A.C.D. work as above. 'B' Coy. packing preparatory to moving to LA MOTTE for hurdle making. Lt. ROBERTSON + 10 men (advanced party) proceeded to MIN FONTAINE to take over billets, stores, etc. from battalion of 8th Div.	E. 19. sheet 36a. C. 21. a. sheet 36 a

1577 Wt. W10791/1773 500,000 1/15 D. D. & L. A.D.S.S./Forms/C. 2118.

Instructions regarding War Diaries and Intelligence Summaries are contained in F. S. Regs., Part II. and the Staff Manual respectively. Title pages will be prepared in manuscript.

WAR DIARY
or
INTELLIGENCE SUMMARY.
(Erase heading not required.)

Army Form C. 2118.

Place	Date	Hour	Summary of Events and Information	Remarks and references to Appendices
	9th		A Coy. resting. C + D Coys. work as before. B Coy. left RUE de BRUGES at 8 a.m. & marched to LA MOTTE, billets E.19.a. sheet 36a. for hurdle making under C.E. 3rd Corps. 2nd Lts Maclaren + Ward returned from leave. 2 Lewis machine guns received to replace the 2 lost.	
			At 2 a.m. gas attack was made by 59th BDE. XIth D.L.I. M.G.O. with 2 Lewis machine guns took up position at N.8.a.3.6 (sheet 36) to bring indirect fire to bear on German communication trenches.	
			2nd Lts. Hopkinson + Wood + 16 men went on leave today at 1.45 a.m.	
	10th		A Coy. left RUE de BIACHE billets + marched to RUE de BRUGES.	
	11th		C + D Coys. rejoined HDQTS. at RUE de BRUGES.	
	12th		Battalion (less B Coy) left RUE de BRUGES at 8.30 a.m. passed SAILLY BRIDGE at 9 a.m. marched via DOULIEU - BLEU - VIEUX BERQUIN to SEC BOIS (E.8.d. sheet 36a) arrived 1.30 p.m. Excellent billets. No men fell out.	
	13th		Resumed march at 8.15 a.m. via LA MOTTE - PAPOTE - MORBECQUE to MIN FONTAINE (C.21.a. sheet 36a). Arrived 1.30 p.m. No men fell out.	
	14th		Time spent in settling down, cleaning rifles + equipment.	
			2nd Lt. Maclaren + 20 men sent to C.E. 1st Army at AIRE (H.28. sheet 36a) for work under R.E. direction.	
			18 men arrived from base (15 men who had been sick or wounded) 3 men who had been left behind on embarkation.	

1577 Wt. W10791/1773 500,000 1/15 D. D. & L. A.D.S.S./Forms/C. 2118.

Army Form C. 2118.

WAR DIARY
or
INTELLIGENCE SUMMARY.
(Erase heading not required.)

Instructions regarding War Diaries and Intelligence Summaries are contained in F. S. Regs., Part II. and the Staff Manual respectively. Title pages will be prepared in manuscript.

Place	Date	Hour	Summary of Events and Information	Remarks and references to Appendices
	15. 16.		As on 14th. 2nd Lt. Bagguley joined 13th Bn. Durham L. I.	
	17th.		Training commenced (in reserve). Physical training, musketry, squad drill, section drill, platoon drill. Fire control etc. 8.30 a.m. – 12.15 p.m. 2 p.m. – 4.15 p.m. Major Hayes + Lt. + Q.M. Tollit went on leave. 2nd Lts. Hopkinson + Wood returned from leave.	
	18.		As above	
	19.		Work in morning as above. Afternoon football matches. Working party of 1 officer + 50 men working at new rifle range C. 24. d. 5. 0. from 9 a.m. till 4 p.m. under C.R.E. orders.	
	20		1 officer + 50 men sent to Blaringhem Canal Bridge for coaling duties – 9 a.m. – 4 p.m.	
	21st.		Lt. Gen. Sir W. Pulteney, 3rd Corps Commander, inspected battalion to say "Farewell" on departure of 20th Division from the 1st to the 2nd Army. Concert to men 5.30 – 7.30 p.m. by officers.	
	22nd		Reveille 5 a.m. Moved off 8 a.m. Marched to Zermezeele via Wallon Cappel (I. 27. a.) Sheet 27. Arrived 1.30 p.m. Best billets we have yet had. No men fell out.	
	23rd		'B' Coy. from LA MOTTE (3rd Corps) rejoined Battalion. Foot inspection of Coys. Gen. Davies (20th Division) visited Zermezeele + enquired if men were comfortable etc.	
	24th.		Parade 8.30 a.m. Physical training 8.45 – 9.45 a.m. Platoon drill etc. 10.30 – 11.30. Afternoon football	
	25th.		Work as per yesterday. Afternoon Rugby football match – Officers v. N.C.Os. (latter won).	
	26th.		As per yesterday. Lt. Tollit returned from leave. Major Hayes' leave extended.	

Army Form C. 2118.

Instructions regarding War Diaries and Intelligence Summaries are contained in F. S. Regs., Part II. and the Staff Manual respectively. Title pages will be prepared in manuscript.

WAR DIARY
or
INTELLIGENCE SUMMARY.
(Erase heading not required.)

Place	Date	Hour	Summary of Events and Information	Remarks and references to Appendices
	27th		Capts. LLOYD + VICK. + Dr. Ward went on leave to England. Work as before.	
	28th		C.O. interviewed Gen. Plumer (2nd Army Commander). Route march via ARNEKE.	
	29th		Major Hayes returned from leave. Our own bootmakers' shop recommenced.	
	30th		Church parades, 10.30 a.m.	
	31st		Route march + inspection by General Plumer. Commenced 11 a.m. marched past + returned at 1.30 p.m.	

[illegible] Collins
Lt Col.
Commanding XIth Durham L.I.
(Pioneers)

Confidential

War Diary

of

XIth (S) Bn. Durham L. I.
(Pioneers)

from Feb. 1st to Feb. 29th 1916

Volume 8

Instructions regarding War Diaries and Intelligence Summaries are contained in F. S. Regs., Part II. and the Staff Manual respectively. Title pages will be prepared in manuscript.

~~WAR DIARY~~
or
INTELLIGENCE SUMMARY.
(Erase heading not required.)

Army Form C. 2118.

XIth Durham L.I. (Pioneers)
Vol. 8.

Place	Date	Hour	Summary of Events and Information	Remarks and references to Appendices
Zermezeele. sheet 27	Feb 1st		Major G. Hayes (2nd in command) + 4 Coy. officers + 8 N.C.O's left by bus for 3 days to inspect new line + work to be taken over from XIth Liverpools (Pioneers) 14th Division. Work as before.	
	2 + 3		Work as before.	
	4		1 officer + 1 platoon with tools marched to A.22.d.8.8 for work in burying cables for 20th Div. Sigs. 15 carpenters + 10 pioneers attached to 96th F. Coy. R.E. at A.22.d. (sheet 28) for hut building. Capts. Pollock + Scott went on leave.	sheet 28
"	5th		Bn. marched to Winnezeele J.17.a.	
	6th		Church parade. Rest from work – cleaning up.	
	7th		Work as before.	
	8th 9th		Col. Collins went on 10 days' leave. Work as before.	
	10th 11th		B + D Coys. under Capt. G. R. Vick marched to ELVERDINGHE Chateau B.14.a sheet 28. Capt. Leeson went on leave. 20th Div. relieving 14th Div. on Yser Canal.	
	12th		A + C Coys. + HQ moved to ELVERDINGHE Chateau. Shelling going on: Coys. held up for an hour. B + D Coys. (less 2 reserve platoons) went to Canal Bank, one attached to each BDE. in front line. 42 shells reported as having fallen in or near Chateau grounds. Gas Alert from 20th Div. HQ. received at 5.20 p.m.	
	13th		Church parade. Inspected Elverdinghe defences. Message received from Sigs. CZH that 2 Zepps. moving east over Trench C.1. at 10.45 p.m.	

Army Form C. 2118.

Instructions regarding War Diaries and Intelligence Summaries are contained in F. S. Regs., Part II. and the Staff Manual respectively. Title pages will be prepared in manuscript.

WAR DIARY
or
INTELLIGENCE SUMMARY.
(Erase heading not required.)

Place	Date	Hour	Summary of Events and Information	Remarks and references to Appendices
	14th		C.O. made out Defence Scheme for Elverdinghe which G.O.C. 20th Div. approved of.	
			1 Officer + 1 platoon sent to Belmont Farm for work under O.C. 84th Fd Cy. R.E.	(B.18.c. Boesinghe sheet 1)
			Received message from 20th Div. S.O.S. from 24th Div. at Hooge.	
	15th		~~Capt. Dawson left for leave~~. Capt. Higgens rejoined this battalion. Oxford + Bucks L.I. relieved the 12th K.R.R.C. who came into rest at Elverdinghe.	
	16th		Capt. Dawson went on leave. Work as before.	
	17th 18th		Work as before. Col. Collins returned from leave.	
	19th		"Gas Alert" sent from Div. HQ.	
	20th		"Gas Alert" sent. Reserve platoon of D Cy. rejoined Cy. under Rt. Sector BDE. orders.	
			" " " B Cy. engaged in burying cables.	
	21st		"Gas Alert" signalled by 60th BDE.	
			A + C Coys. working on Trench 7Y to 7Z + Rotherham Rd C.7.	B.17.b.10 3. Boesinghe sheet 1
	22nd		S.O.S. received 4.45 p.m. Cancelled 6.50 p.m. Work as before.	
	23rd		A+B work as before. D Cy. left Canal Bank for concrete dugouts at BRIELEN (B.28 central)	sheet 28.
	24th		Work as before. All leave cancelled.	
	25th		S.O.S. D20 received 2 a.m. cancelled 2 minutes later. Work as before.	
			2nd Lts. Taylor + Jee joined the Battalion.	

Army Form C. 2118.

Instructions regarding War Diaries and Intelligence Summaries are contained in F. S. Regs., Part II. and the Staff Manual respectively. Title pages will be prepared in manuscript.

~~WAR DIARY~~

or

INTELLIGENCE SUMMARY.

(Erase heading not required.)

Place	Date	Hour	Summary of Events and Information	Remarks and references to Appendices
	26th.		Cpt. Dawson returned from leave. Work as before.	
	27th		Lt. Rigby to Workshops to understudy Lt. Cunyngham who has been running Workshops since Bn. arrived at Elverdinghe.	
			7th K.O.Y.L.I. came into rest in place of King's Liverpool Bn.	
	28th.		Work as before.	
	29th.		Work as before. 20th Div. Artillery bombarded F.34 with 4.5" Howitzers from 3 p.m. till 4.30 p.m.	

[signature]

Lt. Col.

Comdg. XIth Durham L.I.

(Pioneers)

1577 Wt. W10791/1773 500,000 1/15 D. D. & L. A.D.S.S./Forms/C. 2118.

11 DLI
Vol 8

2

Confidential.

War Diary

of

XIth Bn. Durham L. I. (Pioneers)

for March 1916.

Volume IX.

Instructions regarding War Diaries and Intelligence Summaries are contained in F. S. Regs., Part II. and the Staff Manual respectively. Title Pages will be prepared in manuscript.

XIth Durham L.I. (Pioneers)

~~WAR DIARY~~ or INTELLIGENCE SUMMARY

(Erase heading not required.)

Vol. IX.

Army Form C. 2118

Place	Date	Hour	Summary of Events and Information	Remarks and references to Appendices
ELVERDINGHE B.14 central sheet 28.	March 1st		Work: 1 Coy. attached BDE. Right Sector. 1 Coy. attached BDE. Left Sector. 2 Coys. working under orders of C.R.E. 20th Division. 1 platoon burying cables for 20th Div. Signal Coy., cables running across country to Canal Bank West side (Yser).	
	2nd.		Gas alert 9 a.m. Elverdinghe Chateau grounds (HQ. Pioneer Bn.) shelled: 2 R.A. officers wounded.	
	3rd 4th 5th 6th		2 Coys. under C.R.E. orders working on Canal Bank 7Y–7Z (Sheet 28. B.12.d.9.6 – South to B.12.d.9.3) on communication trenches – clearing fire bays. Tramways – repair work continued. Sapping for M.G. emplacement 7Z. making dug outs. Capt. Fisher on leave, reported sick, War Office letter. Later attached to Pioneer Depot, Reading.	
	9th		7 men sent to carry on Well Sinking at A.23.b.5.8. sheet 28.	
	11th		2nd Lt. J.H. Gaudion from Cadet School, Base, posted to this Bn. Chateau grounds shelled 3 King's Shropshire L.I. O.R. wounded. 1 hut wrecked.	
	13th		Posts 7.8.9.10. at (B.20.c.3.3.) (B.19.d.6.6) (B.19.d.4.8.) (B.19.a.5.5.) visited. Trenches badly need repair: rain + frost worked much damage. Only 10 men (caretakers) for repair work. Much of work on 7Y–7Z reported blown in by enemy Trench mortars.	
	15th		Work for last week summarised: 7Z–7Y. 95 yards of work completed, i.e. U frames placed in position; revetted with corrugated iron; trench boards laid. 15 yards blown in on the 14th by enemy Trench mortars. 7Z to French lines. Machine Gun Sap + Emplacement completed with exception of loopholes. Lateral communication Trench 80 yards completed of which 20 yds. were obliterated by Trench mortars. 3 dug outs completed. Trolley System 280 yards of existing Windsor Castle Line has been relaid + Trench boards put down. Existing curves have been removed + for this purpose 42 yds. of New line have been laid.	

1875 Wt. W593/826 1,000,000 4/15 J.B.C. & A. A.D.S.S./Forms/C. 2118.

Instructions regarding War Diaries and Intelligence Summaries are contained in F. S. Regs., Part II. and the Staff Manual respectively. Title Pages will be prepared in manuscript.

~~WAR DIARY~~ ~~or~~

INTELLIGENCE SUMMARY

(Erase heading not required.)

Vol. IX

Army Form C. 2118

Place	Date	Hour	Summary of Events and Information	Remarks and references to Appendices
	16th		Chateau grounds shelled afternoon & evening from 3 - 6 p.m. 1 man + 1 mule wounded.	
	17th		Draft of 20 men (returned wounded & sick) arrived from Base.	
	18th } 19th }		Chateau grounds shelled. Direct hit on Chateau. 2nd direct hit damaged wall outside Orderly Room. Officer (R.A.) wounded in Chateau grounds.	
	20th		2nd. Lts. A. Philip & G. C. Heslop joined Bn. today from Border Regt. 9th Bn.	
	21st		21 blind shells landed north of Chateau.	
	22nd		Lts. Marples & Tollit went on leave to England. Direct hit (4·2) on Chateau.	
	23rd		Lt. Puntin returned from 2 months leave in Canada. North Gate Sentry Box (Chateau) demolished.	
			Summary of Work for last week.	
			Sector YZ - YY. 120 yards traffic trench completed with U frames, C.I. revetment & Trench boards. 30 yards damaged by Trench Mortars. Wiring on X line commenced from road in direction of TALANA Farm, about 50 yards were thoroughly thickened.	B18.c. sheet 28.
			Trolly System. 260 yards of new line laid, packed with ballast and Trench boarded. 200 yards Windsor Castle Line relaid last week, has been packed with ballast.	
			Machine Gun emplacement. Loopholes sited & put in position. Roof of sap has been covered with 15 slabs of concrete to render it shell proof.	
			Lateral communication Trenches, damaged last week, have been repaired.	
	24th		Visual Signalling office at BRIELEN (B.29.a) sheet 28, worked by Sigs. of this Bn. shelled; end of house blown in. Chateau grounds heavily shelled. 2nd. Lt. J. Cooke joined this battalion.	

1875 Wt. W593/826 1,000,000 4/15 J.B.C. & A. A.D.S.S./Forms/C. 2118.

Instructions regarding War Diaries and Intelligence Summaries are contained in F. S. Regs., Part II. and the Staff Manual respectively. Title Pages will be prepared in manuscript.

~~WAR DIARY~~

INTELLIGENCE SUMMARY

(Erase heading not required.)

Vol. IX

Army Form C. 2118

Place	Date	Hour	Summary of Events and Information	Remarks and references to Appendices
	25th		Building dugouts in Chateau Grounds in lieu of tents and huts which are unsafe.	
	26th		Heavy shelling. 9 O.R. King's Liverpool + 1 wounded in grounds.	
	27th, 28th		No shelling: first quiet day + night for 6 weeks.	
	30th		Lt. Pemberton + 2nd Lt. Floyd gone on leave.	
	31st		Summary of work week ending 31st. Trolley System. 160 yds. new line laid + ballasted. Track prepared for extension of line to Brielen Rd. Sector YY – YZ. 17 men + 1 Corp. worked here 3 nights – heavy shelling interrupted work. X line. 2 platoons carrying for R.E. Wiring of field N. of Rotherham Rd. C.T. and between YPERLEE and YPRES – BOESINGHE RD. finished. Dugouts commenced on West Bank of Canal. Lateral Communication Trench: very much damaged: pathway cut through débris + trench boards laid down. At a point adjoining French line following work has been commenced:– (1) Fire bay facing N. (2) Listening post approached by small sap from (1) (3) A loophole traverse. Machine Gun Emplacement + Sap have been badly damaged by Trench Mortars. New Dug Outs. On East bank of Canal about 250x S. of Bridge 4 commencement was made with dugouts.	Rupert Collins Lt Col O/c XIth Batt. [illegible] (Pioneers)

1875 Wt. W593/826 1,000,000 4/15 J.B.C. & A. A.D.S.S./Forms/C. 2118.

11 D L I
Vol. 9

XX

Confidential.

War Diary
of
XIth Bn. Durham L. I. (Pioneers).

from April 1st. to 30th. 1916.

Volume 10.

Instructions regarding War Diaries and Intelligence Summaries are contained in F. S. Regs., Part II. and the Staff Manual respectively. Title Pages will be prepared in manuscript.

~~WAR DIARY~~
~~or~~
INTELLIGENCE SUMMARY
(Erase heading not required.)

Army Form C. 2118

Vol 10

Place	Date	Hour	Summary of Events and Information	Remarks and references to Appendices
ELVERDINGHE CHATEAU B.14. Central Sheet 28.	April 1.		Work: 3 platoons A Coy on dugouts on West Side Canal Bank (Yser canal) C.19.c. sheet 28. 1 platoon on ~~railways~~ B.30. sheet 28. C Coy. 1 platoon cable laying; working under 20th Div. Sigs. 1 platoon making dugouts on East bank of canal. Remainder working at 7Y–7Z. B + D Coys. working under Right + Left Bdes., respectively. ~~Lt. Tollit + Cunninghams returned from leave~~. Chateau grounds shelled.	
	2nd.		Chateau grounds again shelled: 3 K.O.Y.L.I. wounded in grounds. 20th K.R.R.C. Pioneers arrive to take over work on 7Y–7Z. C Coy. D.L.I. then released work on dugouts on East Canal Bank (south of Bridge 4).	
	4th		Major G. Hayes, second in Command, proceeds to Div. HQ. for month's course attached to General Staff.	
	5th		Chateau grounds again shelled: one 4.9 shell through roof 6 men wounded. Draft of 42 N.C.O. arrived from 10th Entrenching Bn. These were all men of this battn. previously wounded or sent to hospital sick. Machine gunners + resting Coys. from Reserve Bde. commence building dugouts in Chateau grounds.	
	7th		"Gas Alert" at 9.30 p.m. from Front line 2 FA.	
	8th		Lt. R.L.S. Pemberton, having commanded B Coy. for 30 days, becomes temp. Capt. Lt. C. Palmer goes on leave.	
	9th		Capt. Pollock + 2nd. Lt. Hopkinson go on leave.	
	10th		Letter from C.R.E. eulogising "B" Coy's work. A + C Coy. men instructing 20th K.R.R.C. in pioneering work near front line	

Instructions regarding War Diaries and Intelligence Summaries are contained in F. S. Regs., Part II. and the Staff Manual respectively. Title Pages will be prepared in manuscript.

~~WAR DIARY~~ ~~or~~

INTELLIGENCE SUMMARY

(Erase heading not required.)

Army Form C. 2118

Place	Date	Hour	Summary of Events and Information	Remarks and references to Appendices
	11th		S.O.S. E 27 received at 7.30 p.m. Stood to arms. Later manned ELVERDINGHE defences.	
	12th		Lt. Rigby returned from leave. All leave suspended.	
	16th		Lt. C. Palmer returned from leave. A & C Coys. + HQ. + Transport marched to Oodezeele J. 14. a. Left Chateau by platoons at 5 min. intervals, commencing at 7.30 a.m. arrived destination 3.45 p.m. 2nd Lt. Hopkinson returned from leave.	J. 14. a. Sheet 27.
	17th		B & D Coys. left Elverdinghe, where they spent night 16/17th marched to Oodezeele	
Oodezeele J. 14. a. sheet 27.	18th		Lt. Cunningham + Workshops detachment arrived. Capt. Pollock returned from leave.	
	19th		Training during Corps Reserve commenced today, from 8.30 a.m. till 12.30 p.m. Afternoons spent in games, sports ~~sports~~. Evening lectures to Junior officers and to N.C.O's.	
	20th		Lt. Marples contracted German measles: removed to Fd Ambulance.	
	21st		2nd Lt. Clough returned to Bn. after 3 mons. above. 2nd Lt. Wardle reported & posted to D Coy.	
	22nd		Route March 9 a.m. till 12.45 p.m. Heavy rain fell en route.	
	23rd	Easter	Church Parades. Leave to be reopened on 26th. 2nd Lt. G. S. Wood understudying Adj.	
	24th		G.O.C. 20th Div. Col. Maddocks. + C.R.E. visited Coys. at work + Transport. 40 men under 2nd Lt. Clough despatched to L 4 lines for work: (near Ypres) 25 men " " Grimshawe " " L 2 " " . (Brielen for billet) Guard of 5 N.C.O's + 35 men sent to Div. HQ.	

1875 Wt. W593/826 1,000,000 4/15 J.B.C. & A. A.D.S.S./Forms/C. 2118.

Instructions regarding War Diaries and Intelligence Summaries are contained in F. S. Regs., Part II. and the Staff Manual respectively. Title Pages will be prepared in manuscript.

WAR DIARY
or
INTELLIGENCE SUMMARY
(Erase heading not required.)

Army Form C. 2118

Place	Date	Hour	Summary of Events and Information	Remarks and references to Appendices
	24th		2nd Lt. Wardle sent to WATOU to relieve Officer i/c. Forbidden Zone Posts.	
			Lecture by Lt. A. I. Ward on "Gas preventatives: Liquid Fire, etc".	
			Riding School for officers commenced today.	
	25th		Draft of 27 N.C.O's & men arrived: all men of this battalion wounded or sick.	
	26th		5 N.C.O's + 35 men attached to 177th Tunnelling Coy. R.E. 2nd Lt. Stubbs + 2 N.C.O's returned from Course on Physical Training + Bayonet Fighting with excellent reports.	
			Lecture at 6.30 p.m. by Capt. Scott on "Lessons from the South African War".	
	27th		6 days' Course for 4 officers + 32 N.C.O's commenced today under 2nd Lt. Stubbs.	
	28th		1 Sergt + 8 men went to Brielen – Elverdinghe Road for work with 14th Corps. Sigs.	
			Battn. attended baths at HORMHOUDT.	
	29th		Bn. Sports held today. 9 N.C.O's + men marched to Div. HQ. ESQUELBECQ to be tested as bandsmen.	
			2nd Lts. Ward + Wood went on leave.	
	30th	Sunday	Church parade 12 noon. Physical Training + Bayonet Practice, and Bombing School continued today.	

Angus Collins Lieut Col
O/C XIth Batt
DLI (Pioneers)

1875 Wt. W593/826 1,000,000 4/15 J.B.C. & A. A.D.S.S./Forms/C. 2118.

11. DLI
Vol 10

Confidential.

War Diary

of

XIth (S) Bn. Durham L. I.
(Pioneers).

from May 1st to 31st. 1916.

Volume XI.

Original

Instructions regarding War Diaries and Intelligence Summaries are contained in F. S. Regs., Part II. and the Staff Manual respectively. Title Pages will be prepared in manuscript.

~~WAR DIARY~~ ~~or~~ INTELLIGENCE SUMMARY

(Erase heading not required.)

Vol. XI

XIth Durham L.I. (Pioneers)

Army Form C. 2118

Place	Date May	Hour	Summary of Events and Information	Remarks and references to Appendices
Oudezeele J.14.a sheet 27	1st to 5th		Bn in Corps Reserve. Training carried out daily 8.30 a.m. till 12.30 p.m. afternoon games, sports etc. Evening – lectures.	
	6th		2nd Lt. J. Cooke attached to R.F.C. 2nd Lts Stubbs & Grimshawe proceeded on 7 days' leave	
	7th		Col. A.E. Collins & Capt. H.W. Ward R.A.M.C. proceed to England on leave	
	8th		Major G. Hayes assumed command of the Bn. in absence of Lt. Col. Collins.	
	9th 10th 11th		HQ. B & D Coys Transport & M.G. Section proceeded to Camp H. for work under 6th Division. 2 Coys. proceeded to L8 defences (Burgomester Farm) H.5.b. sheet 28. 2 Coys. at work on Communication Trenches East of YSER Canal.	
	12th		60 men working at 6th Divl. workshop.	
	13th		17 men with scabbies sent from Detachment at H.5.b. isolated.	
	14th		Capts. Higgens & Nick go on leave	
	16th		2nd Lts. Grimshawe & Stubbs return from leave	
	17th		2nd Lt. F.A. Pickering from 4th Bn. D.L.I. posted to this Bn.	
	18th		Col. Collins returned from leave. Major Hayes proceeded on leave	
	20th		2 Coys. HQ. march from Camp H to Brandhoek, G.12.b. sheet 28. 2 Coys. from L8 marched to " " " . We relieved 4th Bn. Coldstream Guards (Pioneers).	
	21st		Train for Ypres 8.15 p.m. 300 men entrained for work in forward area	

1875 Wt. W593/826 1,000,000 4/15 J.B.C. & A. A.D.S.S./Forms/C. 2118.

Instructions regarding War Diaries and Intelligence Summaries are contained in F. S. Regs., Part II. and the Staff Manual respectively. Title Pages will be prepared in manuscript.

WAR DIARY
or
INTELLIGENCE SUMMARY
(Erase heading not required.)

Army Form C. 2118

Vol XI.
XI D.L.I. (Pioneers)

Place	Date	Hour	Summary of Events and Information	Remarks and references to Appendices
	21st		Work on following Trenches being done. Haymarket I 4 & 5 sheet 28. West Lane I 10 & 11 sheet 28. White Chateau I.10 c. Kaaie Salient I 2 c. Threadneedle St C 27. Garden St C 27 & 28. Reclaiming, draining, wiring, repairing & heightening parapets etc. All night work. Train to Ypres about 8.30 p.m. daily, return from Asylum Ypres at 2 a.m.	sheet 28 N.W. 4 & N.E. 3 (parts of)
	22nd		Capt. Scott & 2nd Lt. Cooper gone on leave	
	23rd		120 men working under 20th Divl Sigs. laying cables from Ypres to Poperinghe	
	24th		Capt. Higgens returned from leave.	
	25th		"C" Coy. proceeded to billets (cellars) in Ypres	
	26th		Visited L8 defences. C.O. XI D.L.I. is responsible for manning these defences in event of attack. Also for L4 defences. Defence schemes drawn up.	
	27th		2nd Lt. Floyd, Sergts. Williams & Lambert proceed to 2nd Army School of Instruction for 1 month. Men with 20th Divl Sigs. released for work on forward area.	
	28th		Gas alert. 2nd Lt. Pickering proceeded to Divl. School of Instruction, Poperinghe.	
	29th		Major Hayes & Capt. Vick returned from leave. 40 men from 177th Tunnelling Coy returned. 30 men Divl. Guard returned for work	
	30th } 31st		Work as above. STRAND (C.4.b.) sheet 28. Work on this Trench is being expedited — cleared, drained, & Trench boards laid.	

Angus ? Collins Lieut Col. Comdg. XI [illegible]

11 D.L.I. Vol 11 June

Confidential.

War Diary
of
XIth (S) Bn Durham L. I.
(Pioneers)

from June 1st — 30th

Volume XII.

Instructions regarding War Diaries and Intelligence Summaries are contained in F. S. Regs., Part II. and the Staff Manual respectively. Title pages will be prepared in manuscript.

Vol. XII

~~WAR DIARY~~ ~~or~~

INTELLIGENCE SUMMARY.

(Erase heading not required.)

Army Form C. 2118.

XIth Durham L. I. (Pioneers)

Place	Date	Hour	Summary of Events and Information	Remarks and references to Appendices
BRANDHOEK sheet 28 G. 12. b.	1st 2nd 3rd		Progress of Work for week ending June 3rd.	
			STRAND. sheet 28. (I. 4. b.) 400^x cleared, drained + made passable. 500^x trenchboarded.	
			HAYMARKET. (I. 4. a. + b. + d) 30^x trench made secure; 6 tiers of sandbags laid.	
			Garden St. (C. 27. d. + 28 a). north side of parapet raised + banked up for distance of 70^x. South side: 9^x revetted with frames.	
			X 8 Extension. (C. 27. d.) Trench dug 50^x + 50 revetting frames put in.	
			Kaaie Salient. (I. 2. c.) 67 Revetting frames put in; opening back of traverse made.	
			West Lane. (I. 9. d. + 10 a + d. + 11 c). 70^x sandbagged 4 ft. high.	
			White Chateau (I. 10 c). 180^x old trench cleaned + deepened to 4 ft. 288 ft. wired. 100^x traverse trench deepened + new traverse cut 5 ft. deep.	
			Draft 30 men from Yorks. + Lanc. Regt. arrived.	
	2nd		S.O.S. sent out from H. 15. at 8.30 pm Cancelled at 9.13 pm	

Instructions regarding War Diaries and Intelligence Summaries are contained in F. S. Regs., Part II. and the Staff Manual respectively. Title pages will be prepared in manuscript.

WAR DIARY
or
INTELLIGENCE SUMMARY.
(*Erase heading not required.*)

Army Form C. 2118.

Place	Date	Hour	Summary of Events and Information	Remarks and references to Appendices
			Train for working parties leaves BRANDHOEK nightly at 8·30 p.m. for YPRES. Returns at 1·15 a.m.	
	4th		C.E. service (voluntary) 150 men attended.	
			Train not able to proceed beyond VLAMERTINGHE, consequently no work done by 3 Coys. 1 Coy. living in cellars in Ypres worked.	
	5th		Defence scheme prepared for L 8. (H.5. central). & L.4. (H.11. central)	
	6th		S.O.S. at 3·45 p.m. from A5. & H20. S.O.S. H.20 cancelled at 4·30 p.m. A5. SOS. cancelled at 10·15 p.m.	
	7th		Test S.O.S. sent out at 4 p.m.	
			Progress Report for week ending June 10th:	
			STRAND. 20 men worked on drainage by day: 120 men by night.	
			White Chateau. 50x trench deepened 3 ft 6 ins. & drained. Revetting frames fixed: stakes driven in.	
			West Lane. 200x of sandbag revetment 2 ft 6 ins. high built up on South side of trench. 50%. completed	
			Muddy Lane. H.21. (I 11 d. sheet 28) 250x new trench zigzag dug.	

1577 Wt. W10791/1773 500,000 1/15 D. D. & L. A.D.S.S./Forms/C. 2118.

Army Form C. 2118.

WAR DIARY
or
INTELLIGENCE SUMMARY.
(Erase heading not required.)

Instructions regarding War Diaries and Intelligence Summaries are contained in F. S. Regs., Part II. and the Staff Manual respectively. Title pages will be prepared in manuscript.

Place	Date	Hour	Summary of Events and Information	Remarks and references to Appendices
			X Line + Congreve Walk. (C. 28. c. + I. 4 a).	
			500x slits. (These require revetting).	
			X Line (C. 27. d. 5. 6) 25x revetted with frames.	
			West Lane — Potijze. 350x new trench dug: 4 ft. wide top 3' wide bottom.	
			Garden St. 70x parapet thickened & sandbagged on North side.	
			Kaaie Salient. 50x parapet + parados thickened + traverses put in.	
			2 entrances to traverses made + revetted.	
			110 men preparing place for gas cylinders working with 83rd + 84th Fd Coy.	
	13th	Noon	Memorial Service for Lord Kitchener, at Poperinghe.	
	14th		Daylight Saving Bill adopted here at 11 p.m.	
	16th		Capt. Scott & 2/Lt Rigby struck off strength of Bn. on being transferred to Machine Gun Coy. Grantham.	

Army Form C. 2118.

Instructions regarding War Diaries and Intelligence Summaries are contained in F. S. Regs., Part II. and the Staff Manual respectively. Title pages will be prepared in manuscript.

~~WAR DIARY~~

~~or~~

INTELLIGENCE SUMMARY.

(Erase heading not required.)

Place	Date	Hour	Summary of Events and Information	Remarks and references to Appendices
			Slits X 2. X 3. X 4. most of work done nullified by heavy rains. Drainage done. Repairing & starting C.I. revetment.	
			New X line (West Lane, southwards) 230x dug to a 3 ft. level. 75%. revetment completed. all excavated earth used for thickening. Parapet blinded.	
	18th		Capt. R.F. Higgons appointed O.C. Salvage Corps. 20th Div. Capt A.J.B Weare to 2nd Army.	
	24th		Wire cutting on 20th Divl. + Guards Divl. front. (Ypres salient).	
			Progress Report week ending 24th.	
			Haymarket day work. Preparation made for lowering trench boards. 2 drains made. Trench cleared at 3 falls. 250x deepened 2 ft. 6 ins. & drained. Parapet rebuilt 20x.	
			Garden St day + night work. Boards lowered for distance of 12x. Trench widened in 2 places. 5 drains widened & deepened. 220x deepened 2 ft. Trench repaired in 3 places demolished by shell fire.	
			Muddy Trench. Parapet built up with sandbags. 1 drain cleared, completely drained & deepend 2 ft. for 120x. 70x deepend 3 ft.	

Instructions regarding War Diaries and Intelligence Summaries are contained in F. S. Regs., Part II. and the Staff Manual respectively. Title pages will be prepared in manuscript.

WAR DIARY
or
INTELLIGENCE SUMMARY.
(Erase heading not required.)

Army Form C. 2118.

Place	Date	Hour	Summary of Events and Information	Remarks and references to Appendices
			X4. 44x revetted with C.I. + strutted. Hollow 5ft. long filled in for depth of 2 ft. 80x slits prepared for revetting.	
			Kaaie Salient. 3 exits completed 25x parados sandbagged + completed	
			X8 Extension (C.27.d.) 124 revetting hurdles placed in position + wired.	
			Slits X4. Much drainage to do. 64x revetted with C.I. 2 slits ready for revetment.	
			STrand. 40x trench deepened 18 ins. Obstructions removed + new cut to main drain made.	
			Further 80x cleared + deepened + trench boards lifted.	
			Another 150x cleared + drained – 10 trench boards raised + improved.	
	25th		Raid by 59th I B. on Salient C.29. central.	
	26th		No work owing to heavy shell fire.	
	27th		2nd Lt. E. R. B. Clough killed – shrapnel on St Jean Rd.	
	28th		Work as usual.	
	29th		No work except by 6 platoons living in Ypres or near.	
	30th		Work as usual	

[illegible signature]

1577 Wt. W10791/1773 500,000 1/15 D. D. & L. A.D.S.S./Forms/C. 2118.

Pioneers.
20th Div.

WAR
DIARY

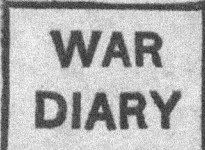

11th BATTN. THE DURHAM LIGHT INFANTRY.

J U L Y

1 9 1 6

Instructions regarding War Diaries and Intelligence Summaries are contained in F. S. Regs., Part II. and the Staff Manual respectively. Title pages will be prepared in manuscript.

Vol. 13.
July 1916

WAR DIARY or

INTELLIGENCE SUMMARY.

(Erase heading not required.)

11th Durham L. I. (Pioneers)

Army Form C. 2118.

Place	Date	Hour	Summary of Events and Information	Remarks and references to Appendices
BRANDHOEK.	July 1		2nd Lt. A. I. Ward + Sergt. McEvoy commence month's course at 2nd Army School, WISQUES.	
G.12.b. Sheet 28.	3.		New trench (CAVAN TRENCH) from WIELTZE FARM to CROSS RDS. (C.22.c. Sheet 28) dug 11 p.m. till 2 a.m. 640 men on the work: 400x trench dug 5 ft deep.	
	5th		2nd Lt. F. A Pickering appointed Bn. Grenade Officer vice 2nd Lt. Clough, killed.	
	8th		Weekly Progress Report of Work done.	
			X.8 line. (C.27.d. sheet 28) 70x revetted. One box drain fitted.	
			X.2 + 3. 2 slits completed - 60x. 20x - 50% completed.	
			Garden St (C.27.d. + 28a. sheet 28) Lowered 50x trench, 22x cleaned, + new boards laid; 10x parapet heightened 1 foot. 4x revetment renewed + trench thereby widened. 30x trench boards lowered 2 ft.	
			STRAND. (I.4.b + d sheet 28) 170x damaged trench cleared, cleaned + drained.	
			Mud Trench. 158 revetting frames placed, of which 82 were wired back. 2 frames repaired. 45x old fire-step removed. 50x trench cleaned. 20x drain deepened. Drainage kept in good order nightly.	

1577 Wt. W10791/1773 500,000 1/15 D. D. & L. A.D.S.S./Forms/C. 2118.

Instructions regarding War Diaries and Intelligence Summaries are contained in F. S. Regs., Part II. and the Staff Manual respectively. Title pages will be prepared in manuscript.

Vol. 13.

July 1916.

~~WAR DIARY~~ or INTELLIGENCE SUMMARY.

(Erase heading not required.)

XI Durham L. I. (Pioneers).

Place	Date	Hour	Summary of Events and Information	Remarks and references to Appendices
			HAYMARKET. (I. 4. a. + b. + d) sheet 28. 150x trench boards lowered, revetting frames over same distance strutted at bottom to prevent collapse; 80x trench cleaned + drained; 25x trench revetted	
			CAVAN Trench. approximately 430x dug to depth of 5ft 25x drained lowered 1ft. 5x drain dug 3ft. deep. 3 firebays cleared out by day for revetting. 31 revetting frames placed, 21 wired, 18 strutted.	
			Kaaie Salient (I 2 c. sheet 28). 8 exit completed 30x trench cleared.	
			West Lane. (I. 9. d. and 11. c. and 10. a + d sheet 28) Daily trench patrol employed on drainage + small repair work. 50x parapet heightened, average of 5 layers + thickened. Trench boards repaired + parapet repaired where blown in	
			New X Line. (C. 27. d. to C. 10. d.) sheet 28.	
			Section I. Digging of trench completed. Firesteps + trench boards laid. 15 firebays revetted in front. 2 new drains commenced + drainage of whole trench completed.	
			Section 2. 220x trench enlarged as follows:– Firebays 4' 3" x 3' 3" x 4' 6" Traverses 3' 6" x 2' 6" x 4' 6"	

1577 Wt. W10791/1773 500,000 1/15 D. D. & L. A.D.S.S./Forms/C. 2118.

Instructions regarding War Diaries and Intelligence Summaries are contained in F. S. Regs., Part II. and the Staff Manual respectively. Title pages will be prepared in manuscript.

Vol 13.
July 1916.

~~WAR DIARY~~ or INTELLIGENCE SUMMARY.

(Erase heading not required.)

XI D.L.I.
(Pioneers)

Place	Date	Hour	Summary of Events and Information	Remarks and references to Appendices
			Section 3. 300x drained: water lowered by 1 ft.	
			Section 4. 250x trench drained. 150x trench boards laid temporarily + 200 ft. fire-steps put in	
	10th		No work tonight – demonstration etc. raid by 59th I.B.	
	14th		H.R.H. The Prince of Wales visited Bn. HQ.	
	15th		All Coys. (less 150 men at L8. + at L4) now in billets at BRANDHOEK. No work done on CAVAN Trench last night – working parties not permitted there on account of operations.	
			Casualties in this sector of YPRES SALIENT – May 20th – July 16th.	
			Officers 1 Killed.	
			O.R. 1 Killed 45 wounded.	
			Evacuated Sick. Officers 1. O.R. 43.	
			Casualties since embarkation:	
			Officers 1 Killed 3 wounded.	
			O.R. 38 Killed 153 wounded.	
			Weekly Progress Report on Work.	
			X 2 + 3. 75x slits dug + revetted.	
			X 8 (extension). (C.27.d.7.9) Sheet 28. 40x trench revetted.	

1577 Wt. W10791/1773 500,000 1/15 D. D. & L. A.D.S.S./Forms/C. 2118.

Instructions regarding War Diaries and Intelligence Summaries are contained in F. S. Regs., Part II. and the Staff Manual respectively. Title pages will be prepared in manuscript.

or

INTELLIGENCE SUMMARY.

(Erase heading not required.)

Place	Date	Hour	Summary of Events and Information	Remarks and references to Appendices
			Kaaie Salient. 50^x trench revetted. 30^x parapet repaired. 150^x trench boards laid. 14 exits completed.	
			Strand. 150^x drain cleared & deepened	
			Cavan Trench. 14 firebays revetted. 198 frames & pickets carried to B 13.	
			West Lane. 30^x parapet heightened & thickened – repaired in 5 places.	
			Mud Trench 9 firebays completed, including sandbagging.	
			New X Line. 230 revetting frames fixed & wired. 1000 sandbags filled & laid. 100^x drain deepened 1ft. 6ins. 25 firebays revetted & sandbagged. Nos. 2 & 3 drains deepened 1ft. for distance of 40^x. No. 1 dug 10ft deep for 40^x. 15 traverses revetted. 150^x trench boards fixed on pickets & transoms.	
			Haymarket. Repaired 100^x trench boards.	
	16th		Bn. (less 150 men) moved by train to WINNEZEELE (J. 17. a. sheet 27)	
	17th, 18th		Training in rest billets. Physical Training, section, Platoon & Coy. Drill.	
	19th		Left Winnezeele at 4 p.m. Arrived M Camp at 7 p.m.	
	20th		Left M Camp 8 a.m. arrived 24th Div School (3 miles East of BALLIEUL at 4 p.m.	

1577 Wt. W10791/1773 500,000 1/15 D. D. & L. A.D.S.S./Forms/C. 2118.

Instructions regarding War Diaries and Intelligence Summaries are contained in F. S. Regs., Part II. and the Staff Manual respectively. Title pages will be prepared in manuscript.

or

INTELLIGENCE SUMMARY.

(Erase heading not required.)

Place	Date	Hour	Summary of Events and Information	Remarks and references to Appendices
	21st. 22nd.		Training contd.	
	23rd		Left School (S.17.b. sheet 28) at 11 a.m. arrived St SYLVESTRE CAPEL (P.17.a) at 4 p.m.	sheet 27
	25th		marched to BAVINCHOVE STATION – entrained for DOULLENS – arrived too late for billets – bivouaced.	
	26th.		marched to COUIN – arrived 7.30 p.m. Billets consist of huts in a filthy condition.	
	27th		Day spent cleaning huts & grounds.	
	28th		Left COUIN for THE DELL (J.17.a. 8.2. sheet 57d). Relieved 19th Bn. Welsh Fusiliers (Pioneers). The dirtiest camp we have yet struck.	
	29th		Officers visit front line + Blue Line + work to be taken over.	
	30. 31st		Coys. commenced work on Blue Line K.34.d.3.1 to K.16.c.0.5. sheet 57 D. Left camp at 5 a.m. Returned at 1 p.m.	

Angus E Collingwood Lt/Col
Offr. Cdg. 1st Batn. ??? (Pioneers)

1577 Wt. W10791/1773 500,000 1/15 D. D. & L. A.D.S.S./Forms/C. 2118.

20th Divisional Troops.

PIONEERS

11th BATTALION

DURHAM LIGHT INFANTRY

AUGUST 1 9 1 6

Instructions regarding War Diaries and Intelligence Summaries are contained in F. S. Regs., Part II. and the Staff Manual respectively. Title pages will be prepared in manuscript.

WAR DIARY
or
INTELLIGENCE SUMMARY.
(Erase heading not required.)

Army Form C. 2118.

11. Durham

Vol 13

Place	Date	Hour	Summary of Events and Information	Remarks and references to Appendices
THE DELL	1.8.16	.	Companies employed repairing support lines and constructing deep dugouts.	
" "	2.8.16	.	" " " "	
" "	3.8.16	.	Companies employed on "deep dugouts", "the improvement of support lines" was continued.	→ Killed O.R 3, Wounded O.R 4
" "	4.8.16	.	Smoke demonstration on 61st Bde front, work of Companies suspended till 10 PM. O.C. 'B' Coy to Hospital. (Capt Pemberton)	
" "	5.8.16	.	No working parties at night. ~~Much cooler all day~~	
" "	6.8.16	.	Church parade. Work at night on dugouts.	
" "	7.8.16	.	Work as usual on dugouts and support line. Lieut Cunningham to hospital.	
" "	8.8.16	.	Bombardment of German wire and trenches opposite our line. D.C.L.I carrying party attached	
" "	9.8.16	.	9 dugouts completed, trenches deepened and improved.	
" "	10.8.16	.	Heavy bombardment by German Batteries during the night. Work as usual for 4 Companies	
" "	11.8.16	.	" " " " Trench Mortars. Two Officers returned from Hospital.	
" "	12.8.16	.	Work carried on by 4 Companies. One Officer (Lieut Lloyd) to Hospital. One Officer proceeds on a course of instruction (Lt Joe)	
" "	13.8.16	.	Work on trenches suspended. Dugouts in the DELL commenced. Church parade at 3 PM.	
" "	14.8.16	.	Under orders for ORVILLE. Work on trenches carried out as usual.	
" "	15.8.16	.	Work on support trenches carried out.	
" "	16.8.16	.	Battalion marched to ORVILLE, no men fell out during the march of 11 miles	
ORVILLE	17.8.16	.	Cleaning equipment & billets and bathing parade.	
"	18.8.16	.	Battalion marched to BERNEUIL. Good billets, no men fell out during the march.	
BERNEUIL	19.8.16	.	Physical training & Bayonet fighting. Transport left by road for NAOURS.	
"	20.8.16	.	Battalion marched to CANDAS station, to entrain enroute to MORLANCOURT, ~~at 3 PM~~ & arrived 3 PM	

1577 Wt. W10791/1773 500,000 1/15 D. D. & L. A.D.S.S./Forms/C. 2118.

Instructions regarding War Diaries and Intelligence Summaries are contained in F. S. Regs., Part II. and the Staff Manual respectively. Title pages will be prepared in manuscript.

WAR DIARY
or
INTELLIGENCE SUMMARY.
(*Erase heading not required.*)

Army Form C. 2118.

Place	Date	Hour	Summary of Events and Information	Remarks and references to Appendices
MORLANCOURT	21.8.16	–	Marched from MORLANCOURT to the CITADEL between FRICOURT & BRAY. The men of the BN made their own bivouac's out of empty shell boxes. One Officer to machine gun Corps. (Capt Leeson)	
CITADEL	22.8.16		Moved into Bivouac's near CARNOY previous to taking over from Notts & Derby Pioneers	
TRENCHES	23.8.16		Moved into Old German front line. Dugouts knocked about a lot on 1st July. OR Killed 1. Wounded 1 C.O and one other Officer reconnoitred ground near GUILLEMONT. 3 Companies digging trenches.	
"	24.8.16		~~Battalion in rest. Artillery demonstration in connection with operations by 4th Army~~ Brigade to connect captured positions with front line. Two Companies Divisional Reserve.	
"	25.8.16		14th Division on our left successful in taking their first objective last night. S.O.S gas at 7.50 PM Cancelled 10 PM 3 Companies digging and improving trenches. German Captain captured.	Wounded OR 9.
"	26.8.16		Four Companies working all night on trenches.	
"	27.8.16		" " " " " " " New communication trench dug.	
"	28.8.16		Batteries near Bn H Quarters shelled last night. Trenches widened and deepened, 3 Companies out on the work.	
"	29.8.16		Very wet day, all work suspended, roads almost impassable, dugouts falling in	
"	30.8.16		Very wet and cold, all work suspended. Artillery very active all day.	
"	31.8.16		Fine bright day. Great activity in the air. German Artillery shelled Batteries near our lines. ~~A busy day with Artillery~~. British Artillery replied strongly to German fire	

1577 Wt. W10791/1773 500,000 1/15 D. D. & L. A.D.S.S./Forms/C. 2118.

To
A. Q.
20th Division

I forward herewith War Diary for month of August 1916. The C.O. & Adjutant are both sick. The diary for the month of September will be more fully recorded.

G. Hayes. Major
Commdg XIth Durham L.I.
(Pioneers)

31/8/16

@200 20th Divisional Troops

11th BATTALION

DURHAM LIGHT INFANTRY (Pioneers)

SEPTEMBER 1 9 1 6

D 174

Headquarters

20th Division

I forward herewith War Diary for September 1916. The delay in sending this in is regretted but was unavoidable owing to continual moves and lack of office accomodation in the trench.

G. Hayes Major

2/10/1916

Comdg 11th D L I Pioneers

Instructions regarding War Diaries and Intelligence Summaries are contained in F. S. Regs., Part II. and the Staff Manual respectively. Title pages will be prepared in manuscript.

WAR DIARY
or
~~INTELLIGENCE SUMMARY.~~
(Erase heading not required.)

Army Form C. 2118.

P/70

14

Place	Date	Hour	Summary of Events and Information	Remarks and references to Appendices
In TRENCHES	31.8.16	6 PM	4 Companies proceeded to work. A Coy under the O.C. 96th F Coy R.E. B & C Companies under the orders of O.C. 11 ELS	
	1.9.16		and D Coy under orders 83rd Coy RE. Casualties night of 31st O.R. Died of Wounds 2. Wounded 9.	
		6 AM	Bright clear morning. British Heavy generally active during the day.	
		6 PM	A & B Companies worked with Right Brigade. C & D Companies with Left Brigade	
			Casualties: Lieut J.H. Marples Wounded, Gas. O. Ranks. Killed 1. Wounded 9.	
" "	2.9.16	6 AM	Fine morning. British Heavy Artillery commenced fire at 8 AM and continued all day. Great activity in the Air	
		6 PM	Work carried out same as night of 1st. Casualties O. Ranks, Wounded 4.	
" "	3.9.16	6 AM	The morning opened fine but cloudy. British Heavies continuing their fire from 8 AM yesterday. Very great Number of British Aircraft up, also Kite Balloons.	
		8 AM	Battalion marched out for operations. A Coy working with 59th Brigade. 'D' Coy with 47th Brigade	
			B. C & HQ Companies in Reserve at BERNAFAY WOOD. Only sick men in camp.	
			A Coy were employed in consolidating positions and making strong points, they went out at Zero hour + 10 the Company worked all day and night. D Company moved to Guillemont at ZERO + 2 hours and assisted 47th (Irish) Brigade to consolidate, worked all the afternoon and most of the night.	
			B & C Companies worked with 84th F Coy R.E at about 7.30 PM, they carried wire etc, dug a new trench east of GUILLEMONT Station and cleared old German trench for communication trench to new front line. Casualties, Lieut W.A. CUNNINGHAM, very slightly wounded. O R 20 Wounded + 4 Missing.	
	4.9.16	5.AM.	The C.O went with Capt V POLLOCK to 1st objective gained after 3rd and found 'A' Company assembling there. Shell fire very heavy. found 5 wounded men in SUNKEN Rd. Men of A Coy were hit by shell fire. No water for men and no stretchers. C.O & Capt Pollock left 2/Lieut WARD digging in with 2 Platoons of A Coy. C.O. returned and reported to C.R.E and then received orders to send 2 Companies to BRIQUETERIE. 12-45 PM C.O & Major LLOYD proceeded to Brigade H.Q at BRIQUETERIE	
		~~12.45~~ PM	B-C Companies H.Q ~~with~~ Lewis Guns moved off at 2.15 PM for BRIQUETERIE	
		1 PM	C.O. went with RSM and Orderlies to front line and reported to Col White in Command. Enemy barraging fairly heavy during afternoon. Received orders to bring the 2 Companies up at dusk	
		9.30 PM	~~Orders sent to~~ Major Lloyd who had remained with 2 Companies near ARROW HEAD COPSE arrived and again received instructions to guide B & C Companies to front line and assist Infantry to consolidate near LEUZE WOOD. At 1-30 AM Major Lloyd and 2 Platoons 'C' Company arrived in front line remainder had lost touch and arrived in support line. Brigade was relieved and the Battalion returned to CRATERS about 6 AM 5th Sept. Casualties Captains POLLOCK & Pemberton Lieut Cunningham on sick list from 1 PM 4th. Lieut Robertson 2/Lt Stubbs and Ward Wounded. O.R Killed 3. Wounded 52 Missing 1.	

1577 Wt. W10791/1773 500,000 1/15 D. D. & L. A.D.S.S./Forms/C. 2118.

Instructions regarding War Diaries and Intelligence Summaries are contained in F. S. Regs., Part II. and the Staff Manual respectively. Title pages will be prepared in manuscript.

WAR DIARY
or
~~INTELLIGENCE~~ SUMMARY.
(*Erase heading not required.*)

Army Form C. 2118.

Place	Date	Hour	Summary of Events and Information	Remarks and references to Appendices
CRATERS	5.9.16	6 AM	Companies resting all the morning. Lieut C. Palmer assumed command of "A" Company, 2/Lieut Wardle placed 2nd C.O. "A" Coy. No work at night. Expecting to go into rest on 7th	
"	6.9.16	6 AM	Resting all day. Capt G. Vick placed on Sick list. Lt A Floyd assumed Command of "D" Company	
Bois-de-Tailles	7.9.16	9 PM	Battalion marched here from CRATERS, arriving at 7-30 PM. All ranks slept in a field, no shelters.	
"	8.9.16	6 AM	Battalion preparing to march to MERICOURT. Marched out at 2.15 PM, arrived MERICOURT at 5-15 PM. ~~[illegible]~~ [illegible] No billets. 100 shelters arrived at 7.30 PM. Bivouaced out in Cornfield.	
MERICOURT	9.9.16	6 AM	General clean up of Equipment. Men paid and allowed into the town for 4 hours.	
"	10.9.16	6 AM	Church parade at 10 AM. G.O.C Division addressed the 61st Brigade, also the Battalion, on the good work done. Bathing in the afternoon and a general holiday.	
"	11.9.16	10 AM	Battalion out under C.O for 4 hours practicing the attack etc. 5PM C.O. lectured Officers and N.C.O's	
"	12.9.16	8 AM	Cleaning camp and getting ready to move away. Marched out at 2.15 PM for Sand Pits and arrived at 4-30 PM. 11 O.Ranks arrived from Base.	
SAND PITS	13.9.16	8 AM	Physical Drill. Maps checked by C.O. Machine Gun Carts arrived. BN ready to move away.	
" "	13.9.16	11.15 PM	Orders arrived for working party 300 strong for Road making	
" "	14.9.16	6 AM	Working party for Road making marched out. C.O inspected Company Wagons at 10 AM	
" "	14.9.16	2 PM	Battalion marched out to CITADEL arriving at 4.15 PM. Conference at C.R.E's 6 PM. BN in hutments	
CITADEL	15.9.16	8 AM	BN getting ready to march out. 12-55 PM marched out strong as possible in Battle order, for TALUS BOIS 2 days rations carried, BN stayed night at TALUS BOIS. No shelters or dugouts.	
TALUS BOIS	16.9.16	6 AM	Battalion standing too. 10 PM still standing too.	
" "	17.9.16	5 AM	Battalion marched away by Companies to BERNAFAY WOOD, accomodated in trenches and a few dugouts. A+B Coys worked on repair of Roads during the afternoon, tracks to TRONES WOOD made very good. A strong party of D Coy worked under the 96th Fld Coy R.E. C Coy worked under the R.E's Casualties 3 men "C" Coy badly wounded by striking a bomb or shell whilst digging in	

Instructions regarding War Diaries and Intelligence Summaries are contained in F. S. Regs., Part II. and the Staff Manual respectively. Title pages will be prepared in manuscript.

WAR DIARY
or
~~INTELLIGENCE~~ SUMMARY.

(Erase heading not required.)

Army Form C. 2118.

Place	Date	Hour	Summary of Events and Information	Remarks and references to Appendices
BERNAFAY WOOD	18/9/16	6 PM	Four Companies = 440 all ranks employed making assembly trenches west of LESBOEUFS. A good nights work mentioned. Party worked all night. Casualties = O.R. Killed 1. Wounded 9.	
"	19/9/16	6 PM	Companies completed work commenced on 18th. All ranks did their utmost to finish the work. 2 men wounded accidentally.	
"	20/9/16	8 Am	Roads in vicinity of Wood shelled. C&D Companies had to move out of their lines. 150 men only working at night.	
		6 PM	Battalion less 150 men marched out to Sand Pits and arrived 12 PM. Officers arrived, 2/Lieuts P. KEMP - J. LIDDELL - R BUSHELL - W. INGLIS - & F. FILLINGHAM. Casualties O.R Killed 2. Wounded 13.	
SAND PITS	21.9.16	7 AM	150 all ranks arrived from BERNAFAY Wood. Draft of 8 O.R. arrived. 9 to 12 cleaning equipment etc.	
" "	22.9.16	8 AM	1 Officer & 80 O.R. on Fatigue at Rail Head. Battalion marched out at 12/30 for billets in ~~M~~	
MEAULTE	" "	1 PM	MEAULTE arriving at 1 PM. Remainder of day spent cleaning up dirty billets.	
"	23.9.16		320 Officers and O.R proceeded to CARNOY at 1-15 PM for Road making. Remainder of BN cleaning Equipment	
"	24.9.16	8 AM	1 Officer & 80 men working at RE Dump. 10 AM Church Parade for remainder. Remainder of day a holiday.	
"	25.9.16	8 AM	D Coy on Physical drill. 80 O.R 1 officer at RE Dump. 4.40 D Coy & Details marched to Citadel arriving 6 PM.	
CITADEL	26.9.16	8 AM	D Coy and Details marched to MALTZ HORN Valley. 10.30 AM Picked up CARNOY party en route	
MALTZ HORN Valley	26.9.16	1/30 PM	Battalion arrived from CITADEL. Lieut A Brown & 2 Lt G Dennes joined BN.	
"	27.9.16	8 Am	Cleaning trenches and improving lines. 12-30 to 4-30 PM Battalion repairing track from GINCHY towards MORVAL. 5-30 PM BN marched out for TALUS BOISE and arrived at 7-30 PM. No shelters, rain. Camped in a field. Lieut W. SEARS arrived	
TALUS BOISE	28.9.16	8 AM	Cleaning Camp and erecting shelters & tents. 45 O.R arrived.	
" "	29.9.16	3/45 PM	Marched out for camp near TRONES Wood and arrived 5/20 PM. Only trenches and shell holes.	
TRONES Wood	30/9/16	2 PM	Battalion commenced to march out, by Platoons, for WATERLOT FARM and 3rd line trenches all settled in by dark. H.Q. & 2 Companies in 3rd line trenches. Very few dugouts. C&D Companies at WATERLOT FARM	
"	"	7 PM	Artillery fairly active on both sides.	

20th Divisional Troops

11th BATTALION

DURHAM LIGHT INFANTRY (Pioneers)

OCTOBER 1 9 1 6

vol 15

11th D. L. I.

Instructions regarding War Diaries and Intelligence Summaries are contained in F. S. Regs., Part II. and the Staff Manual respectively. Title pages will be prepared in manuscript.

WAR DIARY
~~or~~
~~INTELLIGENCE SUMMARY.~~
(*Erase heading not required.*)

Army Form C. 2118.

Place	Date	Hour	Summary of Events and Information	Remarks and references to Appendices
TATLER TRENCH	1.10.16	6 AM	Companies improving accomodation. 11 AM Instruction to Officers on work to be done at night.	
"	"	6 PM	Companies proceeded to work on new Trench. 10 PM Gas shells sent over by the Enemy.	
"	2.10.16	5 PM	A & B Companies proceeded to complete work commenced on the 1st. C & D Companies did not reach their work owing to fault of R.E. Guide. Heavy shelling all night.	
"	3.10.16	9 AM	C.O. went out to hill South of GUEUDECOURT and inspected new Trench dug on 1st & 2nd. No Work at night for Companies. Lieut. A. Brown and 2/Lt F. Pickering admitted to Hospital	
"	4.10.16	5 PM	Companies proceeded to dig an assembly trench. "A & C" Coy worked with 61st Brigade "B & D" with 60th Brigade. All work carried out very well. 2/Lieut. C. Grimshaw sent to Rest Station. Casualties. Killed. O.R. 7. Wounded. O.R. 21	
"	5.10.16	11 AM	"A" Coy left for MONTABAN to join 14th Corps Pioneer Group. 6 PM. 3 Companies proceeded to work and were employed improving newly dug Trenches, making fire steps and a new BN. Headquarters. 7.20 PM S.O.S sent out from 60th Brigade front, Cancelled at 8.10 PM. Casualties. Killed O.R. 1. Wounded O.R. 10.	
"	6.10.16	7 AM	C.O. inspected work done on 5th. "C" Coy came into TATLER TRENCH from WATER LOT FARM at 5 PM. 2 O.R died and were buried at BERNAFAY WOOD. Wounded O.R. 2.	

Instructions regarding War Diaries and Intelligence Summaries are contained in F. S. Regs., Part II. and the Staff Manual respectively. Title pages will be prepared in manuscript.

WAR DIARY
or
~~INTELLIGENCE SUMMARY.~~
(Erase heading not required.)

Army Form C. 2118.

Place	Date	Hour	Summary of Events and Information	Remarks and references to Appendices
TATLER TRENCH	7-10.16	2 AM	"C" Coy moved out to LEEK TRENCH and remained there till 5 PM, the Company were heavily shelled. 5 PM the Coy joined up with the R.E^s for work on new position. B & D Companies employed on new dugouts and Aid posts. Casualties, Killed O.R. 4. Wounded O.R. 28	
" "	8.10.16	2 AM	"C" Coy marched out to WATERLOT FARM. Owing to excellent work done on night of 7th other 2 Coys did not work at night and were relieved. 1 PM "C" Coy marched from WATERLOT FARM to billets in MEAULTE. 3 PM 'B' & 'D' Coys commenced moving to WATERLOT FARM by Platoons. 4 PM S.O.S received. Cancelled at 4-30 PM. 6 PM all at Waterlot Farm.	
WATERLOT FARM	9-10-16 7 AM	7 AM	H.Q. and 2 Companies marched out enroute to billets in MEAULTE and arrived at 12 noon. 2/Lieut Kemp and 24 O.R^s remained at BERNAFAY WOOD for work with C.R.E.	
MEAULTE	10.10.16		A day of rest and cleaning up. Men paid out. 'C' Coy went to baths.	
"	11.10.16	9 AM	Cleaning and inspecting equipment. 2-30 to 4 PM Battalion drill under the C.O.	
"	12.10.16	8-30 AM	Physical drill. 9-30 AM to 2 PM 2 Companies at Baths in VILLE. 2-30 PM to 3-30 PM Battalion drill. 6 PM 2/Lt Kemp and 24 men joined from BERNAFAY WOOD.	
"	13.10.16	9 AM	Corps Commander inspected 61st Brigade and 11th K.L.I. Battalion received very hearty Congratulations from Corps Commander on the excellent work done since the Division came to the SOMME. BN marched past on conclusion of inspection	

T2134. Wt. W708—776. 500000. 4/15. Sir J. C. & S.

Instructions regarding War Diaries and Intelligence Summaries are contained in F. S. Regs., Part II. and the Staff Manual respectively. Title pages will be prepared in manuscript.

WAR DIARY
or
INTELLIGENCE SUMMARY.
(Erase heading not required.)

Army Form C. 2118.

Place	Date	Hour	Summary of Events and Information	Remarks and references to Appendices
MEAULTE	14.10.16	9 to 12 AM	Physical drill – Platoon drill and Company drill	
"	15.10.16	11/30 AM	H.Q. and 3 Companies marched out for new billets in VILLE. on arrival at 12/45 AM it was found that no billets were vacant so the BN marched on to TREUX arriving at 1-30 PM.	
"	"	6 PM	Lieut-Col Collins returned from sick leave and took over command of the BN.	
TREUX	16.10.16	8 AM	Order received to march back to VILLE owing to billets at TREUX being required for H.Q. 8th Division. 2 PM marched out 3 PM arrived VILLE.	
VILLE	7.10.16	9 to 12 AM	Physical training and inspection by Commanding Officer.	
"	18.10.16	6 AM	Orders received for BN to move to CITADEL. 11 AM marched out. arrived 1/30 PM	
CITADEL	19/10/16	8 AM	3 Companies moved off for work on Roads – Railway etc, 5 different groups working under orders of C E 14th Corps. Heavy rain all day. Men soaked	
"	20/10/16	8 AM	3 Companies working under C.E. as for 19-10-16. Fine day. Frosty	
"	21/10/16	8 AM	3 Companies working as for 19th 20th. Frosty.	
"	22/10/16	8 AM	3 Companies working as for 19th 20th & 21st. 20 O.R. went to GINCHY for mining work.	
"	23/10/16	8 AM	3 Companies working as before. Fine day.	
"	24/10/16	8 AM	Work as before. Very dull slight rain at night.	
"	25/10/16	8 AM	" " " Very wet and cold. 4 men repairing huts in camp.	

Army Form C. 2118.

Instructions regarding War Diaries and Intelligence Summaries are contained in F. S. Regs., Part II. and the Staff Manual respectively. Title pages will be prepared in manuscript.

WAR DIARY

~~or~~

~~INTELLIGENCE SUMMARY~~.

(*Erase heading not required.*)

Place	Date	Hour	Summary of Events and Information	Remarks and references to Appendices
CITIDAL	26 10/16	8 Am	3 Companies working, under orders of C.E. 14th Corps, Repairing Roads and Railway generally fine day. C.O inspected work being done by Companies	
"	27 10/16	8 Am	3 Companies worked as for 26th	
"	28 10/16	8 Am	3 " " " " 27th. C.O Visited 'A' Coy at MONTAUBAN.	
			2/Lt Dennis detained in Hospital	
"	29 10/16	8 Am	Companies on same work, Roads etc, A beastly day, Very cold winds and Rain men very wet returning from work.	
"	30 10/16	8 Am	Companies started for work as usual but very little done owing to Violent Rain and Wind storm, men very wet but cheerful. C.O. proceeded to H.Q. of Division to confer with G.O.C.	
"	31 10/16	8 am till 12 Noon	Bright morning, strong wind. Camp thick with mud. Companies went out to work on Roads etc.	
		12 Noon	Diary closed	

Angus Collins Lt Col OC 14th [illegible] (Pioneers)

T2134. Wt. W708—776. 500000. 4/15. Sir J. C. & S.

D 245.

Headquarters

20th Division.

I beg to forward attached War Diary for month of October 1916.

Angus R Collins

Lieut Col

Comdg 11th D.L.I.

Pioneers

31 10/1916

Despatched to D.R.L.S. 12 Noon

20th Divisional Troops

PIONEERS

11th BATTALION

DURHAM LIGHT INFANTRY

NOVEMBER 1 9 1 6

Instructions regarding War Diaries and Intelligence Summaries are contained in F. S. Regs., Part II. and the Staff Manual respectively. Title pages will be prepared in manuscript.

WAR DIARY
or
~~INTELLIGENCE~~ SUMMARY.
(Erase heading not required.)

Army Form C. 2118.

Vol 16

Place	Date	Hour	Summary of Events and Information	Remarks and references to Appendices
CITIDAL	31.10.16	7 Pm	Reinforcements arrived, 80 O.R.	
"	1.11.16	11 Am	Battalion marched out and entrained at EDGEHILL Rail head, train left for SAILEUX at 5-30 PM and arrived at 9 PM, no billets available owing to being in French Area, men bivouaced for night. 2/Lt Hopkinson Sick	
SAILEUX	2.11.16	7 Am	Battalion marched out for BOURDON, 16 mile march, arrived at 3 PM, rather a bad day for a march owing to rain and bad roads.	
BOURDON	3.11.16		The day spent in cleaning equipment and billets. G.O.C Called and saw part of the billets. Men generally comfortable.	
BOURDON	4.11.16	7 Am	Physical Training. 9-30 to 12 noon Company Drill. Major Hayes returned from leave	
"	5.11.16		Church Parades. R.C.s at 10 Am. C of E.s at 11.30 Am.	
"	6.11.16	7 Am	Physical Training. 9 to 12 noon Field training and lectures. 2/Lt Philips returned from leave. Order received that we move on the 8th Nov.	
"	7.11.16	7 Am	Physical Training. 9 to 12 noon Company drill. Reinforcements 20 O.R. arrived.	
"	8.11.16	9 Am	Battalion marched out for PICQUIGNY and arrived at 11 Am, the afternoon was spent in cleaning up dirty billets lately occupied by Anzacs.	
PICQUIGNY	9.11.16		Physical Training and instruction under Company Commanders till 3-30 Pm	

[illegible]

T2134. Wt. W708—776. 500000. 4/15. Sir J. C. & S.

Instructions regarding War Diaries and Intelligence Summaries are contained in F. S. Regs., Part II. and the Staff Manual respectively. Title pages will be prepared in manuscript.

WAR DIARY
~~or~~
~~INTELLIGENCE SUMMARY.~~
(Erase heading not required.)

Army Form C. 2118.

Place	Date	Hour	Summary of Events and Information	Remarks and references to Appendices
PICQUIGNY	10.11.16	7 Am	Physical Training, and Baths till 4 PM Platoon drill.	
"	11.11.16	9 Am	Battalion drill. Rev WALTON joined.	
"	12.11.16	10 Am	Church Parade, remainder of day a holiday	
"	13.11.16	10 Am	Battalion drill. 2-30 PM Inspection by G. O. C. 4th Army.	
"	14.11.16	7 Am	Physical Training. 9 to 11 Platoon drill. 11 till 4 PM Battalion Sports.	
"	15.11.16	9 Am	Company Parades. 2 till 5 PM final of Battalion Sports.	
"	16.11.16	8 Am	Transport marched out for CORBIE. 9 Am Battalion embussed for CORBIE and arrived at 1 PM. Transport arrived at 4 PM. Very dirty billets.	
CORBIE	17.11.16		Training programme continued till 4 PM.	
"	18.11.16		A very wet day, Lectures and indoor work till 12.30 PM	
"	19.11.16	10 Am	Church Parade, remainder of day a holiday	
"	20.11.16	7/30 Am	Physical Training. 9-30 to Noon Field Training by Companies. 2 PM Commenced to change billets so as to get better accomodation.	
"	21.11.16	7/30 Am	Physical Training. 9-30 to 12-30 Am Bayonet fighting. 2-30 to 3-30 PM Lectures	
"	22.11.16	9 Am	200 men working under order of CRE remainder of Battalion on drill and musketry. Lt Wardle returned from leave. Capt PALMER went on leave.	

A. J. A. Collins Lt Col
OC X1 [illegible]

T2134. Wt. W708—776. 500000. 4/15. Sir J. C. & S.

Army Form C. 2118.

Instructions regarding War Diaries and Intelligence Summaries are contained in F. S. Regs., Part II. and the Staff Manual respectively. Title pages will be prepared in manuscript.

WAR DIARY
or
~~INTELLIGENCE~~ SUMMARY.

(*Erase heading not required.*)

Place	Date	Hour	Summary of Events and Information	Remarks and references to Appendices
CORBIE	23-11-16	9 Am	150 Men working under C.R.E. Remainder of Battalion on Company drill and Bombing.	
"	24-11-16	9 Am	Battalion on drill less 200 men working under the C.R.E. Orders received that we move to CITADEL.	
CITADEL	25-11-16	3 Pm	Battalion arrived from CORBIE, heavy rain all the way, men very wet and cold. huts very wet and all leaking. Camp inches thick in mud	
"	26-11-16	9 Am	Commenced to move out by Companies for MONTABAN, another wet march, took over shelters from 18th BN Middlesex Regt.	
MONTAUBAN	27-11-16	8 Am	3 Companies proceeded to work under RE's constructing a light railway. 1 Company worked in Camp draining and generally improving bad accomodation	
"	28-11-16	8 AM	3 Companies proceeded to work under R.E.s. as above 1. Coy remainded in Camp, and worked on track leading into Camp. Orders received from "Q" 14 Corps to move Camp to A 4 a central.	
"	29-11-16	8 AM	3 Companies as above. 1 Coy remained behind to load Wagons and clean Camp. New Camp taken over 11. AM Transport moved off to new Camp. Dug outs filthy. Road into Camp practically impassable to Transport	

August [illegible] Lt Col
O.C. 11th DLI

T2134. Wt. W708–776. 500000. 4/15. Sir J. C. & S.

D333.
H.Q.

20th Division.

Herewith War Diary for Month of November 1916.

[signature]

Lt. Col.
Comdg. XI D.L.I.

29/11 1916.

20th Divisional Troops.

11th BATTALION

DURHAM LIGHT INFANTRY (Pioneers)

DECEMBER 1 9 1 6

Instructions regarding War Diaries and Intelligence Summaries are contained in F. S. Regs., Part II. and the Staff Manual respectively. Title pages will be prepared in manuscript.

December 1916

WAR DIARY

~~or~~

~~INTELLIGENCE~~ SUMMARY.

(Erase heading not required.)

Army Form C. 2118.

~~Volume XI~~ 18 DL 1

Vol 17

Place	Date	Hour	Summary of Events and Information	Remarks and references to Appendices
	Dec.			
Montauban	1.	9a.m.	4 Coys. out working under R.E. (84 men per Coy.) Remainder working on dugouts preparing footpaths out of camp, & a track into camp for transport. Foot inspection by M.O.	
	2.		Major H.P. Lloyd returned from Hospital & assumed appointment as 2nd in command. Lieut. Wardle to hospital, sick. 3 Coys. at work under 280th Coy. R.E. (84 men per Coy.) Remainder making tracks etc. in camp as on Dec. 1st. Mr. Stubbs returned from leave.	
	3.		Work as for 2nd Dec. 2nd Lt. Cooper & R.S.M. Cox proceed on leave.	
	4.5.6.		Work as on 2nd Dec.	
	7.		" " " " C.O. 1/2 Monmouth Regt. visited C.O. this battalion re handing over work. Left copies of orders & maps. Instructions from CRE. to take over Monmouth work on 12th inst.	
	8.		Work as on Dec. 2nd. Officers i/c. Coys. went with representatives Monmouth Regt to view billets occupied by that Bn. & to see work, roads etc. leading thereto. Capt. Palmer returned from leave.	
	9.		Work as before. Leave party of 20 O.R. left for England.	
	10.		B.C.D Coys. sent advanced parties to take over accomodation in forward area. Work as above.	

G. Hayes Major
Comdg. 11th Durham Lt. Inf.

T2134. Wt. W708—776. 500000. 4/15. Sir J. C. & S.

December 1916.

WAR DIARY

or

~~INTELLIGENCE SUMMARY~~.

(*Erase heading not required.*)

Army Form C. 2118.

Volume 18.

Instructions regarding War Diaries and Intelligence Summaries are contained in F. S. Regs., Part II. and the Staff Manual respectively. Title pages will be prepared in manuscript.

Place	Date	Hour	Summary of Events and Information	Remarks and references to Appendices
	11		B + C Coys. each 100 strong went to HOGSBACK Trench. D Coy. into dugouts MORVAL Road.	
			48 tins of water sent by Pack mules. 30 tins by train. Rations by rail.	
			A Coy. + remainder of B + C Coys. acted as carrying party for above.	
	12		B Coy + C Coy. 100 strong each, D Coy 130 strong in forward area. 50 men A Coy. as fatigue to B Coy.	
	~~12~~		Remainder of B Coy. acted as carrying party – trench stores. 3 G.S. wagons of trench boards sent to GINCHY Dump. Orders to explore cellars in GINCHY, LES BOEUFS, and MORVAL. Telephone communication to forward area interrupted.	
	13.		As on 12th. Capt. Ward R.A.M.C., + Lt. Q.M. Tollit returned from leave.	
	14.		Work as on 12th. Also small party wood-cutting for troops in forward area.	
	15.		A Coy. relieved B Coy. in forward area.	
	16.		B Coy. resting. C+D Coys. at work on FLANK Avenue. A Coy. on OZONE trench.	
	17		A. C. D Coys. as on 16th. B Coy. work in camp. C.E. Vol. Church Parade 2.30 p.m.	
	18.		Work as on 17th. 30 men B Coy. working under 83rd Fd Coy. R.E. 5 O.R. proceeded on Lewis Machine Gun Course. 1 Corpl. proceeded on Gas Course.	
			2nd Lt. Liddell returned from Lewis Gun Course.	
	19.		B Coy. relieved C Coy. in HOGSBACK. A. C. D. Coys. as above. Major Lloyd went on Leave.	

C. Hayes Major
Comdg 11th Durham Light Infantry

December, 1916.

Instructions regarding War Diaries and Intelligence Summaries are contained in F. S. Regs., Part II. and the Staff Manual respectively. Title pages will be prepared in manuscript.

WAR DIARY

~~or~~

~~INTELLIGENCE SUMMARY.~~

(Erase heading not required.)

Volume 18.

Army Form C. 2118.

Place	Date	Hour	Summary of Events and Information	Remarks and references to Appendices
	20.		Capt. A W Dawson rejoined Bn. and assumed duties as Adjutant. 2nd Lts. Pugh & Adams from the 4th Bn. D.L.I. joined the battalion. Work as before.	
	21.		2nd Lts. Rees & Morton from 35th I.B.D. joined this battalion. All available men of A, B, D Coys. (less men on OZONE & FLANK) engaged in digging Intermediate Line.	
	22.		Work as on 21st. at night. Trench completed to 18" depth. 50 C Coy. assisting. Draft of 52 men arrived: only 3 of these men were suitable for a Pioneer Bn, grocers, agents, musicians etc are not fitted for the hard work of pioneering. O.C. 4th Y & L. Regt. visited C.O. this battn. re taking over of work.	
	23.		Work on Intermediate Line completed. Intermediate Line. Work done as follows:–	
			A Coy. T. 11. c. 8. 7. to T. 11. d. 1. 5. Length of trench 200x.	
			B Coy. T. 11. a. 0. 3 to T. 11. a. 4. 4. " " " 150x	
			D Coy. T. 10. b. 2. 3. to T. 10. b. 2. 8.	
			C Coy. assisted. " " " 150x	
			20th Divn. go into rest. 11th D.L.I. remain at work under XIVth Corps.	

G. Hayes Major
Comdg 11th Durham Lt Infty.

December, 1916.

WAR DIARY
or
INTELLIGENCE SUMMARY.
(Erase heading not required.)

Volume 18.

Army Form C. 2118.

Instructions regarding War Diaries and Intelligence Summaries are contained in F. S. Regs., Part II. and the Staff Manual respectively. Title pages will be prepared in manuscript.

Place	Date	Hour	Summary of Events and Information	Remarks and references to Appendices
	24.		C Coy. worked under 280th A.T. (Coy. R.E.). A B D Coys. remained in camp improving bivouacs. Bathing.	
	25.		All Coys. working under 280th Coy. R.E. till 12 noon. 3 Coys. on COMBLES Extension Railway – 1 Coy. on railway near GUILLEMONT. 2nd Lt. Buslell + 11 men proceeded on leave. Men removing putrid German Corpses.	
	26		Work as on 25th. Men still removing piles of decaying corpses. Message from Army Commander wishing Happy Christmas, also best wishes from C in C.	
	27.		" " " ". Owing to long journey to + from work under bad weather conditions, long hours of work + bad condition of bivouacs, men appear to be run down + are in real need of a rest.	
	28.		Work as above. Major G. Hayes, visited 20th Divl. HQ. with reference to work and the condition of the men.	
	29.		Work contd. The men are thoroughly weary on arrival in bivouacs after work. They parade daily at 7.15 a.m. carry haversack rations, + return at 4.30 p.m. They take both breakfast + dinner in the dark. Some are too tired to eat dinner – others too weary to turn out for rum rations. The C.O. + 2nd Lt. Rees proceeded to CORBIE to attend Court-Martial on 30th inst.	

G. Hayes Major
Comdg 11th [illegible]

T2134. Wt. W708–776. 500000. 4/15. Sir J. C. & S.

December, 1916.

Instructions regarding War Diaries and Intelligence Summaries are contained in F. S. Regs., Part II. and the Staff Manual respectively. Title pages will be prepared in manuscript.

WAR DIARY
or
INTELLIGENCE SUMMARY.
(*Erase heading not required.*)

Volume 18.

Army Form C. 2118.

Place	Date	Hour	Summary of Events and Information	Remarks and references to Appendices
			O.C. 280th Coy. R.E. called at Bn. H.Q. at 10 p.m. re tomorrow's work.	
			B Coy. to work at Flank Avenue Railhead (proceed by train from TRONES).	
			Remaining Coys. to complete drains on paths already made for Combles Extension Railway. Orders received for Bn. to proceed on 30th inst. to VILLE by train from TRONES WOOD siding for a few days' rest.	
			Rain fell heavily during the night, flooding many of the dugouts. Men slept little, having to continually bale out the dugouts.	
	30.		Work as above cont'd till midday.	
			2 parties working on dugouts at GINCHY recalled. Transport proceeded at 12 noon to VILLE. Owing to appalling condition of camp, 2 hours were occupied in getting transport clear of camp on to the road.	
			G.O.C. Guards Division, & O.C. 4th Coldstream Guards visited this camp during the morning. They were astonished at men being quartered in such a place & are not likely to take over the camp.	
			Bn. quitted camp by 3.15 p.m. & entrained for GROVETOWN. Here Bn. detrained & marched to VILLE arriving at 9.15 p.m. The men have	

G. Hayes Major.
Comdg. 11th Durham L.I.

T2134. Wt. W708—776. 500000. 4/15. Sir J. C. & S.

December, 1916

Instructions regarding War Diaries and Intelligence Summaries are contained in F. S. Regs., Part II. and the Staff Manual respectively. Title pages will be prepared in manuscript.

WAR DIARY
or
INTELLIGENCE SUMMARY.
(Erase heading not required.)

Volume 18.

Army Form C. 2118.

Place	Date	Hour	Summary of Events and Information	Remarks and references to Appendices
			~~only~~ once in their 18 months in France been so thoroughly done up.	
			2nd Lts. Liddell & Fillingham + 15 men proceeded on leave.	
	31.		The brief period at VILLE is being spent in cleaning clothing equipment etc., refitting, bathing and resting, before proceeding to Combles & Wedge Wood on Jan. 3rd. 1917.	
			The billets in VILLE are not clean.	
			Reinforcements 4 O.R. arrived.	
			C.E. service in Y.M.C.A. at 3 p.m.	
			G. Hayes Major Comdg 11th Durham L Infty.	

D. 430

To

Head Quarters
20th Division

Enclosed herewith War Diary for
December 1916

G. Hayes Major
Commdg. XIth Durham L.I.
(Prs.)

31/12/16

WAR DIARY

Vol 18

of the.

11th Bn. DURHAM. L.I.

(Pioneers)

January 1917.

Instructions regarding War Diaries and Intelligence Summaries are contained in F. S. Regs., Part II. and the Staff Manual respectively. Title pages will be prepared in manuscript.

Vol. XIX.

WAR DIARY

~~or~~

~~INTELLIGENCE SUMMARY.~~

(*Erase heading not required.*)

XIth D. L. I.

Army Form C. 2118.

Place	Date	Hour	Summary of Events and Information	Remarks and references to Appendices
VILLE	1st		Battalion in rest. Adjutant to hospital sick: duties assumed by 2nd Lt. Dennes	
	2.		Bn. resting & cleaning. The Quartermaster to hospital sick.	
	3.		Bn. left VILLE at 8.30 a.m. in motor lorries. A.C.D Coys. debussed at TRONES WOOD & marched to WEDGE WOOD (T.26.c.0.4). B. bussed to COMBLES.	
			3 Lewis handcarts broke down on the road. Major Lloyd returned from leave.	
			2nd Lt. Rees proceeded to 4th Army School for one month's course.	
	4.		Adjutant, & Lt. Stubbs both returned from hospital & resumed duties.	
			2nd Lt. Kemp + 19 men proceeded on leave.	
	4+5.		Work: A & D Coys. in reserve work under CRE 20th Divn. A Coy. work on dumps at TRONES WOOD, the Divl. Dump, + tunnelling at Dump on GINCHY-WEDGEWOOD Rd.	
			D Coy. work on COMBLES-BOIS de la HAIE Rd., repairing.	
			B Coy. attached to I. B. Left Group: billeted in COMBLES.	
			C Coy. attached to I. B Right Group: billeted at MOUCHOIR COPSE.	
			Chateau Avenue:	
			215x trench cleared. Digging + revetting & drain at strong point V. 14. d. 2. 2.	
			Durham Trench. Communication trench to front line.	

G. Hayes. Major
Comdg. XIth D. L. I.

T2134. Wt. W708—776. 500000. 4/15. Sir J. C. & S.

Instructions regarding War Diaries and Intelligence Summaries are contained in F. S. Regs., Part II. and the Staff Manual respectively. Title pages will be prepared in manuscript.

WAR DIARY
or
~~INTELLIGENCE SUMMARY.~~
(Erase heading not required.)

Army Form C. 2118.

Place	Date	Hour	Summary of Events and Information	Remarks and references to Appendices
			295^x^ dug. 50^x^ drainage dug. depth 2'.6" to 6'6" to suit slope of hill.	
	6th.		16 V frames (large) set & revetted behind with expanded metal. 120^x^ trench deepened.	
			Night work: B Cy. 2 platoons carrying material from HAIE WOOD dump to Durham Trench.	
			2 platoons clearing trench & revetting – 85^x^ revetted.	
			Day: C Cy. Draining & clearing BETTY TRENCH	
			Night: " " " " " 40^x^ dug 5' deep. 10^x^ revetted.	
	7th.		C Coy. Betty Trench Drain. Revetted 37^x^. cleared 30^x^. dug 36^x^. deepened 10^x^ of trench.	
			A Cy. Durham Trench. Revetted 70^x^ with V frames – wired back 28 frames.	
			C of E. service at Wedge Wood for A & D Cys. & HQ. & Transport.	
	8th		2. O.R. casualties rejoined Battn. today.	
	& 9th.		work: B Cy. Revetted 40^x^. 110 V frames set & wired back. ~~50~~ 100^x^ trench boards laid.	
			C. Cy Betty Trench Drain. 28^x^ dug 3'x3'. 76^x^ deepened. 59^x^ revetted.	
			15^x^ drain N. end widened.	
			Orders issued for Inter Coy. Relief on 14th.	
	10th		2nd Lt. Dennis + 19 O.R. proceeded on leave. 10 cases scabies in C Coy.	
			4 O.R. wounded C Coy.	
			G. Hayes. Major Comdg. XIth D	1.

T2134. Wt. W708—776. 500000. 4/15. Sir J. C. & S.

Instructions regarding War Diaries and Intelligence Summaries are contained in F. S. Regs., Part II. and the Staff Manual respectively. Title pages will be prepared in manuscript.

WAR DIARY

~~or~~

~~INTELLIGENCE SUMMARY.~~

(Erase heading not required.)

Army Form C. 2118.

Place	Date	Hour	Summary of Events and Information	Remarks and references to Appendices
			B Cy	
	10th (contd)		63 U frames set & revetted	
			C Cy. Night 49x revetted.– 60x wired back – 34x dug 3' x 3' – 34x deepened 3' x 5' 2 falls cleared – shell holes drained.	
	11th		6 officers arrived & were attached to Bn.:– 2nd Lt. H.S. PARKIN & W.G. CRAIG, 3rd Bn, posted to A Cy. 2nd Lt. J.R.A. BRANCH & C.K. MOORE, 3rd Bn, posted to B Cy Lt. H.S. BYERS, & 2nd Lt. B.H. WOOD, 3rd Bn, posted to D Cy.	
			C Cy. moved from MOUCHOIR COPSE to FREGICOURT (T.24. C. 6½. 0.).	
			Orders received to cut & stack wood for fuel, in FAVIERE WOOD – 40 infantry to assist	
	12th		4 N.C.O's & 10 men under Lt. Sear take charge of work in FAVIERE WOOD. 2 Sergts. sent to superintend Bde. Dumps at HAIE WOOD. Men's clothing sent to BRONFAY FARM to be exchanged for clean clothing – not satisfactory: clothing received was not clean.	
			Work. C Cy Betty Trench drain. 22x dug 3' x 3' – 35x deepened to 5ft – 35x revetted.	
			B Cy. 145 U frames set & revetted. 64x trench dug. 100x trench boards laid & nailed down. FAVIERE WOOD party felled 55 trees.	
			G. Hayes. Major Comdg. XI D. Cy.	

T2134. Wt. W708–776. 500000. 4/15. Sir J. C. & S.

Army Form C. 2118.

Instructions regarding War Diaries and Intelligence Summaries are contained in F. S. Regs., Part II. and the Staff Manual respectively. Title pages will be prepared in manuscript.

WAR DIARY

or

~~INTELLIGENCE SUMMARY.~~

(Erase heading not required.)

Place	Date	Hour	Summary of Events and Information	Remarks and references to Appendices
	13th		Work: C Coy. Night 12th/13th: Betty Trench drain. 25x deepened to 5ft. 40x dug. — 32x revetted — 87x wired back. new drain from V14.c.8.2 35x drain dug.	
	14th		~~C~~ + B Coys. relieved by A + D Coys. C of E. Service 6 p.m. at Wedge Wood (voluntary). Work: D Coy. Night 14/15th: 65x new drain dug + cleared ready for revetting. 6x old drain cleared + revetted.	
	15th		Capt. Taylor, 2nd Lt. Inglis + 17 O.R. went on leave tonight. Work: D Coy. Night 15/16th: 55x new drain revetted + wired on one side. 56x cross wiring finished.	
	16th		2nd Lt. Liddle returned from leave. Work. Night 16/17th: 45x new drain revetted + wired back. 14x new drain dug. 50x cross wiring finished.	
	17th		2 Coys. hitherto attached to I.Bs. Right + Left Groups come under orders of C.R.E. for a special task. Owing to heavy fall of snow, work on special task was suspended + the previous work is being continued. Night 17/18th: Repairing parapet in Left Sector. 100x cross wiring done.	

G. Hayes. Major
Comdg. XI D.L.I. 1.

T2134. Wt. W708–776. 500000. 4/15. Sir J. C. & S.

Instructions regarding War Diaries and Intelligence Summaries are contained in F. S. Regs., Part II. and the Staff Manual respectively. Title pages will be prepared in manuscript.

Vol. XIX

WAR DIARY

~~or~~

~~INTELLIGENCE SUMMARY.~~

(Erase heading not required.)

XIst D.L.I. (Pioneers)

Army Form C. 2118.

Place	Date	Hour	Summary of Events and Information	Remarks and references to Appendices
	17.		FAVIERE Wood. Weekly report. Trees felled 100. Timber sawn, split + stacked 100' x 6' x 3' 6" Rough estimate 30 tons. Wood at A.22.a.8.3. 11 limber loads disbursed.	
	18th		2nd Lt. Pugh + Corpl. Mole proceeded to 20th Div[l]. School for 2 weeks' course. 2nd Lt. Fillingham returned from leave.	
	19th		Lt. Sear takes over charge of erection of huts at Maricourt Siding, under orders of Q. 14th Corps. 2nd Lt. Brand relieves Lt. Sear at FAVIERE-Woodcutting party. Work: D Coy. night 19/20th. 40[x] drain cleared + revetted. 30[x] drain dug.	
	20th		2nd Lts. Devey + Philip + 17 O.R. proceed on leave. Sergt. Jones + 7 O.R. returned to this unit from 35th I.B. Work. Night 20/21st. C Coy. Trench at Sailleisel. 110[x] dug - 75% completed. A Coy. Drains 3.4.5.6. completed (U.14 d.4.6). D Coy. Bean - Bread Line. 4 drains dug.	
	21st		2nd Lts. Towlson + Andrews from 3rd Bn. joined this unit + were taken on strength. Work. Night. 21/22nd A Coy. Drains 3.4.5-6 improved.	

C. Hayes. Major
Comdg. XIth D.L.I.

T2134. Wt. W708—776. 500000. 4/15. Sir J. C. & S.

WAR DIARY

~~or~~

~~INTELLIGENCE SUMMARY~~.

(Erase heading not required.)

Army Form C. 2118.

Instructions regarding War Diaries and Intelligence Summaries are contained in F. S. Regs., Part II. and the Staff Manual respectively. Title pages will be prepared in manuscript.

Vol. XIX.

XI D. L. I. (Pioneers)

Place	Date	Hour	Summary of Events and Information	Remarks and references to Appendices
	22.		Capt. H. W. Ward RAMC. to hospital. OO 133 received from 20th Div. This unit to move on 28th. 2 D Cy. O.R. wounded.	
			Work: Night 21/22nd. D Cy. Drains on Bread & Bean Line. cleared, deepened & widened.	
	23.		Draft of 82 N.C.Os & men arrived. N.C.Os appear to be a good set; they are men of over 12 months Home Service, & have attended month's course at N.C.Os school, Easton Common.	
			Work: A Cy. 220x new support trench dug. D Cy. Bean & Bread Line. 262x dug. 4 x 3 x 2.	
	24		2nd Lt. R. Tee rejoined unit today. Work: A Cy. new Support Line from CUSHY Sq. to BEAN support Line deepened, widened & revetted. D Cy. 92x new trench completed. 5' x 4' x 2'	
	25th		Wounded 1 OR A Cy. Enemy aeroplane brought down at Wedgewood near Bn. HQ. German airmen sent under guard to Divl. HQ. 20 OR. went on leave tonight.	
	26th		Work continued as above. 1 off. & 5 OR. arrived from Y & L Regt. Pioneers to take over from Cy. at FREGICOURT.	
	27th		2nd Lt. Dennis returned from leave. 28th Bn. moved to MANSEL Camp. 29th moved to MEAULTE	
	30th		Orders from 20th Divl. that this unit is to remain at Meaulte whilst Divn is in G.H.Q. Reserve.	
	31st		Bn. training. Physical exercises - drill with & without arms. Lectures.	

C. Hayes. Major

Comdg. XI D. L. I. (Pioneers)

T2134. Wt. W708—776. 500000. 4/15. Sir J. C. & S.

Original.

Vol 19

Confidential.

War Diary

of

XI[e] Bn. The Durham L. I. (Pioneers)

from Feb. 1st to Feb. 28[e] 1917

Volume 20.

Instructions regarding War Diaries and Intelligence Summaries are contained in F. S. Regs., Part II. and the Staff Manual respectively. Title pages will be prepared in manuscript.

WAR DIARY ~~or~~ ~~INTELLIGENCE~~ ~~SUMMARY~~.

VOL. XX — XIth Durham L.I. (Pioneers)

(Erase heading not required.)

Army Form C. 2118.

Place	Date	Hour	Summary of Events and Information	Remarks and references to Appendices
	February.			
MEAULTE	1 to 4		Battalion in rest. Physical Training, Platoon & Coy. drill during morning – bayonet fighting in the afternoon. Baths in use at Meaulte.	
	5 6.		Training contd. Battalion drill.	
			Bn. OO 36 issued regarding move to forward area on 8th inst.	
	8.		Bn. marched from Meaulte – A Coy. to GUILLEMONT – HQ. Transport & B C D Coys. to MONTAUBAN. (S.28. c. 2. 6)	
	9.		B Coy. moved to HOGSBACK (T. 16. a. central) C Coy. to SUNKEN Rd. (T. 16. a. 7. 9.)	
			D Coy. partly in HOGSBACK & partly in SUNKEN RD.	
			Leave cancelled. 1 officer + 89 OR. reinforcement arrived from 35th I. B. D.	
	10.		2/LT. M. COOPER to Hospital.	
	11		2/LT. REES returned from 4th Army School, FLIXECOURT. Wounded 2 O.R.	
	13.		List of Stores taken over from 1/2 Monmouthshire Regt. & receipt forwarded to Division.	
			Court of Inquiry into accidental burning of the Tombling C Coy. at Meaulte. President: Capt. C. Palmer + 2 subalterns of A Coy.	
			2/LT. Lascelles, 3rd Bn. D.L.I. joined this battalion.	
			C.S.M. McEvoy came to HQ. as Acting R.S.M. vice S.M. Cox to England.	

T2134. Wt. W708–776. 500000. 4/15. Sir J. C. & S.

Instructions regarding War Diaries and Intelligence Summaries are contained in F. S. Regs., Part II. and the Staff Manual respectively. Title pages will be prepared in manuscript.

Vol XX

WAR DIARY
~~or~~
~~INTELLIGENCE SUMMARY~~.
(*Erase heading not required.*)

XIth Durham L. I. (Pioneers)

Army Form C. 2118.

Place	Date	Hour	Summary of Events and Information	Remarks and references to Appendices
	February			
	15.		Bn. 0037 issued to A + B Coys. for Inter-Coy. relief on the 16th.	
			2/LT. Branch returned to Bn. from hospital.	
	17		1. O. R. wounded.	
	18.		1 officer + 30 O.R. B Coy. (Reserve Coy.) met R.E officer at BULL DUMP for special work under C.R.E. orders. Orders received to fix knife rests in gaps in wire in Intermediate Line. C Coy responsible for Right Bde. Sector, D Coy. for Left Bde. Sector.	
			1 N.C.O + small party in charge of work in each sector.	
	19		2/LT. Parkin proceeded to Lewis Machine Gun Course at Meaulte.	
			S.O.S. D.17 received at 7.15 p.m. "STAND DOWN" received by Bn. HQ. at 12.40 a.m. 20th. B Coy. at GUILLEMONT + A & D Coys. in SUNKEN RD. "stood to" under Left Bde. orders until 4 a.m. 20th inst..	
	20.		Acting Capt. Devey's leave extended till 20th by War Office letter. 1 O.R. wounded.	
			19 O.R. casuals rejoined Bn. from No 2 Base.	
	21		Extract from List 122 appointments etc.. Major G. Hayes to be Acting LT. Col. 13th Dec. 1916.	
			2/LT. Devey to be Acting Capt. 6th Dec. 1916.	
			LT. Floyd relinquishes acting rank of Capt. Nov. 22nd. 1916.	

T2134. Wt. W708—776. 500000. 4/15. Sir J. C. & S.

Instructions regarding War Diaries and Intelligence Summaries are contained in F. S. Regs., Part II. and the Staff Manual respectively. Title pages will be prepared in manuscript.

Vol. XX.

WAR DIARY
~~or~~
~~INTELLIGENCE~~ SUMMARY.

(Erase heading not required.)

XIth Durham L.I. (Pioneers).

Army Form C. 2118.

Place	Date	Hour	Summary of Events and Information	Remarks and references to Appendices
	February. 21.		Progress Report of Work during last fortnight.	
			1. Large Dugouts T. 4. c. sheet 57 S.W. C	
			9 entrances started 5'x3' at dip of 1 in 2. Average distance along dip is now 35'. The 9 saps are nearly all far enough down for the galleries to be turned off right & left.	
			2. 140x of double track duck walk has been constructed down the SUNKEN Rd. T. 4. c. leading to these dugouts. This work is proceeding.	
			3. Four Camouflage Screens have been erected across this road: dugout entrances have been similarly screened. Work has been delayed 28 hours owing to shortages of material & owing to "Stand to". Considerable improvements have been made to GINCHY AID POST.	
			4. Accomodation. Sunken Rd. (about T. 16. a. 8. 8. to T. 10. c. 9. 2.). Shelter built for 25 men.	
			5. New Deep Dugouts. T. 16. a. 7. 9. Four entrances No 1. 8' long. No 2. 9 ft. long. No 3. 26 ft. long. No. 4. 16 ft. long.	Slope 1 in 1.
			6. Intermediate Line Wire across T. 10 b. 4 Knife rests for gaps. 10 yds. repaired.	

Instructions regarding War Diaries and Intelligence Summaries are contained in F. S. Regs., Part II. and the Staff Manual respectively. Title pages will be prepared in manuscript.

WAR DIARY or ~~INTELLIGENCE SUMMARY~~.

Army Form C. 2118.

(Erase heading not required.)

Vol. XX. XIth Durham L. I. (Pioneers)

Place	Date	Hour	Summary of Events and Information	Remarks and references to Appendices
	February.			
	21.		7 Extension of old German Saps in SUNKEN RD. T. 10. a.	
			a. One chamber 12 ft. × 6'6" × 6'	
			b. Reclamation of second ~~entrance~~ 9 setts.	
			8 Splinter proof shelters erected in Sunken Rd. T. 10. a. One shelter holds 7 men: improvement to existing shelter holding 8 men. 4 shelters to hold 15 men	
	23		2. O. R. C Coy accidentally killed in train accident on 14/2/17 3. O. R. wounded in the line.	
	24		4 O R reinforcement rejoined Bn.	
	25.		0038 issued to Coys. for relief of C Coy by B Coy.	
	26		0039 issued to Coys. reference to operations in connection with 59th I. B. operations on the 28th inst. 2/LT. Parkin returned from Lewis M. G. Course.	
	27.		0040 and supplement issued with reference to operations in connection with 59th I. B.	
	28		2/LT. Pugh invalided to England.	
			Orders re work tonight following on 59th I. B. operations cancelled.	
			Coys. ~~to~~ resume work on dugouts in SUNKEN Rd. T. 4. c.	

H. B. Lloyd [illegible] Comdg. XI D. L. I.

T2134. Wt. W708–776. 500000. 4/15. Sir J. C. & S.

SECRET COPY No 7

XIth Durham L. Inf. (Pioneers)

Operation Order No 35

Jany 25th 1917

1.(a) The battalion will be relieved by Pioneer Bn. (York. & Lancs. Regt.) 17th Division on January 28th, and will proceed to BUSSY-Les-DAOURS.

(b) On 26th 1 Officer & 2 N.C.Os of the York. & Lancs. Regt. will be attached to each Coy. & will be shown by the O.C. concerned the works & all dumps, etc, to be taken over.

(c) On relief the Bn. will move to MANSEL CAMP on CARNOY-MONTAUBAN Road.

2. (a) On 27th at 11 am D Coy will return to Wedgewood. They will hand over all dugouts etc, previous to vacating.

(b) A Coy. will leave Combles at 8.15am on the 28th & will march direct to MANSEL CAMP with its transport. They will hand over all dugouts etc, by 8 am.

3. B Coy. will hand over Leuze Wood Dump at 5pm on 27th to

the Officer & N.C.Os of the relieving Coy. concerned, but will leave the Guard & signallers there till 8 a.m. on the 28th.

4.(a) The Bn. (less A Coy.) will move off from Wedge Wood at 8.15 a.m. marching across country in the following order:–
B, C, & D Coys & H.Q.
There will be an interval of 250 yds. between Coys.

(b) The Transport will move to MANSELL CAMP by road at 8 a.m. on the 28th.

5. One blanket per man will be carried on the man. The remainder, in bundles of 10, will be carried on the G.S. Wagons. Tools are to be carried in the Limbers.
Gumboots, trench stores, etc, are to be handed over and receipts taken.

6. The Transport Sergt. will arrange the transport for 'D' Coy on the 27th & for A Coy on the 28th.

7. Men absolutely unable to march

to MANSEL CAMP will be sent for the M.O's inspection at Wedge Wood at 11 a.m. the 27th. M.O. will make arrangements for these.

8. O's C. A and D Coys. will arrange for suitable parties to work on night 27th/28th until 10 p.m. to complete & clean up work if required. The party of D Coy. will return direct to Wedge Wood on completion. The work is to be left in a tidy condition.

9. 2/Lieut. R. Tee & Qr. Mr. Sergt. with 1 N.C.O. per Coy. will proceed from Wedge Wood to MANSEL CAMP at 7 a.m. on the 28th. & take over the camp.

10. Orders for move to BUSSY-LES-DAOURS by Rail will be issued later.

11. Acknowledge

A. W. Dawson
Capt. & Adjt.
XI. D. L. I.

Copies to –
No 1 – A Coy. No 2 – B Coy
No 3 – C " No 4 – D "
" 5 Transpt Sgt. No 6. M.O.
" 7 Retained

SECRET. Copy No. 9

OPERATION ORDER No. 36

Feby 6th 1917

XIth Bn. Durham L. I. (Pioneers)

Map Reference. FRANCE. 62D and ALBERT (combined sheet) 1/40000.

1. (a) The 20th Division (less Artillery) will relieve the 29th Div. (less Artillery) in the left sector of Corps Front, commencing Feby. 8th and finishing Feby. 9th

(b) The 17th Div. will be on the Right

(C) The 5th Australian Div. will be on the left.

2. The Divl. Front will be held by two Brigade Groups as follows:-

Right Bde. Group (Morval Sector)

61st I.B. and 2 Battns. 60th I.B.

Bde. H.Q. GUILLEMONT QUARRIES

Left Bde. Group (Les Boeufs Sector)

59th I.B. and 2 Battns. 60th I.B.

Bde. H.Q. GUILLEMONT STATION

Advanced Div. H.Q. T.9.b.3.3.

3. The XIth D.L.I. (Pioneers) will relieve the 1/2 Monmouthshire Pioneers quartered at MONTAUBAN on the 8th inst, moving forward on that date.

Bn. H.Q. will be at dug out vacated by 256th Tunnelling Co. at GUILLEMONT.

4. (1 Officer, C.Q.M.S., & 1 O.R.) per Coy. and Sergt.

Sergt. Rowding for A.Q. will go forward on the 7th inst, as an advanced party, to take over forward area billets, marching from Meaulte at 8 a.m.

This party will be billeted and rationed by the 1/2 Monmouthshire Regt.

The Officers will make themselves acquainted with the work to be taken over.

Qr Mrs will proceed with the above party to MONTAUBAN to arrange billets for the 3 Coys. (B, C & D) for the night of the 8th inst.

5. The Battalion will move off from Meaulte in the following order, commencing at 8 a.m. on the 8th inst.—
A Coy & H.Qrs, B Coy, C Coy, D Coy, Transport.

A Coy. & H.Qrs with their Transport will move to GUILLEMONT.

The remainder will move to MONTAUBAN CAMP.

There will be an interval of 1/4 hr. between Coys.

6. One blanket per man will be carried on the man. The remainder in

in bundles of 10, will be carried on the G.S. wagon.

7. Men unable to march will be inspected by the M.O. at 3 p.m. on the 7th inst.
The M.O. will make arrangements for this.

8. On the 9th inst. B, C, & D Coys. will move as follows:—
B Coy. at 8.15 a.m. to dugouts T.16.a. Central
C Coy. at 8.30 a.m. to Gurkha Road T.16.a.7.9. & dug outs in BOVRIL TRENCH T.16.a.4.8.
D Coy. at 8.45 a.m. to dug outs near BULL DUMP Flank Avenue Railhead T.9.b.3.3.
The Transport Officer will make necessary arrangements for Transport.

9. ACKNOWLEDGE.

Copies to.
1. A Coy.
2. B.
3. C.
4. D.
5. M.O.
6. Transport Officer
7. C.R.E. } For information
8. 1/2 Monmouthshire Regt }
9. Retained

A W Dawson
Capt. & Adjt.
N D (?) (Pioneers)

SECRET. Copy No. 5

15/2/17

XIth Bn. Durham L. I.
(Pioneers)

OPERATION ORDER No. 37.

1. 'B' Coy. will be relieved in HOGS BACK Trench by 'A' Coy. on the 16th inst.

2. O.C. 'A' Coy. will arrange for Officers & N.C.O's to be acquainted with the work of 'B' Coy. before the 16th inst.

3. There is to be no break in the continuity of work on dugouts in Sunken Road during relief.

4. All tools, stores, etc., for forward area on charge of 'B' Coy. will be handed over, and a similar quantity of tools on charge of 'A' Coy. will be handed over to 'B' Coy.
Receipts will be given for these.
Duplicate copies of receipts are to be sent to Bn. H. Qrs.

5. Coys. will report to Bn. H. Qrs. by wire as soon as relief is completed.

6. Times of relief to be arranged between Coy. Commanders who will inform the T.O.

7. Work on all dugouts at T. 4. c. central will be under the direction of Capt. Palmer from 12 noon on the 16th.

8. Acknowledge.

A W Dawson Capt. & Adjt.
XIth Durham L. I.
(Pioneers)

Copies to:-
1. 'A' Coy.
2. 'B' "
3. T.O.
4. C.R.E. (for information)
5. Retained.

COPY No.

SECRET 24/2/17.

XIth Bn Durham L. Infantry (Pioneers)

OPERATION ORDER No. 58.

1. C Coy will be relieved in SUNKEN ROAD by B Coy on the 25th inst.

(a) C Coy will return to SUNKEN ROAD on completion of their special work on PRUSSIAN TRENCH, on the 25th.

(b) They will arrange to take over work in Reserve Area from B Coy, on the 26th inst.

(c) C Coy will move into FLORIN CAMP & huts at BUCKINGHAM PALACE.

(d) B Coy will leave parties for work in Reserve Area on 25th. These parties will proceed to forward area on completion of their work.

2. All tools, stores, ammunition bombs etc in forward area on

on charge of 'C' Coy. will be handed over & a similar quantity of tools on charge of 'B' Coy. will be handed over to 'C' Coy. Receipts will be given for these & duplicate copies sent to Bn. H.Qrs.

3. Coys. will report to Bn. H.Qrs by wire as soon as relief is completed. Use (B.A.B. Code)

4. Times of relief will be arranged between the two Coy. Commanders who will inform the T.O.
Relief must be completed by 4 p.m.

5. Work on all dugouts in the Sunken Rd. is under the direction of Capt. Palmer.

6. Acknowledge.

Copies to:-
1 & 2 B & C Coys.
3. Capt. Palmer for information
4. T.O.
5. C.R.E. for information
6. Retained.

A W Lawson
Capt & Adjt
XIth D.L.I.
(Pioneers).

SECRET Copy No.

11th Durham L.I. (Pioneers)

OPERATION ORDER No 35

26.2.17

1. At dawn on Zero day a Battn. of the Right Brigade will attack the German salient in N.36.d with the object of capturing the portion of trench marked green on the attached plan C.A.B.

They will also attack the German post & dug outs in the Sunken road up to point marked P.

2. On the following night a series of posts will be dug marked 1, 2, 3, 4, 5 & 6 also two C.Ts. to the German trench K.A. and N.F.

These C.Ts. & posts will be dug by parties of the 11th D.L.I. as follows:—

(a) N.F. about 70 yards by 70 men 'D' Coy under O.C. 'D' Coy with two officers.

Capt. Heslop will be in command of 'D' Coy.

(b) K.A. about 150 yards long by 120 men A Coy & 70 men 'D' Coy.

These distances do not allow for waves in the Trenches.

3(a) Posts I, II III & IV will be dug by 'B' Coy.

These will consist of angle posts, thus 

The sides will be at an angle of about 70°

These posts must be able to cover each other by cross fire; one side of No IV covering post at P.

Wire will be erected in front of these posts by the R.E.

These posts will be, as nearly as possible on the line P.X.

Each side of these posts will be 16 yards long, i.e. 32 yards for each post.

25 men diggers will work on each post.

Parties will have to go out independently, but in touch, & pick up each other and adjust the alignment on the line of posts to be dug.

Congestion in assembling & moving ~~up~~ out will have to be avoided.

(b) Posts 5 & 6 of same type & dimensions as above will be dug by C Coy.

Careful reconnaissance will be made by O.C. Companies & selected Officers & N.C.Os.

Compass bearings will have to be taken, both off the map & on the ground.

The bearings and ground where C.Ts are to be dug will have to be reconnoitred from the present front line.

The lie of the ground, its condition & especially the ways up to this part of the line will have to be carefully noted.

4. O.C. B Coy will probably be able to [illegible] one or two small patrols if necessary in the direction of the site for [illegible] 2 & 3.

5. The C.O. will issue detailed instructions after he has [illegible] reconnoitred the area and on receiving Coy Commanders reports.

6. Routes & times of parties will be detailed later.

7. This reconnaissance will

will be made during the early hours of the morning of the 27th. Times for meeting, etc., will be arranged later.

O.C. "C" Coy. will send the Coy. officers who are going with his parties to meet the C.O. at "B" Coy's H.Q. in the Sunken Road. The C.O. will meet Coy. Commanders & officers who are making reconnaissances here at the same time to arrange any further details.

8. In the event of the posts, 1, 2, 3, 4, 5, & 6 not being dug, "A" Coy. will construct posts 1 & 2, "B" Coy. posts 3 & 4, "D" Coy. posts 5 & 6.

Parties of "D" Coy. will move via Derby Lane to H. post.

Parties of A & B Coys. will assemble in trench dug by A & B Coy. from present post in Sunken Road to "PRUSSIAN" Trench.

ACKNOWLEDGE

(Sd) A.W. Dawson
Capt & Adjt.
XIth D.L.I.

Copies to O.C. A Coy.
B
C
D
1 retained

SECRET

COPY No 6

XIth Durham L. I. (Pns.) 27-2-'17

OPERATION ORDER No 40.

1. In connection with O.O. 39 issued yesterday the following will take place on the 27th

2 (a) O.C. A Coy. XIth D.L.I. will detail a party of 2 Officers and 100 men to meet representatives & guides of 96th Fd Co R.E. at BULL DUMP at 5pm. today

(b) A party of 150 men will be supplied by the 59th I.B.

(c) These 250 men will be divided into 2 parties of 125. Each party will carry 24 coils of french wire, 108 long screw pickets 24 short screw pickets & 24 coils of barbed wire.
The guides will lead the parties to about 400 yards beyond Right Bn. H.Q. (in ANTELOPE Trench) at about T 5 d. 5. 8 and wait near the duckboards for other 96th Coy guides who will in the meantime have taped out lines from the duckboard track to site where the material

will be dumped, namely at about T.6.b.1.8 & T.6.a.4.7. The two carrying parties will then be guided, one to each proposed advanced dump, & dump the material.

~~On 28th evening - i.e. after the operation G.O.C. 57th Brigade is arranging for patrols to be out in front of the line to be wired; the patrols will be out by 8.30 pm.~~

3. Orders re carrying parties etc. on the 28th will be issued later.

4. ACKNOWLEDGE.

Capt & Adjt
XIIth D. L. I. (Pio)

Copy No 1 to 'A' Coy
" No 2 " B "
" No 3. " C "
" No 4 " D "
" No 5 retained

SECRET

Copy No 4

XIth D.L.I. (Pioneers)

Supplement to O.O. 40.

1. The following with reference to operations etc. on the 28th is an extract from C.R.E's O.O.

"The 11th D.L.I. will dig 4 posts on the right of the Sunken Rd. + about 40 yds. behind the wire, + similarly 2 posts on the left of the Sunken Rd.

Para. 5a On the 28th evening - i.e. after the operation - G.O.C 59th Brigade is arranging for patrols to be out in front of the line to be wired; the patrols will be out by 8.30pm.

(b) The O.C. 96th will arrange to detail officers + N.C.Os to tape out the line to be wired and this is to be done with a view to a line of posts (ultimately to be connected up) being dug about 40 yds behind the wire; then officers will also tape a guiding line from the two dumps at about T.6.b.1.8 + T.6.a.4.7) to the starting points at about N.36.d.½.1 + N.36.c.30.15 respectively.

(c) The O.C. 11th D.L.I. will detail 6 parties of 20 men for carrying wire. Three of these parties will be at the dump at T.6.b.18 (made on the evening of 27th as in para. 4 above) + three at the other dump at T.6.a.4.7. Each party will pick up 4 trench coils, 18 long screw pickets, 4 short screw pickets and 4 coils of barbed wire. The parties will dump their loads by parties on each side first at the two starting points at N.36.d.½.1 and N.36.c.30.15. + then at 40 yds intervals; they will then return to the dumps (i.e. 3 parties to T.6.b.1.8 + 3 parties to T.6.a.4.7). + pick up the same load as on the previous carry + continue to dump along the line to be wired at 40 yds interval.

Thus at the end of the second carry there will be dumps at 40 yds intervals along the line to be wired and previously taped out by the 96th Company. These carrying parties will arrive at the dumps (3 at T.6.b.1.8 + 3 at T.6.a.4.7) at 8.30 p.m. on 28th evening.

(d) The O.C. 11th D.L.I. will also detail 6 parties each 20 strong to dig 4 posts, at about equal intervals + about 30 to 40 yards behind the line to be wired, between N.36.d.½.1 + N.36.c.6.3 and also 2 posts between N.36.c.6.3 and N.36.c.30.15.
The posts will each have 4 bays of 20 feet each + will not be traversed. They will be shaped

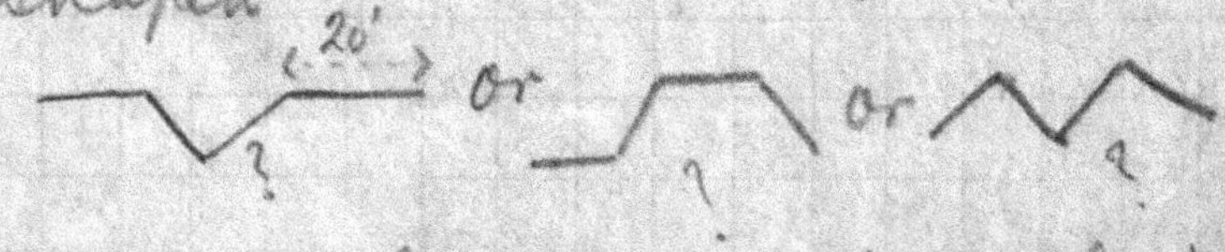

or any other such shape having 4 lengths of 20' and there a decided bend. Parties 20 strong should give 4 men spare per party at 5' per man; then 4 men can if available dig a fifth bay of 20'."

6.. These parties should be at or near the starting points N.36.d.½.1 and N.36.c.30.15 at about 9.30 pm."

Ref. 5(c) above.

(a) 'D' Coy will furnish 2 carrying parties of 20 men each. to be at dump at T.6.b.1.8.

(b) A Coy will furnish 2 carrying parties of 20 men each, to be at dump T.6.a.4.7.

(c) B Coy will furnish 2 carrying parties of 20 men each: one of these parties will go with each of the above (a + b)

There will be 1 officer with each group (a) (b).

Ref. 5(d) above.

The arrangement as in para. 8. O.O.39 issued by O.C. XIth D.L.I. holds good.

* The posts will be shaped

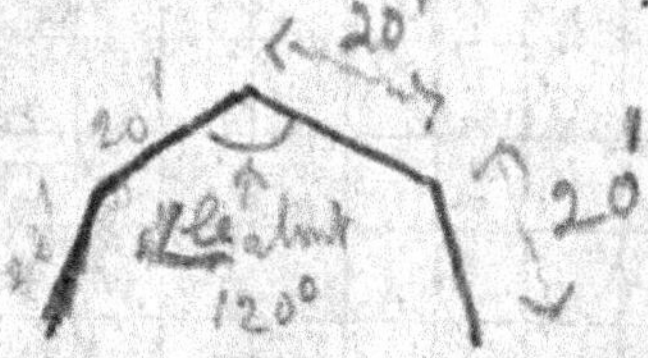

60 sandbags, 6 picks, 6 shovels, will be left in each post by parties.

This plan of post may have to be modified somewhat in shape according to the nature of the ground.

The officers on the spot will draw a plan of whatever shaped post is constructed.

acknowledge.

A W Dawson
Capt. & Adj.
XI

27/4/17

Original.

Vol 20

Confidential.

War Diary
of
XIth Durham L. I. (Pioneers)

from March 1st to 31st 1917.

Volume XXI.

Original

Army Form C. 2118.

WAR DIARY

~~or~~

~~INTELLIGENCE SUMMARY.~~

(Erase heading not required.)

Instructions regarding War Diaries and Intelligence Summaries are contained in F. S. Regs., Part II. and the Staff Manual respectively. Title pages will be prepared in manuscript.

Vol. XXI. XIth Durham L. I. (Pioneers)

Place	Date	Hour	Summary of Events and Information	Remarks and references to Appendices
	March ~~February~~.			
MONTAUBAN.	1st.		A/LT. Col. G. Hayes proceeded to England on 10 days' leave. Major H. P. Lloyd in temporary command of the battalion. Trench dug by D.L.I. on night 24/25 (N. 35. d. 6. 2) to be wired by 96th Fd Coy. 120 men D.L.I. provided for carrying party.	
	2nd.		Capt. A. W. Dawson (adjt.) left to take temporary command of 20th Divl. Works Bn. during the absence of the C.O. 2/LT. Dennis assumed duties of Adjutant vice Capt. Dawson. 2. O. R. wounded whilst carrying as above. 2/LT. Inglis + 20 OR. sent to take over WEDGEWOOD Camp from 1/2 Monmouth Regt.	
	3rd.		1 OR. wounded. 2/LT. Devey struck off strength – medically unfit. 2/LT. Woods reported back from Divisional School, DAOURS.	
	4th.		1 OR. died in hospital (pneumonia)	
	5th.		C Coy. relieved D Coy. in forward area. Divl. Gas Officer fitted HQ. + Transport with Box Respirators. Wiring Report Intermediate Line. 1 double apron from T.11.a. 3. 45 to T.11. a. 8. 2. Total length completed 1050 yards.	
	6th.		2/LT. Lascelles + 20 OR. detailed as digging party to report at Right Bn. HQ. Left Sector. Owing to bright moonlight, this work was cancelled. Party carried up Lewis Gun ammunition instead of digging. Wiring Intermediate Line – 1450^x completed. 600^x remain to be done.	

T.2134. Wt. W708–776. 500000. 4/15. Sir J. C. & S.

Army Form C. 2118.

Instructions regarding War Diaries and Intelligence Summaries are contained in F. S. Regs., Part II. and the Staff Manual respectively. Title pages will be prepared in manuscript.

WAR DIARY
~~or~~
~~INTELLIGENCE SUMMARY~~.
(Erase heading not required.)

VOL. XXI. Contd.

XIth Durham L. I. (Pioneers)

Place	Date	Hour	Summary of Events and Information	Remarks and references to Appendices
	March			
	7th		Lt. Byers 2/LT. Morton + 1 Corpl. proceed to course at Divl. School, DAOURS.	
			2/LT. Andrew took over duties of D.O.R.E. 20th Div. 1 Sgt. + 15 OR. to work under D.O.R.E. All to live at CARNOY CAMP. 2/LT. Fletcher killed whilst on working party 1 OR. slightly wounded. Wagons + harness inspected by A.S.C. officer.	
	8th		Reports on dugout made by XI D.L.I. in Sunken Rd. T. 4. c. rendered to C.R.E.	
			1 officer 20 OR reported to 59th Bde. for work at 10 p.m. — Trench dug to depth of 5ft. length 50x.	
	9th		Work contd. as for 8th. Box respirators fitted for A Coy.	
	10th		1 OR. Killed (shell). 1 seriously wounded, 1 wounded, 1 shock. Signal dugout blown in.	
			6 men sent to CORBIE to work on baths. 00141 received from 20th Divn.	
	11th		2/LT. Philip returned from Machine Gun Course at LE TOUQUET. 5 OR. report to Right + Left Sectors at 8 p.m. to act as supervisors for infantry digging party.	
	12th		Bn. 0042 issued. 20th Divl. Defence Scheme received. Bn. Lewis Gun Course commenced.	
	14th		A/LT. Col. G. Hayes returned from leave.	
	15th		D Coy. working near SLEET Trench on M.G. dugouts.	
	16th		20th Divl. 00142 received. moves as follows:- A Coy. + Bn. HQ. to FLORIN CAMP r. to MONTAUBAN B+C Coys from Morval to Montauban. Bn. (less 1 Coy.) come under orders of C.E. XIVth Corps.	

WAR DIARY

~~or~~

~~INTELLIGENCE SUMMARY~~.

(Erase heading not required.)

Instructions regarding War Diaries and Intelligence Summaries are contained in F. S. Regs., Part II. and the Staff Manual respectively. Title pages will be prepared in manuscript.

Vol. XXI, Contd.

XIth Durham L. I. (Pioneers)

Army Form C. 2118.

Place	Date	Hour	Summary of Events and Information	Remarks and references to Appendices
	March.			
	16.		D Cy. work under orders of 96th Fd. Cy. R.E. 5 O.R. reinforcement arrive.	
			Report on dugouts constructed in Sunken Rd. T.4.c. attached.	See D702
	17.		A & C Cys. stripping Corduroy Rd. at MONTAUBAN. Capt. Heslop proceeds to England on special leave.	
			Sergt. Gardner awarded Italian Bronze Medal for Military Valour.	
	18.		A Cy. clearing road GINCHY – LESBOEUFS. B & C Cys. on Corduroy Rd. as for 17th.	
			2/LT. Kemp returned from Course.	
	19.		A Cy. salving timber at MARICOURT. B & C Cys. on road GINCHY – LESBOEUFS.	
			2/LT. Branch returned from Lewis M. G. Course at MEAULTE.	
	20.		A Cy. work under 259th Cy. R.E. on standard gauge railway at LEUZE crossing.	
			C Cy. on GINCHY – LESBOEUFS road. & move to dugouts T.4.c.	
			Lt. Pemberton & 2/LT. Towlson return to Bn. Former assumes command of D Cy.	
	21.		A & B Cys. to 259th Cy. R.E. for work.	
	23.		A.B.D Cys. move into No 2. Camp GUILLEMONT. C Cy. remain at T.4.c.	
	24		A & B Cys. working under 96th Fd. Cy. R.E. on DECAUVILLE extensions. OO45 (Bn) issued.	
	25th.		Bn. moved to LE TRANSLOY. C.O. & 1 officer per Cy. met C.R.E. at SAILLISEL & proceeded to inspect work to be done. Bn. working under instruction C.R.E. but not under R.E. supervision.	
	26th		Capt. Dawson returned to Bn. from 20th Divl. Works Bn. & resumed duties of Adjutant.	

Instructions regarding War Diaries and Intelligence Summaries are contained in F. S. Regs., Part II. and the Staff Manual respectively. Title pages will be prepared in manuscript.

Vol. XXI Contd.

WAR DIARY ~~or~~ ~~INTELLIGENCE SUMMARY~~.

(*Erase heading not required.*)

XI Durham L.I. (Pioneers)

Army Form C. 2118.

Place	Date	Hour	Summary of Events and Information	Remarks and references to Appendices
	March			
	26		D Coy. move to LE MESNIL. ½ C Coy to ROCQUIGNY.	
	27.		Reinforcement 50 OR. arrive. One of the best drafts received - good, strong, hardy-looking men - all from Durham. Work as per attached copy of letter to C.R.E.	See D 145 attached
			2/LT. Adams to hospital.	
	29th		A Coy. move to BUS. B+C Coys. in ROCQUIGNY. D Coy. in MESNIL.	
			Work: A, B (less 2 platoons) C Coy. clearing BUS - YTRES road.	
			D Coy. clearing MESNIL - MANNANCOURT Rd. 1 officer + 25 OR. B Coy. keeping mule track open from SAILLISEL to LE MESNIL. 25 OR. making bivouacs at ROCQUIGNY.	
			Remainder B Coy. carrying road repairing material for D Coy. All transport now at LE TRANSLOY.	
	30th		B Coy. moved to YTRES (P. 20. d. 5. 7). Transport now at LE TRANSLOY.	
			Report on work done on roads LE MESNIL - MANANCOURT, BUS - YTRES attached.	See D 146 attached
	31st			

G Hayes Lt Col
Comdg. 1/4/17

D702. To:- C.R.E.
20th Division.
Report to 6pm. 14-3-17

Dug Outs T. 4. C.

Chamber	Completed to date.	Completed since last report.
A	Nil	Nil.
B	Nil	Nil.
C_1	17½'	5½'
C_2	16'	2'
passage between shafts 3+4		Complete
D	Nil	Nil
passage between shafts 4+5		— 32' Complete.
E_1	35' (Complete)	2'
E_2	35' (")	2'
passage between shafts 5+6		complete.
F	Nil	Nil
passage between 6+7		— 9' complete
G_1	33' (Complete)	Nil
G_2	33' (")	"
(30 bunks in each chamber.)		
passage between shaft 7+8 complete		
H_1	33' (complete)	Nil
H_2	33' (" except for lagging)	Nil.
passage between shafts 8+9 Completed		
A_3	Nil.	Nil
B_3	Nil.	Nil.
C_3	Nil	Nil.
D_3	Nil	Nil,
E_3	14'	8'
(Complete except for lagging)		
G_3	14'	2½'
(Complete 4 bunks in)		
H_3	12'	12'

14/3/17

To
C.R.E.
20th Division D745

SAILLY-SAILLISEL - LE MESNIL Road.

From road junction U.14.B.9.4 to U.14.B.9.8 earth and debris removed and road level obtained. Not yet passable. There are patches of good metal though the road is much broken up.

The big holes in the roadway are being emptied & filled in, & holes at the side are being drained.

From U.14.B.9.8 to U.9.C.5.2 the road has been partially cleared & many shell holes filled up. From U.9.C.5.2 to LE MESNIL the road is being cleared and drained.

This portion of Road could be used as a mule track now.

From U.4.D.3.2 to LE MESNIL 100 yards cleared and shell holes filled in. The road is very bad, this is being proceeded with, & tomorrow 2 platoons from the Coy on ROCQUIGNY - LE MESNIL road will be employed here.

There is a passable road through now from O.27.D.8.7 to O.34.D.5.3.

Shell holes have been filled in &

road surface cleared to width of 10ft. throughout.

Mine craters at O.27.D.7.7 and O.27.D.8.5 filled in and passable.

Two platoons are being employed in this road to keep it passable for horse traffic.

(Sd) J. Hayes
a/Lieut. Col
Comdg. 11th. D.L.I.
(Pioneers).

27-3-17

D. 746

To

C.R.E.
20th Division

LE MESNIL - MANANCOURT

Road cleared & shell holes filled in from LE MESNIL to where railway crosses road at U.18.a.5.8; beyond this the Artillery have been working.

BUS - YTRES

Track made by D.L.I. to-day for wagons round crater at O.24.c.9.9 now passable: crater being filled in by Infantry under R.E.

Corduroy road being constructed round big crater, P.19.b.5.8 should be open after tomorrow: limbers can get past now.

Trees being cleared, & main road in YTRES also.

BUS - LECHELLE

Big crater at O.30.a.8.9 and another

at O.24 d 2.2 ; trees felled from here south for about 30 yards.

Another crater at O.30.b.5.5

In LECHELLE several craters and many felled trees. Craters are being worked on by Infantry

This road is at present quite impassable for G.S. Wagons. Am sending Company from LE MESNIL tomorrow to open this road up and will report.

Wagons will be able to pass by midday tomorrow through BUS via YTRES to LECHELLE Station, but the BUS-YTRES road is soft at the YTRES end.

One company YTRES, one BUS, one LE MESNIL, one ROCQUIGNY, H.Q. still at LE TRANSLOY.

(Sd) C Hayes

a/Lieut. Col

Comdg XIth Durham L.I.
(Pioneers)

30/3/17

OFFICE

Copy No. 6

SECRET

March 4th 1917

XIth D.L.I. (Pioneers)

OPERATION ORDER No. 41.

1. 'C' Coy. will relieve 'D' Coy. tomorrow 5th March.

2. 'D' Coy. will move to camp vacated by C Coy.

3. Details will be arranged between O.C. Coys concerned. There must be no break in the work on dugouts

4. S.A.A. Grenades, Tools & Trench Stores will be handed over to relieving Coy. Duplicate of Receipts given to be sent in to Bn. H.Q.

5. O.C. Coys will arrange with T.O. for Transport.

6. Report to Bn. H.Q when relief is complete.

7. Acknowledge.

Copies to:-

1 – O.C. 'C' Coy.
2 – " 'D' "
3 – Transport Office.
4 – O.C. 'A' Coy.
5 – Diary.
6 – Retained

4/3/17.

G. S. Dennis
2/Lt for Capt & Adjt
XIth D. L. I.
(Pioneers).

Copy No. 3

SECRET.

XIth Durham Light Infantry (Pioneers)

OPERATION ORDER No. 42

1. D Coy will relieve A Coy in the HOGSBACK Trench on Wednesday the 14th March. Relief to commence at 8 a.m.

2. A Coy, less parties detailed in (a) & (b) will move into camp vacated by D Coy (FLORIN)

(a) 1 Officer & 20 O.R. will proceed direct to WEDGEWOOD to relieve party of D Coy. under 2/Lt Wood.

(b) 1 Sergt. and 15 O.R. (to include 2 carpenters) will proceed to D.O.R.E CARNOY; party will call at Bn. H.Q. for a guide.

(c) 2/Lt Wood with party will rejoin his Coy. at HOGSBACK Trench.

(d) At 8 a.m. D Coy. party at CARNOY will proceed to rejoin Coy. in HOGSBACK Trench.

3. Details of relief will be arranged between O.C. Coys. concerned. There must be no break in the work on dugouts.

4. S.A.A, Grenades, Tools + Trench Stores will be handed over to relieving Coy. Duplicate of Receipts given to be sent in to Bn H.Q.

5. OC. A Coy. will arrange for Baggage etc being sent down by DECAUVILLE notifying T.O. time of departure. The T.O. will arrange to load D Coys Baggage in DECAUVILLE conveying water to forward area.

6. Baggage for officer detailed from WEDGEWOOD by O.C. A Coy will be taken by T.O from TRONES WOOD, who will also bring back relieved officers (2/Lt Woods) and forward same.

7. Report to Bn HQ. when relief complete.

8. Capt Taylor will be in charge of all work in forward area.

ACKNOWLEDGE

Copies to :-
1 – OC A Coy
2 – OC D ..
3 – TO
4 – D.O.R.E (for information)
5 – C.R.E " "
6 – Retained.

G. [illegible]
2/Lt for Adjt
XI th [illegible]
(Pioneers)

12/3/17.

SECRET — Copy No. 2

XIth Durham Light Infantry (Pioneers)

— OPERATION ORDER No. 43 — March 19th. 17.

1. A Coy. will move into FLORIN Camp this afternoon.

2. A. Coy. will be at the disposal of 295th Coy. R.E. for work on Standard Gauge Railway TRONES WOOD — LES BOEUFS.

3. A. Coy. will report at 8 a.m on Tuesday 20th inst. to Capt. E.G. Matheson 295th Coy. R.E. at Level crossing near LEUZE Siding T. 20.c. 4.4 for work.

4. Working Parties will take 75% shovels, and 25% picks with them.

Acknowledge.

Copies to :-
1 — OC A Coy.
2 — Retained

[illegible]
2/Lt. for Adjt.
XIth Durham L.I.
(Pioneers)

SECRET

Copy No.

XIth DURHAM LIGHT INFANTRY
Pioneers.

OPERATION ORDER No. 44

1. Coys. will move tomorrow as follows:-

2. 'A' Coy. will finish work at 2·30 p.m and move to No. 2 Camp GUILLEMONT at 3·30 p.m.

3. 'B' Coy will finish work at 2·30 p.m. and move to No. 2 Camp at 3·30 p.m.

4. 'C' Coy. – no change.

5. 'D' Coy. will finish work at 2 p.m. and move to No. 2 Camp at 3 p.m. No water tins to be left behind.

6. BATTN. HQRS will move to No. 2 Camp at 2 p.m.

7. One Officer & the C.Q.M.S. per Coy. & 1 N.C.O for Hd. Qrs. will meet 2nd in Command

at No 2 Camp at 2 p.m.

8. Transport Wagons will be at the present Coy. Quarters ½ hour before the time stated for Coys. to move.

9. Kits will be packed before proceeding to work.

10. Men to carry blankets.

11. Coy Commanders will render report certifying that Billets etc were left clean.

Acknowledge

Copies to:—
1 – A Coy
2 – B "
3 – C "
4 – D
5 – T.O
6. – Q.M.S.
7 – Retained
8. – Diary

G.S. Dennis 2Lt
Actg Adjt.
XIth. D.L.I.

SECRET

XI

[illegible]

OPERATION ORDER No 45

1. The XI Bn. [illegible] will move into camp at LE TRANSLOY tomorrow the 25th inst.

2. Advanced Parties consisting of 1 officer & 2 O.R. per Coy will report to [illegible] at 10 a.m at the LES BOEUFS Crossroads.

3. Two men per Coy will be detailed to lead Pack animals. Four men per Coy will be detailed to accompany Limber Wagons.

4. Transport will report to O.C. Coys one hour before schedule starting time.
Limbers with Tools will move at 10 a.m.
Pack animals will move at [illegible]

5. Tools to be taken per Coy. are:-
1 shovel per man + 30% picks,
4 crowbars, Cross cut saws,
Proportion of hand saws, axes, +
mauls. (8 Camp kettles)

6. Water. An allowance of 1 quart per
man per day will be drawn
from D.A.C. normally 144 gals.
extra will be supplied by Batt.
Transport. Tomorrow 72 gals. extra
will be supplied.

7. Coys. move off as follows:-
'C' Coy + 'A' Coy at 1 p.m.
'B' " " 1.20 p.m
'D' " " 1.40 p.m
Men will have dinners before starting

8. C.Q.M.S + 2 Storemen to remain at
MONTAUBAN.
All tools left at MONTAUBAN are to be
loaded on G.S. wagons.

9. C.Q.M.S will report to
O.C. Coys. daily at LE TRANSLOY.

XIth [illegible] Copy No.

Secret

28·3·17

OPERATION ORDER No 46.

1. All Transport (less 2 G.S. Wagons + 2 Limbers) will be at LE TRANSLOY from 29th inst. inclusive.
All stores clothing, boots etc. now at MONTAUBAN will be removed to LE TRANSLOY by Transport.

2. R.Q.M.S. [illegible] [illegible] Aswick 1 [illegible] Ptes. McDonald and Horsburgh will remain at MONTAUBAN. All [illegible] will return to their units.

3. All boys' [illegible] kit, gramophones, boxes &c. will be left at MONTAUBAN.
All [illegible] will be checked by the Adjutant at LE TRANSLOY & anything excessive will be left behind.

A W Dawson [illegible]

28-3-17

XIth [illegible]

([illegible])

10. Spare kit and Stores will be collected at 11 a.m and taken to Q.M. Stores.

11. All times stated are new time

ACKNOWLEDGE

Copies to:-
1 - O.C. A Coy
2 - " B "
3 - " C "
4 " D "
5 - Transport
6 - Retained.

G.J. Dennis 2Lt
Act Adjt.
XI L.G.

Battalion OO. 41 – 46
(inclusive)

Original

Vol 21

Confidential.

War Diary

of

XIth Bn. Durham L. I.
(Pioneers)

from April 1st to April 30th 1917

Volume XXII.

Original

Instructions regarding War Diaries and Intelligence Summaries are contained in F. S. Regs., Part II. and the Staff Manual respectively. Title pages will be prepared in manuscript.

Vol XXII

WAR DIARY
~~or~~
~~INTELLIGENCE SUMMARY.~~
(*Erase heading not required.*)

XI Durham L. I. (Pioneers)

Army Form C. 2118.

Place	Date	Hour	Summary of Events and Information	Remarks and references to Appendices
	April.			Sheet 57C.
	1.		Bn. HQ. moved from LE TRANSLOY to BUS. 2 platoons A Cy. moved to YTRES.	
	2.		2 platoons D Cy. moved to LECHELLE. 20th Divl. OO154 received, dealing with future operation against METZ-EN-COUTURE (P. 19 + 20.) + southern edge of HAVRINCOURT Wood. Present Main Line of Resistance, 20th Divn'l Front: EQUANCOURT – YTRES – BERTINCOURT. O.C. D Cy reports: "mine went up at V.1 b.7.6. sheet 57c. at 8.30 a.m. today. Road blocked. Mine on South side of road". Work of refilling crater commenced.	
	3.		2/LTs. W. W. Freeman; H. Padley; J. F. Gardiner, posted to this unit, arrived today. 2/LT. T. A. ATLAY posted but not arrived – gone to hospital. Gas: Orders received to wear Gas Helmet or Box respirator in Alert position at all times east of BUS – LECHELLE.	
	4.		C.S.M. Williams + Sergt. Dawson, candidates for commissions, interviewed by G.O.C. 20th Div. Work Report to 4th inst.. BUS – YTRES road. Now passable. Still being repaired. Shell holes + craters filled in. ROCQUIGNY – DROMORE Corner (O.31. central). Drainage being carried on. BUS – LECHELLE – YTRES station. Road now open to traffic. MENIN – MANANCOURT Rd.. new mine crater being repaired.	

T2134. Wt. W708–776. 500000. 4/15. Sir J. C. & S.

Army Form C. 2118.

WAR DIARY
~~or~~
~~INTELLIGENCE~~ SUMMARY.
(Erase heading not required.)

Instructions regarding War Diaries and Intelligence Summaries are contained in F. S. Regs., Part II. and the Staff Manual respectively. Title pages will be prepared in manuscript.

Vol. XXII. XIth Durham L. I. (Pioneers)

Place	Date	Hour	Summary of Events and Information	Remarks and references to Appendices
	4.		YTRES – LECHELLE Rd. now passable.	
			Craters completed: V.1.a.6.9. P.25.c.2.3. O.24.d.6.3. V.1.b.3.6.	
			Craters being completed: P.32.d.4.9. V.1.a.4.6. O.24.d.4.5. 4 craters in LECHELLE Village.	
			Court of Inquiry held at BUS for purpose of inquiring into circumstances of injury to 14964 Pte. G. Brown. President Capt. C. Palmer. members. 2/LTS. Lascelles & Rees.	
	5.		20th Div. 00157 received, dealing with establishment of new main Line of Resistance to be known as the BROWN LINE.	
	6.		C.O. & 2nd in command reconnoitred FINS – NEUVILLE Rd. Passable for wheeled traffic but needs immediate attention. Road is used by artillery.	
			L/t. Byers & 2/LT. Morton returned from Course at 20th Div. School of Instruction, DAOURS.	
			L/t. Sear returned to Bn. He had been supervising erection of hutments at MARICOURT BOIS Siding.	
			2/LT. Padley (recently commissioned from the ranks) proceeded on 10 days' leave to England.	
	8.		C of E., and R.C. Services at 8 a.m. & 8.30 a.m. respectively at BUS.	
	9.		2 platoons A Coy. moved from BUS to YTRES. 2 platoons C Coy moved from ROCQUIGNY to BUS.	
			2/LT. Adams returned from hospital. Capt. Stubbs to hospital.	
	10.		2/LT. Cooper returned from hospital.	

T2134. Wt. W708–776. 500000. 4/15. Sir J. C. & S.

Army Form C. 2118.

WAR DIARY

~~or~~

~~INTELLIGENCE SUMMARY~~.

(*Erase heading not required.*)

Instructions regarding War Diaries and Intelligence Summaries are contained in F. S. Regs., Part II. and the Staff Manual respectively. Title pages will be prepared in manuscript.

Vol. XXII.

XIth Durham L. I. (Pioneers)

Place	Date	Hour	Summary of Events and Information	Remarks and references to Appendices
	12.		20th Bde. OO161 received. Main Line of Resistance will be advanced tonight.	
			2/LTS. Fitzsimmons & Atlay reported their arrival on being posted to this unit.	
	13.		Progress of Work Report.	
			BUS-YTRES-RUYAULCOURT Rd. Road being repaired & widened; light drains being made. BUS-YTRES section drained with sumps. Road passable for all wheeled horse traffic.	
			ROCQUIGNY-LE MESNIL-MANNANCOURT Rd. Shell holes filled in & road open for wheeled horse traffic as far as U.12.c.0.8.	
			RUYAULCOURT-NEUVILLE Rd. & NEUVILLE-FINS Rd. to P.35. central. Clearing villages. Filling in craters & shell holes & draining road. Road cleared of wreckage from P.22.d.0.7 to P.22.d.2.5. Road now passable for wheeled traffic from RUYAULCOURT to P.35. central. Working on corduroy road at P.29.c.25.45 – this road now being used by vehicles.	
			YTRES-NEUVILLE. Clearing & preparing road, putting rubble on surface & widening. Road passable for all wheeled transport.	
			F.G.C.M. held on Pte. Myers of this battn. S.I.W. Acquitted.	
			Capt. Heslop to hospital.	

Instructions regarding War Diaries and Intelligence Summaries are contained in F. S. Regs., Part II. and the Staff Manual respectively. Title pages will be prepared in manuscript.

Vol. XXII

WAR DIARY
~~or~~
~~INTELLIGENCE SUMMARY.~~
(Erase heading not required.)

XIth Durham L. I. (Pioneers)

Army Form C. 2118.

Place	Date	Hour	Summary of Events and Information	Remarks and references to Appendices
	14.		2/LT. Rees detailed to act as Adjt. & Qr. Mr. to the 20th Divl. Works Bn.	
	15.		C.S.M. Williams & Sergt. Dawson left for England – candidates for commissions.	
			B Coy. HQ. Officers' mess Room & Coy. Signal Office at YTRES blown up by German mine. 4 O.R. killed 4 O.R. wounded. Reinforcement 18 O.R. arrived.	
	16.		Lt. Lear attached to C.R.E. for duty as Officer i/c Water supply & repair of wells.	
			Battn. machine gun course commenced (recruits). Stretcher bearers class commenced.	
	17.		2/LTS. Gardiner & Freeman proceed to England on 10 days' leave.	
	18.		Bn. Signalling Class for recruits commenced. 2/LT. Fleming reported his arrival on being posted to this Battn.	
	20.		Lt. Byers detailed as assistant Instructor at XVth Corps School, 1st course commencing May 1st.	
			Weekly Progress of Work Report.	
			RUYAULCOURT. Craters at P.10.c.3.5. & P.10.c.8.5. filled in: roads on either side cleared.	
			RUYAULCOURT – METZ Rd. Cleared, drained, metalled, from P.17.d.6.6 to P.24.d.5.8.	
			From RUYAULCOURT to P.17.d.6.6. 500 yds. road cleared, drained & metalled.	
			From P.24.d.5.8 to Q.19.b.8.1. cleared. Road passable.	
			NEUVILLE – RUYAULCOURT Rd. 200^x cleared from NEUVILLE Church towards RUYAULCOURT.	

Instructions regarding War Diaries and Intelligence Summaries are contained in F. S. Regs., Part II. and the Staff Manual respectively. Title pages will be prepared in manuscript.

Vol. XXII

WAR DIARY

~~or~~

~~INTELLIGENCE SUMMARY~~. XIth Durham L. I. (Pioneers)

(Erase heading not required.)

Army Form C. 2118.

Place	Date	Hour	Summary of Events and Information	Remarks and references to Appendices
	20.		YTRES Station – towards ETRICOURT. Road made passable.	
			BUS – ROCQUIGNY ; ROCQUIGNY – BARASTRE ; BARASTRE – BUS ; Repairs.	
			NEUVILLE – P.17.d. central. Cleared, drained & bricked. Road round crater at P.17.d. central widened. Road through NEUVILLE cleared.	
	22		Reinforcement 10 OR. (casualties) rejoined. 2/LT. Padley returned from leave.	
	24.		Lt. Sear returned from C.R.E. to duty with Bn.	
	26.		Lt. Byers & Sergt. Shepherd proceed to 15th Corps School, DAOURS as instructors.	
	27.		Bn. HQ. moved to YTRES. 3 Coys. A.B.D in Ytres. C Coy in BUS. Transport in BERTINCOURT. new work commences 28th.	
			A Coy on track P.12.a.1.3 towards P.12. central; thence across country to Q.1.c.5.9. thence to PLACE MORTEMART about Q.8.d.3.7.	
			B Coy. METZ to Q.15.a.7.5. and on to Q.8.d.3.7.	
			C Coy On roads west of BUS. D Coy. NEUVILLE P.17.d. to METZ.	
			1 platoon B Coy} 3 platoons A Coy} will work at night from 9 p.m. till 3 a.m. Filling in shell holes & making roads & tracks passable for traffic.	
	28		Work as detailed for 27th.	

Instructions regarding War Diaries and Intelligence Summaries are contained in F. S. Regs., Part II. and the Staff Manual respectively. Title pages will be prepared in manuscript.

Vol. XXII.

WAR DIARY

~~or~~

~~INTELLIGENCE SUMMARY.~~

(Erase heading not required.)

XIth Durham L. I. (Pioneers)

Army Form C. 2118.

Place	Date	Hour	Summary of Events and Information	Remarks and references to Appendices
	April			
	29		Officers & Senior N.C.O^s. attended lecture by D.A.D.M.S. on "Sanitation."	
	30th.		1 officer + 2 O.R. sent to Bombing Course, 15th Corps. School DAOURS. Course May 1st – 16th. Siting of Reserve Line on Right Bde. Front takes place tonight. Roughly the Line is:– Q.11.a.25.00. Q.10.a.7.4. Q.10.a.4.6. to 2nd O in WOOD at about Q.3.c.3.3. 1 officer, 1 N.C.O. 10 men per Coy. will drive in pickets along Reserve Trench Line at 20^x to 30^x intervals. ~~The party~~ Coys will wire this line on night 1st/2nd May, at distance of 35^x to 55^x in front of trench line, leaving gaps every 100^x.	

G Hayes a/Lt Col
Comdg 11th D.L.I.

Original Copy.

Vol 22

Confidential.

War Diary

of

XI Bn. Durham L. I
(Pioneers)

from May 1st. to May 31st. 1917.

(Volume 23)

Instructions regarding War Diaries and Intelligence Summaries are contained in F. S. Regs., Part II. and the Staff Manual respectively. Title pages will be prepared in manuscript.

VOL. XXIII

WAR DIARY
~~or~~
~~INTELLIGENCE SUMMARY.~~
(Erase heading not required.)

Army Form C. 2118.

XIth Durham L. I.
(Pioneers).

Place	Date	Hour	Summary of Events and Information	Remarks and references to Appendices
	May			
YTRES.	1.		Bn. HQ. at YTRES. P. 20. d. 35. 90. (sheet 57) 3 Coys at YTRES. 1 Coy. BUS. Transport at BERTINCOURT.	
			1 officer + 2 OR. for Bombing Course; 3 N.C.O.s for Infantry Course. All proceeded to XVth Corps School at DAOURS.	
			20th Divl. OO 171 par 5 (c) states: "The wiring of the Reserve Line will be carried out entirely by the Pioneer Bn., under arrangements to be made by the C.R.E."	
			Reserve Line runs roughly Q. 11. a. 0. 0 – Q. 2. central – K. 31. b. 8. 4 sheet 57 C.	See 0047 attached.
			Wiring postponed as no small screw pickets are available (1200 wanted).	
	2.		Reserve Line wired this evening. Right Bde. Sector completed with a double apron 16 ft. wide + loose wire. 1700 yds. done. Left Bde. Sector 650 yds. done.	
	3.		2/LTS. Gardner + Freeman returned from leave. C Coy. moved from BUS to YTRES.	
			A C.T. will be started tonight along line K. 32. d. 3. 0. – Q. 2. a. 7. 7 – Q. 2. a. 7. 3. – Q. 2. c. 5. 7 – Q. 8. a. 0. 7. Trench will be 6 ft. deep exclusive of parapet. Width will be 2 ft. at bottom with occasional passing places. Width at top will depend on the proportion between chalk + clay. Drains will be dug at intervals towards road on West side. Trench will be camouflaged. Berm 1 ft. with height of 1½ ft.	See 0048 attached
			2/LTS. Atley + Fitzsimmons (recently commissioned from the ranks) proceed on leave to England.	

Instructions regarding War Diaries and Intelligence Summaries are contained in F. S. Regs., Part II. and the Staff Manual respectively. Title pages will be prepared in manuscript.

Vol. XXIII

WAR DIARY

~~or~~

~~INTELLIGENCE~~ SUMMARY.

(Erase heading not required.)

XIth Durham L. I. (Pioneers)

Army Form C. 2118.

Place	Date	Hour	Summary of Events and Information	Remarks and references to Appendices
			Gas alarm received 9.50 p.m. HQ. + Reserve Coy "stood to" with Gas Respirators fixed. at 11 p.m. following wire received:– "Gas alarm cancelled are alarm caused by golden rain rocket which proved subsequently to have been fired from enemy lines".	
			2/Lt. Liddell wounded. Slight, shrapnel. Remained at duty.	
	4.		Progress report on C.T. last night. 520^x trench dug, average depth 4ft. Camouflaged.	
			"Gas. D.99" received at 10.50 p.m. Cancelled at 11 p.m. False alarm.	
	5.		Progress report on C.T. 520^x dug on night 3rd/4th deepened to 6ft. 180^x more dug to 6ft. 75^x dug to 5'9". All work camouflaged.	
			Fighting Strength of Battalion: Officers 36, O.R. 903 Details away from Bn.: 6, 112 With the Battn.: 30, 791 = 821 all ranks. Working strength 540	
	6.		Progress Report on C.T. 60^x new trench dug 6×4×2. 60^x commenced depth 3'3". 670^x old ~~track~~ work deepened + widened. 4 passing places under construction.	
			Bn. order re Reserve Line wire issued.	See 0049 attached.

T2134. Wt. W708–776. 500000. 4/15. Sir J. C. & S.

Instructions regarding War Diaries and Intelligence Summaries are contained in F. S. Regs., Part II. and the Staff Manual respectively. Title pages will be prepared in manuscript.

WAR DIARY
or
INTELLIGENCE SUMMARY.
(Erase heading not required.)

Army Form C. 2118.

Place	Date	Hour	Summary of Events and Information	Remarks and references to Appendices
	7.		Progress Report on wiring last night. ① 280ˣ wired from Q.3.c.6.3 to Q.3.c.8.5	
			② From Q.2.b.8.5 to Q.3.a.3.3. 200ˣ completed with gaps (overlapping) every 50 yds.	
			③ 100 yds. fence & wire completed but aprons not laid.	
			C.T. (reference May 3rd) deepened & widened. 2 passing places cut to 18' X 5'.	
			2 switch passing places taped out 100ˣ apart.	
			Ref work tonight see	0050 [illegible]
	8.		Progress Report on C.T. 215ˣ new trench dug. 4'6" X 3'9" X 2'.	
			70ˣ old work completed. One passing place 15ˣ long width 7 ft.	
			METZ – TRESCAULT Rd. Road now in good condition (except for culvert) from METZ to crater Q.10.d.1.8. Passage is being constructed round Northern tip of crater width 14 ft. 35% completed. Shell-holes filled & blinded with dust.	0051 [illegible]
	9.		Progress report on C.T. work 8/9th. 160ˣ new work average depth 4 ft.	
			150ˣ old work widened & deepened to 6 ft. 4'6" top. 2 ft. bottom. 75ˣ old work deepened to 4 ft. 115ˣ new work 3'3" X 4' X 3'	
			Reserve Line wire repaired from Q.10.a.5.6. to Q.3.a.8.4	
			Work on crater at Q.10.d.1.8. cont'd. A Coy. moved to HAVRINCOURT Wood P.18.a.8.0.	

T2134. Wt. W708—776. 500000. 4/15. Sir J. C. & S.

Instructions regarding War Diaries and Intelligence Summaries are contained in F. S. Regs., Part II. and the Staff Manual respectively. Title pages will be prepared in manuscript. Vol. XXIII

WAR DIARY
~~or~~
~~INTELLIGENCE SUMMARY.~~
(Erase heading not required.)

Army Form C. 2118.

XI Durham L. I. (Pioneers)

Place	Date	Hour	Summary of Events and Information	Remarks and references to Appendices
			1 officer 4 OR. with hand axes assisting in a reconnaissance for a road to join on to the road at about Q.8.a.1.6. 1 officer + 8 O.R clearing out well at BERTINCOURT. 2 officers detailed to make an accurate plan of all Trenches + wire in front of Reserve Line (inclusive). Compass + pacing.	
			2/LT. C.K. Moore having returned from Musketry Course at CAMIERS took over duties of Signalling Officer vice Capt. A.W. Dawson.	
	10.		Progress Report. Passage round crater Q.10.d.1.8. Passable for G.S. wagons. C.T. as before. Deepening existing trench between Reserve Line Wire + western edge 250ˣ. Between Reserve Line & Wood 500ˣ. B Coy. moved to HAVRINCOURT Wood P.18.a.8.0.	
	11		Progress Report. (1) Road Q.10.a.3.3 – Q.4.c.6.2. – Q.4.c.5.6 sheet 57C S.E. Passable for G.S. wagons. (2) Work on C.T. contd. widened, deepened, + passing places completed. D Coy. ~~moved~~ moved to HAVRINCOURT Wood P.18.a.8.0.	
	12		Fighting Strength of Battn. Officers 36, O.R 902. Away from Bn. 3, 95. With the Bn. 33, 807 = 840 all ranks.	

Instructions regarding War Diaries and Intelligence Summaries are contained in F. S. Regs., Part II. and the Staff Manual respectively. Title pages will be prepared in manuscript.

Vol XXIII

WAR DIARY
~~or~~
~~INTELLIGENCE SUMMARY~~.
(*Erase heading not required.*)

XI Durham L. I. (Pioneers)

Army Form C. 2118.

Place	Date	Hour	Summary of Events and Information	Remarks and references to Appendices
			C.T. Work train - forward portion of trench 40x long average depth 2' 6"	
			old work. Widening + deepening. Extension of trench westward 410x to depth 3 ft.	
			A/LT. Col. G. HAYES to hospital. Major H. P. Lloyd in temporary command of the Battn.	
	13		Work contd on C.T. Bn. HQ. moves to HAVRINCOURT WOOD P.18.a. 8.0.	
			C Coy. moves to GOUZEAUCOURT, attached to 60th I.B.	
			15 OR reinforcement arrived. A/Capt. R.L.S. Pemberton to be Temp. Capt. from	22/6/16.
	14.		Progress Report. Old C.T. Contd.	
			new C.T. Left Bde. Area. K.31.c. 180x dug from canal rearwards depth 4 ft.	
			new C.T. from Q. 11. a. 1. 1. 246x dug. (depth 4 ft) towards Reserve Line, south of BILHEM FARM	
	15.		Same work contd	
	16.		" " " . 2/LT. Fleming to hospital.	
	17.		" " " . Capt. Duffy RAMC. transferred to 2nd. Lebon Group.	
			2/LT. Adams proceeded to PERONNE to be interviewed by R.F.C.	
	18.		20th Div. O0175 received. Reference Divl move to new area.	
	19.		Work as above contd.	

WAR DIARY

~~or~~

~~INTELLIGENCE SUMMARY~~. XIth Durham L. I. (Pioneers)

(Erase heading not required.)

Army Form C. 2118.

Instructions regarding War Diaries and Intelligence Summaries are contained in F. S. Regs., Part II. and the Staff Manual respectively. Title pages will be prepared in manuscript. Vol. XXIII

Place	Date	Hour	Summary of Events and Information	Remarks and references to Appendices
	19.		Fighting Strength of Bn. — Officers 36, O.R. 910. Away from Bn. — 5, 92. With the Bn. — 31, 818 = Total all ranks 849	
	20.		Progress Report: C.T. Q.11.a.1.1. ; C.T. K.31.b. ; C.T. Q.5.c.8.3 — new support line BILHEM. } completed.	
	21.		Bn. moved from HAVRINCOURT Wood to YTRES. C Coy. returned from GOUZEAUCOURT. 2/Lt. Lascelles reported to 14th D.L.I.	
	22.		Bn. moved from YTRES to BANCOURT. H.36.c sheet 57C.N.W. Capt. Vick + Lt. Marples struck off the establishment.	
	23.		Bn. rested. C.O. + Adjt. visited 5th Australian Pioneers to arrange relief.	
	24.		Bn. HQ. + 2 Coys. moved to H.6.c.3.8. D Coy. to C.19.d. C Coy. to I.1.1. Small party working under Tunnelling Coy. at Front Line. 1 platoon pushing mining sets by rail to NOREUIL C.10.c. 3 men wounded (sniper). 1 man died of wounds.	57C N.W. See move order attached.

Instructions regarding War Diaries and Intelligence Summaries are contained in F. S. Regs., Part II. and the Staff Manual respectively. Title pages will be prepared in manuscript.

Vol. XXIII

WAR DIARY
~~or~~
~~INTELLIGENCE SUMMARY.~~ XIth Durham L. I. (Pioneers)

(Erase heading not required.)

Army Form C. 2118.

Place	Date	Hour	Summary of Events and Information	Remarks and references to Appendices
	25.		Progress Report. (1) Timber & sandbags carried to old German Trench.	
			(2) Dugout Railway Embankment C.4.b. Mining sets carried.	
			(3) Right C.T. (C.10.c.9.9.) six places blown in, cleared & Trench repaired.	
			(4) Decauville railway between 2 sunken Rds. C.16.c & b. 40 yds. sleepers laid at intervals of 6 yds. 150x drain dug on one side.	
			(5) No 6 dugout. C.9.d.8.6. } 3 ft. excavated & timbered.	
			" 7. " C.15.b.2.0. } Dimensions 6'x3'x3'.	
			1 O.R. Killed. 2 O.R. wounded.	
	26.		Fighting strength of Battn. Officers 35, O.R. 907	
			away from Bn.. Officers 4, O.R. 90	
			with the Battn. Officers 31, O.R. 817 = Total all ranks 848.	
			Progress Report. (5) as above contd. Road from C.26.a.9.6. to C.20.d.3.8. repaired.	
			C.T. from IGGAREE Corner C.10.c.7.9 (sheet 57c N.W) to Embankment C.5 central repaired.	
			Accomodation for 1 Coy. being made at C.20.b.7.5.	
			Pioneers not to provide carrying parties – to work on C.T.	

Instructions regarding War Diaries and Intelligence Summaries are contained in F. S. Regs., Part II. and the Staff Manual respectively. Title pages will be prepared in manuscript.

Vol. XXIII

WAR DIARY

~~or~~

~~INTELLIGENCE SUMMARY.~~

(Erase heading not required.)

XI Durham L.I. (Pioneers)

Army Form C. 2118.

Place	Date	Hour	Summary of Events and Information	Remarks and references to Appendices
	27.		The following are mentioned in despatches :-	
			A/LT. G. Hayes; T/Capt. C. Palmer. T/2nd Lt. A. Philip.	
			13308 Sgt. J. Dawson. 16009 L/Sgt. W. Johnston 21508 Corp. J. A. Boyne 18814 Corp. H. Seggar.	
	28.		Progress Work. 1 platoon with 91st Bde. R.F.A. } making deep dugouts.	
			1 platoon with 92nd. " " " }	
			1 platoon on upkeep of Decauville track between VAULX & NOREUIL.	
			Upkeep of following roads:- C.25.b.o.6 – C.10.c.2.0. C.26.b.0.6 – C.16.a.4.4.	
			C.16.a.6.6 – C.10.c.2.0. C.10.c.2.0 via C.10.c.6.9 to C.5.c.5.7.	
			Remainder of Bn. on C.T. SIDNEY AVENUE between Railway Embankment at	
			C.5.a.9.0. and C.10.b.4.4. thence southwestwards to C.10.b.1.1. thence	
			West to C.10.a.6.1. then West by South to join Sunken Rd. LONGATTE – NOREUIL	C.9.d.6.8
			This C.T. taped by XI D.L.I. morning 28th.	
	29.		A Coy. move to C.20.b.7.5. B Coy. move to VAULX VRAUCOURT.	
			Accomodation for Bn. HQ. being provided in vicinity of B Coy.	
			R.QM.S. Quayle to hospital. Lt. Sear acting as Q.M. 2/Lt. Cooper to hospital.	
	30		Reinforcement 12 O.R. arrived – all casuals.	

Instructions regarding War Diaries and Intelligence Summaries are contained in F. S. Regs., Part II. and the Staff Manual respectively. Title pages will be prepared in manuscript.

Vol. XXIII

WAR DIARY
~~or~~
~~INTELLIGENCE SUMMARY.~~
(Erase heading not required.)

XIth Durham L. I. (Pioneers)

Army Form C. 2118.

Place	Date	Hour	Summary of Events and Information	Remarks and references to Appendices
	30.		G.O.C. 20th Div. visited HQ this morning Progress Report. C.T. SIDNEY AVENUE (see date 28th). 110x complete. 2 exits steps completed. 44x dug. 4' deep. 160x dug 5'6" deep. 170x dug 3ft. deep. Roads see (May 28th). Being repaired – will be passable in two or three days.	
	31.		Bn. HQ. moved to VAULX-VRAUCOURT. C 26. c. 9.5. sheet 57c N.W. H. J. Lloyd Major Comdg. XI D. L. I. (Pioneers)	

Secret

Copy No. 8.

XIth Durham L. Inf. (Pioneers)

OPERATION ORDER No. 47.

Reference Map; France 57C 1/40,000.
Reference to Divl. order. Wiring of Reserve Line

1. Total material available for each Coy is:-

Long S.P.	Short S.P.	Coils of barbed wire
200.	400.	150.

2. At the dump at Q.15.C.3.8. there will be

Long S.P.	Coils of barbed wire
650.	150.

3. 100 men per Coy will take 100 Long Pickets & 50 coils of barbed wire from this dump & carry them straight on to the work.
The remainder of this material (Par 2) will be carried up by the remainder of the men of Companies.
O.C. 'A' Coy will detail an officer & 2 NCOs to be at this dump at 5.30pm. This officer will issue the material to Companies.

4. The material being brought up by wagons is:-

Short. S.P.	Coils of barbed wire
1200.	400.

This will be unloaded on the TRESCAULT Rd. and 3 separate Coy dumps will be formed. This will be done under the direction of an officer to be detailed by O.C. 'B' Coy. He will have entire charge of the unloaded material.
The material from the wagons will be distributed as follows.

	Short. S.P.	Coils barbed wire
'D' Coy	400.	135.
'B' Coy	400.	135.
'C' Coy	400	130.

This will be issued equally as it arrives.
Congestion of carrying parties will be avoided.

5. O.C. 'A' Coy will detail a loading party under an officer to be at the R.E. Dump YTRES at 7.30 pm to load the above material (S.S.P. 1200 Coils barbed wire 400) on to the G.S. wagons.
If there is not enough material at YTRES this will be obtained from the dump at NEUVILLE.

6 Coys will move off from METZ at the following times:-

D Coy at 8.30 pm.
'B' " " 8.45 "
'C' " " 9.0 "

Wagons will move off from METZ at 9.15 pm.
These times are to be adhered to: otherwise congestion will occur at the Dump & on the roads.

7 Acknowledge:

1/5/17.

A W Dawson
Capt & Adjt
XIth DLI (Pioneers)

Copies to:-
1. A Coy
2. 'B'
3. 'C'
4. 'D'
5. T.O.
6 Retained.
7 } Diary.
8 }

SECRET

Copy No.

XIth Bn. Durham L. Infantry

OPERATION ORDER No. 48.

Reference Map 57c. 3rd May 1917

1. A C.T. will be started tonight roughly along the line K.32.d.3.0 – Q.2.a.7.7 – Q.2.a.7.3 – Q.2.c.5.7 – Q.8.a.0.7.

2. This has been partly pegged out and the whole will be taped out tonight by an officer of the 84th Field Coy. by 9.30 p.m.

3. The trench will be 6 ft. deep exclusive of parapet.
The width will be 2 ft. at the bottom with occasional passing places.
The width at the top will be 4 ft. (This may vary later)
The trench will be commenced at the front line & will work westwards.
Every effort will be made to dig the portion of trench allotted to a uniform depth of 5 ft. tonight.

The portion from the front line to the reserve line wire is especially important. This can be deepened by a few men later.

The parapet will have a berm of 1ft. & will be 1ft. 6ins. high.

Care will be taken to keep the earth or chalk compact, as this trench has to be camouflaged.

4. O.C. D Coy. will detail a party under an officer to camouflage this trench from the front line as far back as possible on completion of the work tonight.

The officer detailed will arrange for small pegs to be cut in the wood for fastening the camouflage down. The camouflage is at the Bde. dump & in charge of a N.C.O. of 'C' Coy.

5. Coy. Commanders or 2nd in Command of Coys. will meet the 2nd in Command

at the Left Bde. dump at 9 p.m. tonight.

6. Coys. will pass the Left Bde. dump (Q. 1. c. 2.8) at the following times:-
'A' Coy - 9.20 p.m.
B Coy - 9.30 p.m.
D Coy - 9.40 p.m.

7. Officers Commanding Coys will make their own arrangements re guides.

8. 50% picks will be taken as the ground is chiefly chalk.

9. Acknowledge.

3/5/17.

A W Dawson
Capt & Adjt
XIth D.L.I.
(Pioneers)

Copies to:-
1 - A Coy
2 B Coy
3 D Coy
4
5
6

Copy No 4

Reference OPERATION ORDER 48

Work tonight 4th May 1917

1. B, C & D Coys. will work tonight, 'C' Coy taking over the work commenced by A Coy.

2. These Companies will (except 'B' Coy) employ 2 platoons to finish the work commenced last night. 'B' Coy will employ one platoon for this. This work is to be dug to a full depth of 6 ft. (measured)

3. O.C. 'C' Coy. will arrange to replace the camouflage on completion of work.

4. The remainder of the platoons will carry on the trench from the point where the work ended last night & will work westwards in the following order, 'C', 'B', 'D'.

5. O.C. 'D' Coy will detail an Officer to mark the limits of Company tasks by 9.30 pm. These lengths will be allotted at 1½ yds. per man. The

strengths of the parties for the new work will be sent to O.C. 'D' Coy. by 6 pm. tonight

6. All N.C.O's below the rank of Sergeant will dig with their sections except Corporals who may be acting Sergeants.

7. Coys. will pass Left Brigade Dump at the following times:- 'C' Coy 9-15 pm. 'B' Coy 9-25 pm. 'D' Coy. 9-35 pm.

8. March discipline will on no account be allowed to relax on the way back from work. This was noticeable this morning in one case. If men are tired they must be brought in properly & not allowed to string out over the road.

9 ACKNOWLEDGE

A W Dawson
Capt. & Adjt.
XIth D.L.I. (Pns)

Copy No 1 - O.C. 'B' Coy
" No 2 " 'C' "
" No 3 " 'D' "
" 4, 5, & 6 retained.

Secret. Copy No. 2

XIth Durham L.I. (Pioneers)

OPERATION ORDER No. 49. 6.5/17.

Reference Map 57C. 1/20,000.

1. The Reserve Line wire is too far forward. From about Q.4.c.3.1. it will run to Sap junction at Q.3.c.o.w., to meet the old German wire not far from the WATER COPSE Road. These corrections will be marked out by 9.30 pm tonight.

2. A & B Coys will wire this line tonight.

3. The following material will be required:–

    250 Long screw pickets
    500 short "
    100 coils of German wire or 200 coils British

The Transport Officer is responsible for the collection & the transport of this material (6 GS wagons & 3 limbers). These wagons will leave the dump at NEUVILLE at 7.15 pm and will leave METZ at 9.30 pm at 3 mins intervals

The wagons will take material to advanced dump at Q.10.a.2.3.

4. The Coys will leave METZ as follows:-
'A' Coy 9.20 pm.
'B' " 9.30 "
O.C. Transport will arrange to have wagons with long screw pickets & small proportion of wire in METZ by 9.10 pm.
The Coys will carry on the screw pickets by hand & pick up what wire there is on the TRESCAULT Rd.
This will enable the fence to be started.

5. 'B' Coy will detail 1 Officer to issue material on TRESCAULT Rd.

6. O.C. 'D' Coy will detail 1 Sergt & 15 men to load wagons at NEUVILLE under the Transport Officer.

7. 1 Officer 'A' Coy & 1 Officer 'B' Coy will meet representatives of 96th Fd Coy to accompany the marking out party.
The Officer detailed by OC 'B' Coy will fix the inter Coy boundaries.
The time & place of meeting will

be notified later.

8. O.C. 'C' Coy. will detail a carrying party of 1 Officer + 50 men for the left Bde. 74 Fd Coy RE. This party will be at PLACE ST. HUBERT at 9.0 pm. Remainder of 'C' Coy will be employed in improving the C.T. Instructions have been given to O.C. 'C' Coy about this.

9. The wire will be a similar fence to that already erected. It will be a four strand fence with double apron, 16 ft. wide, 4 strands each apron & with loose wire on & between the aprons. This wire will be completed tonight.

10. Coys will make their own arrangements re guides.

11. Acknowledge.

A W Dawson
Capt & Adjt
XI DLI (Pioneers)

Copies issued to:-
1 A Coy
2 'B'
3 'C'
4 'D'
5 T.O
6 } War Diary
7 }
8 Retained.

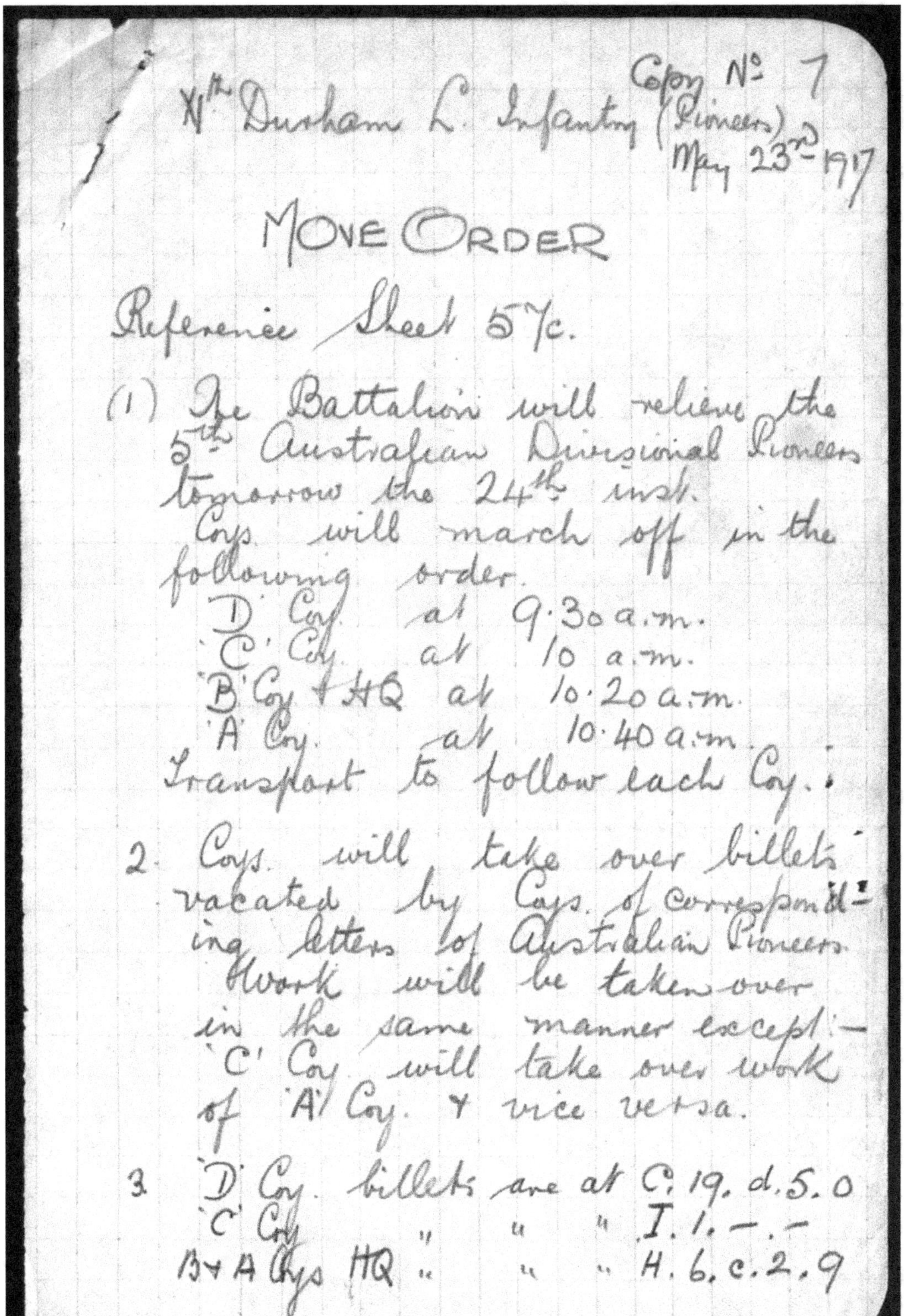
Copy No 7

XIth Durham L. Infantry (Pioneers)

May 23rd 1917

MOVE ORDER

Reference Sheet 57c.

(1) The Battalion will relieve the 5th Australian Divisional Pioneers tomorrow the 24th inst.

Coys. will march off in the following order.

'D' Coy. at 9.30 a.m.

'C' Coy. at 10 a.m.

'B' Coy & HQ at 10.20 a.m.

'A' Coy. at 10.40 a.m.

Transport to follow each Coy.

2. Coys. will take over billets vacated by Coys. of correspond^g ing letters of Australian Pioneers.

Work will be taken over in the same manner except:—

'C' Coy will take over work of 'A' Coy. & vice versa.

3. 'D' Coy. billets are at C.19.d.5.0

'C' Coy " " " I.1.–.–

B & A Coys HQ " " " H.6.c.2.9

Guides for each Coy. will be at Cross roads at ~~I.6.c.5.9.~~ H.17.b.7.8.

4. 1 Officer + 2 N.C.Os per Coy. of the 5th Australian Pioneers will remain behind for 1 day or longer if necessary to show the Coys. the work in hand.

5. The usual report will be made to Bn HQ after vacating billets in the morning

6. Special precautions will be taken against gas as the enemy uses gas shells very freely on this front.
Box respirators will be carried invariably in the alert position by working parties at night, whatever the direction of the wind.

7. Acknowledge.

23/5/17

A W Dawson

Capt. + Adjt.
XI DLI (Pnrs).

Secret. Copy No. 5

11th Durham L. Inf. (Pioneers)

OPERATION ORDER. No. 61.

May 8th 1917.

1. O.C. 'D' Coy will arrange for two platoons to work on the crater at TRESCAULT & also on road repair if any is required.

2. O.C. 'D' Coy will detail 8 O.R. to work under Lt Sear tomorrow under instructions already issued to Lt Sear.

3. 'A' & 'B' Coys will carry on the work on new portions of C.T. westwards. The remainder of 'D' Coy will carry on the work on C.T. that A & B Coys did last night, to the correct dimensions.

4. O.C. 'D' Coy will detail a party to camouflage the above C.T. with brushwood.

5. O.C. 'A' Coy will detail an officer 2/Lt Craig if available, and 12 O.R. to repair the wire in 'C' Coys

portion of the work in the Right Bde section which was done on the night 1st/2nd. There is a portion which has no apron. Care must be taken that the portion of the German wire used for Reserve Line is not confused with that which is in front. The Officer will make a reconnaissance of the German wire which is being used for the Reserve Line wire. The C.R.E. reports a weak place or places in it somewhere in R2.b. This party will probably be employed on strengthening this wire for 3 or 4 nights, which can be done with screw pickets and wire.

6. Reference Para 3. O.C. "B" & "D" Coys will forward to O.C. "A" Coy their working strengths by 7.0 pm and will arrange for an Officer of each Coy to accompany the Officer of "A" Coy who marks out the tasks.

A W Dawson Capt & Adjt
XIX D.L.I.
(Pioneers)

7. Acknowledge.
Copies to:- 1, 2, 3, 4 to Coys.
5 & 6 War Diary.

Diary.

SECRET. Copy No. 6

XIth Durham L.I. (Pioneers)

OPERATION ORDER No. 52

May 20th 1917.

1. The battalion less 'C' Coy will move to YTRES tomorrow afternoon 21st inst in the following order. A, 'B' & 'D' Coys & Battn Headquarters.

'A' Coy will move off at 1.0pm
'B' " " " " " 1.30 "
D " " " " " 2.0 "
Bn HdQrs " " " " 2.30 "

2. Transport will follow each company. Transport officer will send 3 limbers for H.Q. baggage also conveyance for Lewis Guns.

3. Bivouac sheets, tents & petrol tins will be dumped outside the wood. A Coy will detail an officer & each coy. 2 men to remain behind. The officer will report to the Adjutant tomorrow morning for instructions.

The Transport officer will arrange for conveyance of sheets etc. to Bertincourt as soon as possible after move is compleat.

4. Blankets will be rolled on top of the valise & waterproof sheets folded underneath the flap.

5. 2nd Lt Allay 'D' Coy & 1 Sergt per Coy will proceed to YTRES at 11am to arrange billets with the Town Major.

6. Coy Commanders will see that the camp is left perfectly clean.

7 March discipline will be strictly maintained.

8. Acknowledge.

Copies to:-
1. 'A' Coy
2. 'B'
3. 'C'
4. 'D'
5. T.O.
6. War Diary
7. Retained.

H K Moore 2/Lt
for Capt [illegible]
[illegible]

SECRET. Copy No 8

XIth Durham L.I. (Pns)

OPERATION. ORDER. No 53.

21st May 1917

Reference Map France 57C. 1/40,000.

1. (a) 20th Division (less Artillery) will relieve 5th Australian Div. (less Artillery) in the left sector of 1st Anzac Corps front between 21st & 26th May.

(b) 49th Divn will be on the right & 57th Divn (Corps) on the left.

2. (a) The Pioneer Battn of 5th Australian Divn will be relieved by XIth D.L.I (Pioneers)

(b) XIth D.L.I will work under orders of C.R.E.

3. (a) Advanced Divl Headquarters will be established at VAULX at 10am on 26th inst.

(b) Rear Hd Qrs will remain at the MONUMENT (H.13.C) near BAPAUME.

4. The XIth D.L.I will form part of the 59th I.B. group from 6 pm on the 21st until further orders.

5. The battalion will move from YTRES on the 22nd inst & march via P.19.c.7.9. - BUS - ROCQUIGNY - new junction O.31.b.4.0. - LE TRANSLOY - BEAULENCOURT.

6. (a) The battalion will march off at 10.40 am in the following order:-
A Coy, B Coy, C Coy, D Coy, H.Q. & Transport.

(b) Head of the column will be at P.19.c.7.9.
There will be 100 yds intervals between Coys on the march.

7. All tents & bivouac sheets will be loaded on wagon at the H.Q. Orderly Room at 7.30am & conveyed to Town Major, BERTINCOURT.
2/Lt Liddell will hand over to Town Major BERTINCOURT the tents & 40 bivouac sheets, & will obtain 2 receipts.

8. O's C. Coys will obtain the official time from the acting adjutant at 10am, & watches must be synchronised.

9. O.C. Coys will inspect billets immediately after vacating in YPRES & will report to acting Adjutant.

10. Supplies – Refilling will be as under
22nd – N.11.d.4.3 on completion of march. 23rd – Same at 2 pm
24th 25th 26th Ditto.

11. Strict attention will be paid to march discipline during the move to new area.

12. Acknowledge:

F.K. Moon for
Capt & Adjt.
XIIth D.L.I. (Pioneers)

Copies to:-
1, 2, 3, & 4 to Coys.
5. Transport officer
6. H.Q.
7. C.R.E. for (information)
8 & 9 W.D.
10 retained.

Original

Vol 23

Confidential

War Diary - June 1917

11th Bn Durham L I
(Pioneers)

Army Form C. 2118.

Instructions regarding War Diaries and Intelligence Summaries are contained in F. S. Regs., Part II. and the Staff Manual respectively. Title pages will be prepared in manuscript.

VOL XXIV.

WAR DIARY
~~or~~
~~INTELLIGENCE SUMMARY.~~
(Erase heading not required.)

Place	Date	Hour	Summary of Events and Information	Remarks and references to Appendices
VAULX	June 1st		Bn H.Q. - VAULX C26.c.9.5. (sheet 57C N.W.) 2 Coys VAULX. 1 Coy VAULX-VRAUCOURT. 1 Coy Death Valley about C25.b.6.5.	
			A/Lt Col. G. Hayes returned from hospital & resumed command of the Battalion.	
			Weekly Progress Report - ① C.T. SYDNEY AVENUE - 900x new trench dug from C9.d.6.8. to existing trench at C10.b.3.4. - Completed except for trenchboards & [illegible] repairs. ② C20.a.7.8. - C26.c.5.8. ④ C26.a.9.6. - C5.c.4.2. ③ Artillery Dugouts - C23.a.6.4. - C29.a.3.2. - C29.a.1.1. - C29.d.3.9.	
			Right Group commenced, accomodation 5 officers 110 ORs. - C27.b.4.6. - C26.a.6.6. - C19.d.8.8. Left Group commenced, accomodation 10 officers 110 ORs. - ④ Dugouts. No 6. C9.d.8.6. No 7. C15.b.2.0. Completed. ⑤ Decauville Railway - Vaulx Vraucourt - Noreuil. Maintained. ⑥ R.E. Dump - 1 Platoon employed. ⑦ Accomodation for 1 Coy dug in Bank Side about C25.b.6.5.	
	2.		Lt Wardle wounded admitted to Hospital. - 2/Lt Adams left to join R.F.C. & struck off the strength.	
			Fighting Strength of Bn. 35 Officers 903 ORs. Away from Bn. 4 Officers 100 ORs. - Actually with Bn. 31 officers 803 ORs. - 4 officers are. 2/Lt Cooper & 2/Lt Fleming in Hospital. Capt Hopper OC Reinforcement Camp. Lt Byers a/Instructor 4th Army School. - Lt & QM Tollet rejoined Bn. from England.	
			1 Sgt. & 6 men engaged on well sinking at FAVREUIL.	
	3rd		13 ORs. wounded by explosion of dump in VAULX (Shell). Bn. visiting Baths at B30 [illegible]. C of E services (voluntary) for Companies at 2.30pm & 3.30 pm.	

T2134. Wt. W708—776. 500000. 4/15. Sir J. C. & S.

Instructions regarding War Diaries and Intelligence Summaries are contained in F. S. Regs., Part II. and the Staff Manual respectively. Title pages will be prepared in manuscript.

VOL XXIV

WAR DIARY
or
INTELLIGENCE SUMMARY.
(Erase heading not required.)

Army Form C. 2118.

Place	Date	Hour	Summary of Events and Information	Remarks and references to Appendices
VAULX	June 4		Bn HQ is situated in a large garden, not [illegible] anything but comfortable. Our batteries being in fairly close proximity, the Bn HQ billets come in for more than a fair share of splinters from hostile shells bursting NE + SE of us, although the shells drop fully 500 to 600x away. The Coys are exceedingly uncomfortable except perhaps D Coy in VRAUCOURT.	
	5th		Reinforcements 6 ORs arrived (4 casuals 2 draft) – 1 OR wounded. shrapnel slight	
	6th		ORs wounded – 2. (includes 1 at duty). – Progress Report. SYDNEY AVENUE extension to C5.b 7.7 deepened to 6' throughout. Embankment cut through + camouflaged. Now passable under cover from commencement to Sunken Road + front line. – Extract from 3rd Div. No G 913. Communication – "Very good work has been carried out by the Divisional Pioneer Battalion in the MORCHIES sector, who have constructed in the last few days a deep + trenchboarded communication trench from C9 d 6.8 through C10 a 65.10 to C10 b 4.4 where it joins a communication trench commenced by the 5th Australian Division.	
	7th		Vicinity of Bn HQ shelled early in the morning by German long range guns. – News of 2nd Army attack. Messines captured. Wytschaete. 7000 prisoners 3 guns + 2 large T.Ms so far reported. Later Prisoners now 4500.	
	8th		Weekly Progress Report. SYDNEY AVENUE. (1) 1490x of old trench 4' deep deepened to 6'3" + widened	

T2134. Wt. W708–776. 500000. 4/15. Sir J. C. & S.

Army Form C. 2118.

Instructions regarding War Diaries and Intelligence Summaries are contained in F. S. Regs., Part II. and the Staff Manual respectively. Title pages will be prepared in manuscript.

VOL XXIV

WAR DIARY
or
~~INTELLIGENCE SUMMARY.~~

(Erase heading not required.)

Place	Date	Hour	Summary of Events and Information	Remarks and references to Appendices
VAULX	8th		(C) cont. (2) 140x trench dug along embankment to average depth of [illegible] (3) 100x [illegible] along embankment average depth 3'. (4) 1350x SIDNEY AVENUE trench [illegible] from commencement at C9d 6 8 towards front line. (5) 500 x [illegible] CT [illegible] at C5d 2 8 to Sunken Road at C5b 65 55. [illegible] of [illegible] the embankment is cut through & camouflaged with boards at the [illegible]. The front line can now be reached via SIDNEY AVENUE in daylight [illegible] in the [illegible] sitting. (6) 350x new CT dug [illegible] of 5' [illegible] from C18c 2 9 to C17d 75 70. (7) Rifle Supports (a) C24c 6 4 (b) C29a 1 1 (c) C26d 3 9 Right Group 60% complete. (d) C27 [illegible] (e) C21c 6.6 [illegible] 60% complete. (8) [illegible] Railway VAULX to MORCHIES – [illegible] to [illegible] [illegible] of the [illegible].	
	9th		8 [illegible] proceeded to [illegible] CORNER [illegible] TMK [illegible] proceeded to BOYES [illegible] School [illegible]. Fighting Strength 23 offrs. 897 ORs.	
	10th		[illegible] proceeded on leave. Capt Philips + 10 ORs proceeded to [illegible] for [illegible] at sea side – [illegible] Church services. [illegible] by [illegible].	

(A7092). Wt. W12839/M1293. 750,000. 1/17. D. D. & L., Ltd. Forms/C.2118/14.

Instructions regarding War Diaries and Intelligence Summaries are contained in F. S. Regs., Part II. and the Staff Manual respectively. Title pages will be prepared in manuscript.

Vol XXIV

WAR DIARY
or
INTELLIGENCE SUMMARY.
(Erase heading not required.)

11th [illegible] (Pioneers)

Army Form C. 2118.

Place	Date	Hour	Summary of Events and Information	Remarks and references to Appendices
	June			
VAULX	11th		Enemy shelling [illegible] [illegible] [illegible] - [illegible] [illegible] of [illegible] [illegible] [illegible] [illegible]	
			he is preparing for further [illegible] in this sector	
	12th		Lt Sear [illegible] party to continue work for 3-4 days in [illegible] [illegible] at [illegible]	
	13th		Nil.	
	14th		Capt Palmer left Bn for 10 days leave. [illegible] 25 [illegible] [illegible] [illegible] [illegible] 10 [illegible] [illegible] [illegible]	
			recalled for work in [illegible] of operations commencing at 2.30 a.m. [illegible]	
	15th		Weekly Progress Report - Continuation of the one on 8th inst.	
	16th		Heavy firing on [illegible] front early [illegible] morning till about 4.30 a.m. [illegible] [illegible] [illegible]	
			33 Offs. 903 OR [illegible] from Bn 5 Offs 110 OR.	
	17th		Bn [illegible] [illegible] [illegible] [illegible] [illegible] [illegible] + Church services. A/30/10/6 [illegible] [illegible]	
			[illegible] [illegible] [illegible] for 30 Div [illegible] Div. Cmdr [illegible] [illegible] [illegible] [illegible] [illegible] [illegible]	
			is excellent [illegible] [illegible] [illegible] [illegible] [illegible] [illegible] [illegible] [illegible] [illegible] [illegible] [illegible]	
	18th		Lecture at BAPAUME to [illegible] 4th Corps [illegible] [illegible] [illegible] 6 officers + 8 NCOs [illegible] [illegible]	
	20th		12 men released from RA[illegible] [illegible] - [illegible] [illegible] [illegible] [illegible] for [illegible] work.	
	21st		Capt [illegible] [illegible] [illegible] [illegible] leave. [illegible] [illegible] [illegible] [illegible] [illegible] [illegible]	
			1 OR killed + 2 ORs wounded.	

Instructions regarding War Diaries and Intelligence Summaries are contained in F. S. Regs., Part II. and the Staff Manual respectively. Title pages will be prepared in manuscript.

VOL XXIV

WAR DIARY ~~or~~ ~~INTELLIGENCE SUMMARY.~~

(Erase heading not required.)

11th Border Regt [illegible] (Pioneers)

Army Form C. 2118.

Place	Date	Hour	Summary of Events and Information	Remarks and references to Appendices
VAULX	22nd		Commencement of [illegible] weeks. Progress Report [illegible] AVENUE [illegible] 250× [illegible] land. [illegible] + drains [illegible] 21× [illegible] of trench [illegible] C9 a 4 7 completed + steps fixed – New CT running [illegible] from C 4 c 3.1 120× [illegible]. Dugouts [illegible] 1300× dug [illegible] C 17 c 2.0 + C 22 [illegible] [illegible] from 4 [illegible] C 23 [illegible] 20 [illegible] [illegible] working [illegible]	
	23rd		[illegible] from C 24 [illegible] 7.9 to C 30 [illegible]	
	24th		B[illegible] [illegible] 2 platoons [illegible] [illegible]	
	25th		[illegible] to DOMART [illegible] [illegible] Lt Col G [illegible] [illegible] attended CO's conference [illegible] Div HQ	
	26th		[illegible] completed. Capt [illegible] [illegible] for leave.	
	27th		[illegible]	
	28th		Bn concentrated at Transport lines near BEUGNATRE – moved off at 4 pm. Marched past Divisional General near FAVREUIL arrived at Camp near BIHUCOURT G 18. central at 6 pm.	
	29th		Inspections in the morning – Holiday in the afternoon.	
	30th		Battalion moved to DOMART.	

H P [illegible] Major
Cmdg XI [illegible]

(A7092). Wt. W12839/M1293. 750,000. 1/17. D. D. & L., Ltd. Forms/C.2118/14.

Vol 24

War Diary

11th (P) Bn Durham L. I.

July 1917

Instructions regarding War Diaries and Intelligence Summaries are contained in F. S. Regs., Part II. and the Staff Manual respectively. Title pages will be prepared in manuscript.

WAR DIARY

~~or~~

~~INTELLIGENCE SUMMARY.~~

(Erase heading not required.)

Army Form C. 2118.

11th Bn Durham Light Infantry

Place	Date	Hour	Summary of Events and Information	Remarks and references to Appendices
	July			
DOMART	1st	10am	Church Parade.	
"	2nd	8am	Section and Platoon drill. Inspection of Companies by C.O.	
"	3rd	8am	Section and Platoon drill. 2pm Sports till 5pm.	
"	4th	8am	Platoon drill. Leave allotment increased to 25 men per week.	
"	5th	8am	Training Continued till 12/30pm.	
"	6th	8am	Training Continued till 10/30am. 2pm G.O.C Division inspected the Battalion, a very good report received.	
"	7th	8am	Company drill. 10am lecture by Adjutant. 2pm Sports by Companies.	
"	8th	10am	C of E Church Parade. 2pm Conference at the C.R.E's Office. 5pm Nonconformist Church Parade. 16 NCO's sent away for training in Rifle Bombing.	
"	9th	7am	6 NCO's and men went to assist Farmer in getting in hay. 8am Companies on drill and Musketry. Inoculation of N.C.O's and Men proceeded with	
"	10th	8am	Field firing and Company Training. Lieut HOPKINSON joined Battalion leave allotment increased to 46 per week.	
"	11th	8am	Company drill. Tactical scheme in Trench and open Warfare. Sports in afternoon. Adjutants lecture to N.C.O's	

T2134. Wt. W708–776. 500000. 4/15. Sir J. C. & S.

Instructions regarding War Diaries and Intelligence Summaries are contained in F. S. Regs., Part II. and the Staff Manual respectively. Title pages will be prepared in manuscript.

WAR DIARY
or
INTELLIGENCE SUMMARY.
(Erase heading not required.)

Army Form C. 2118.

Place	Date	Hour	Summary of Events and Information	Remarks and references to Appendices
	July			
DOMART	12th	8a	Musketry - Field firing and bombing practice till 12/30 Pm.	
"	13th	8am	Training of Platoons in attack. Bombing practice and Field firing. Capt + Adjt AW. Dawson assumed Command of "C" Coy. Lieut + QM G.H. TOLLIT assumed duty as acting Adjt. All leave to U.K. stopped.	
"	14th	8am	Company Training. Battalion Sports in afternoon. A party of 1 Officer* and 71 O.R. Reinforcements arrived. 8 Pm 5 mile Race. *: 2/Lieut Fleming	
"	15th	9am	9 am to 12/30 Pm inspection of arms by D.A.D.O.S. of Division. 10 to 12 noon inspection of billets by C.O. 3 Pm lecture in Rifle Bombing.	
"	16th	8a	Rifle bombing and bombing, Musketry and Field firing. 50 O.R at work filling in trenches at BARLETTE. 2/30 Pm Battalion Sports.	
"	17th	8am	Company training. Field firing. 10/30 Pm to Midnight Night operations including marching with box Respirators on.	
"	18th	8a	Company training. 2 Pm Revolver practice. Advanced party left for CANDAS	APPEN 1.
"	19th	12/30Pm	Battalion proceeded by March Route to DOULLENS and arrived 5.45 Pm.	12 miles
DOULLENS	20th	8/15am	A Transport of A B & D Coys proceeded to entrain at DOULLENS SOUTH. 100 O.R loaded the train in 65 minutes. A. B & D Coys with H Q entrained at 11 am	

T2134. Wt. W708–776. 500000. 4/15. Sir J. C. & S.

Instructions regarding War Diaries and Intelligence Summaries are contained in F. S. Regs., Part II. and the Staff Manual respectively. Title pages will be prepared in manuscript.

WAR DIARY
or
INTELLIGENCE SUMMARY.
(*Erase heading not required.*)

Army Form C. 2118.

Place	Date	Hour	Summary of Events and Information	Remarks and references to Appendices
	July			
DOULLENS	20th	12/19pm	Train left for HOPOUTRE. 4/19 Pm "C" Coy and Company transport left by train for HOPOUTRE. 1st train arrived 6 Pm, 2nd train at 12 midnight on arrival marched to Camp at PROVEN. Map sheet 27. F 7. c 5 8.	APPENDICE "2"
PROVEN	21st	8am	Cleaning equipment. 2/30 PM "C" Coy proceeded to Camp at E.11 B central. and reported for duty with Railway Construction Party.	
"	22nd	9/30am	9/30 to 10/30 inspection of Camp by C.O. 11am Church Parade.	
"	23rd	8/30am	Physical training. Musketry instruction. Lectures. 9. O Ranks arrived from Base	
"	24th	8/30a	" " " " "	
"	25th	8/30a	" " " " " 4 O Ranks proceeded on leave to U.K	
"	26th	8/30am	" " " " " "C" Company proceeded to Camp at A 8.d.0.1.	sheet 28.
"	27th	8/30a	" " " " . Anti gas. 2/Lt ELLWOOD joined from Base	
"	28th	8/30a	Parades as for 27th. "C" Company moved from A 8.d.0.1 to A 14.b. central and returned same day.	
"	29th	8/30a	Church Parades.	
"	30th	10am	Inspection of Companies in Battle order. 9-30 Pm Battalion less 1 Coy proceeded to "C" Camp A16.b 2.4.	APPENDICE "3"
Camp A16.b.2.4	31st	1/30am	Battalion, less 1 "C" Coy arrived at Camp. 8am "B" & "D" Company proceeded to Canal Bank at B.24.b.9.3. Sheet 28. "A" Company marched out for same place at 2 Pm.	

T2134. Wt. W708–776. 500000. 4/15. Sir J. C. & S.

Instructions regarding War Diaries and Intelligence Summaries are contained in F. S. Regs., Part II. and the Staff Manual respectively. Title pages will be prepared in manuscript.

WAR DIARY
or
INTELLIGENCE SUMMARY.
(*Erase heading not required.*)

Army Form C. 2118.

Place	Date July	Hour	Summary of Events and Information	Remarks and references to Appendices
G Camp A 16 b 2.4 Sheet 28	31st	4 pm	Companies on Road making from Canal Bank B 24 b 9 3 to Trenches Captured from the enemy.	
"	31st	4 pm	Closed.	

Strength

	Officers	O Ranks
June 30th	35	924
July 31st	36	980
Increase	1	56

31st July 1917

H P Lloyd Major
for O/C 11th Durham Light Infantry

(A7092). Wt. W12839/M1293. 750,000. 1/17. D. D. & L., Ltd. Forms/C.2118/14.

XI Durham L.I. (Pioneers) Appen 3

OPERATION ORDER 58

30th July 17.

Ref. Map. Sheet 27 - 1/40,000.
28 - 1/40,000.

1. The Battalion with Transport (less C Coy. & Coy. Transport) will move to Canada Farm Area on night 30th/31st July.

2 The Battn. will parade in 'Battle Order' without packs at 9.30 pm. During the march an interval of 200yds will be kept between Coys. Transport will be in rear of last Coy.

3 Water Bottles & Water Carts will be filled

4. Packs will be taken by Motor Lorry. These will be stacked by Coys. at F.7.b.2.2. under the supervision of 2/Lieut. P.V. Kemp. One man per Coy will be left in charge; these 3 men will proceed by Lorry and unload the Packs at Canada Farm.

(5 men A.Q. will load packs on lorry). Packs must be marked, Mess Tins must not go with Packs.

5. A Billeting Party consisting of Lieut. W.G.L. Sear & 1 N.C.O. per Coy, H.Q. & Transport will parade at 1.30 pm and proceed to A.18.b.0.8 (Sheet 28) and there report to Staff Captain 59th Bde.

6. Rations for consumption on 31st (less Breakfast ration) will be carried on the man.

7. After arrival at CANADA FARM all Companies must be prepared to move at 15 minutes notice

8. This afternoon the men are to rest & all possible rest is to be obtained at CANADA FARM.

9. Breakfasts will be issued at CANADA FARM prior to moving off from there. Time not yet known: probable time of moving about 6 a.m.
This will be communicated to Coy. Commanders as soon as it is known.

10 Further orders will be issued later re move from CANADA FARM.

Acknowledge.

Issued at 9/50 a.m.

G.N. Rocket Lieut & a/Adjt.
XI D.L.I.
(Pioneers)

Copies to:-
O.C. "A" Coy.
" B
" D
2nd in Command
T.O.
H.Q.
W.D. (2)
Office

XI Durham L. I. (Pioneers)

July 19th 17.

MOVE ORDER N° 56.

Appen I

1. The Battalion will parade in marching Order tomorrow 19th inst. and proceed by march route to DOULLENS. Caps will be worn.
Helmets will be carried on packs.
The Battn. will move off in the following order:-

A, B, C, D Coys. H.Q., Traffic Control.

The Head of the Column will pass the X roads on BERNEUIL RD. at E. end of DOMART at 12·30 p.m. Coys. will time their arrival at X roads accordingly.

2. The T.O. will arrange to have necessary wagons at Coy. H.Qrs. tomorrow morning at 9 a.m.
All wagons will be loaded by 11 a.m.
O.C. Coys. will furnish a brakesman for each Coy wagon, cooker, & also 2 men per Coy. for pack animals.

HQ will furnish 2 men for Lewis Gun Limbers, 1 for each vehicle.

3 The Billeting Party consisting of 2 Lieut. Moore, Coy Q.M. Sgts and 1 N.C.O. from HQ will parade at HQ at 12.15 pm. and proceed on bicycle to DOULLENS & on arrival will report to the Town Major for billeting instructions.

4 Rations for consumption on the 20th will be drawn by hand as soon as they are ready for issue (about 10.30 a.m) and will be placed in Coy Cookers. Rations for consumption on 21st will be carried by the A.S.C. wagons.

5. The usual billeting certificate as to cleanliness of billets will be handed in to the Orderly Room by 11.30 a.m.

6. A Stragglers' Party consisting of 1 N.C.O. & 4 men per Coy under the charge of Sgt. McMenam

will march in rear of the Traffic Control Party. This party will not wear packs.

Acknowledge.

Issued at:- 5 p.m.

Lieut & Adjt.
XI. D. L. I.

Copies to:-
O.C. A. Coy.
" B
" C
" D
" H.Q.
" Transport.
" 2nd in Command.
" Office

XIth. Durham L. I. (Pioneers)

July 19th. 17.

MOVEMENT ORDER No. 57.

Appx 2

1. MOVE. The Battalion will entrain tomorrow 20th inst at DOULLENS South Station.
A, B & D Coys. Hd. Qrs. and all Transport including bicycles, stretchers etc not mentioned below will proceed by No. 2 Train leaving at 12 hrs. 19 mins.
The Coys. will parade at 10 a.m.

2. TRANSPORT. C. Coy. 2 G.S. wagons 'C' Coy. 2 G.S. wagons 'D' Coy., and 'C' Coys Cooker will proceed by No. 5 train leaving at 16 hrs. 19 mins.
'C' Coy. will be at station 1½ hrs before this hour.

3. UNLOADING and LOADING PARTIES. A loading party consisting of 1 officer and 50 men of 'A' Coy & 1 Officer and 50 men of 'B' Coy. will report to the 2nd in Command at DOULLENS South Station at 8.45 am
A loading party of 2 officers & 100 O.R from 'C' Coy., will report

to Capt. Webb 6th K.S.L.I. at
at DOULLENS South Station at 12.45pm
This party will load No. 5 Train.
An unloading party of 1 officer
+ 50 men of 'A' Coy. and 1 officer +
50 men 'B' Coy. will unload No. 2 train
on arrival at destination.
2 Officers + 100 men of D Coy.
will unload No. 5 train on
arrival at destination.

4 WAGONS All wagons, less those proceeding
with 'C' Coy., will be loaded by
8.15 a.m. and will be at
DOULLENS South Station by 8.45 am.
Transport going with 'C' Coy.
will be at DOULLENS South
Station by 12.45 pm.

5 RATIONS. Water Carts will travel full.
Water bottles will be filled
& the days rations carried on
the man.
Tea will be made on arrival
at destination.
Horses will be watered before
departure

6. DESTINATION — On arrival at Detraining Station 'C' Coy., with Transport will proceed direct to Training Camp at E.11.a.5.0. and report to A.D.L.R.

O.C. 'D' Coy., will detail a guide to conduct unloading party to Camp.

7. DETACHMENT — 'C' Coy & 'C' Coy. Transport will be a detachment from 8 a.m. tomorrow under Captain Dawson.

8. Acknowledge.

Issued at:- 10 oclock p.m.

19/7/17.

Lieut & a/Adjt.
XI D.L.I.
(Ps).

Copies to:- O's C. A, B, C, D. Coys.
H.Q.
2nd in Command
T.O.
Office.

Confidential

War Diary - Aug 1917

Vol 25

11th Durham Light Infantry

Instructions regarding War Diaries and Intelligence Summaries are contained in F. S. Regs., Part II. and the Staff Manual respectively. Title pages will be prepared in manuscript.

WAR DIARY
or
~~INTELLIGENCE SUMMARY.~~

Army Form C. 2118.

(Erase heading not required.) 11th Bn Durham Light Infantry (PIONEERS)

Place	Date	Hour	Summary of Events and Information	Remarks and references to Appendices
"G" Camp. A16. b. 2.4 Sheet 28	31/7/17	4 Pm	Very heavy rain stopped work on road making. A. B & D Coys remained on the work all night. 6 Pm Rations and Water sent up to Coys at B24. b. 9.3. Heavy enemy Artillery fire on EAST side of PILCKEM Ridge. 8.30 Pm all guns on Corps front opened fire which continued for some time. A few gas shells sent over during the night.	
A 16 b. 2.4 Sheet 28	1/8/17	2 Pm	"B" & "D" Coys returned to Camp. 7.30 Pm "A" Coy returned to Camp, men all very wet and tired. "C" Coy employed with Light Railway Coy, 100 yds of track made, very heavy work under shell fire.	
A 16. b. 2.4 Sheet 28	2/8/17	6/30 am	"B" & "D" Coys proceeded to BARD CAUSEWAY, C 13. c, Sheet 28 for road making. "A" Coy followed at 12/30 Pm. Men now have a march of 14 miles daily and in addition have 6 hours work to do. "C" Coy continued work on Railway from 11 am to 7 Pm.	
A 16. b. 2.4 Sheet 28	3/8/17	6/30 am	"B" & "D" Coys proceeded to Canal Bank for work on roads. "A" Coy followed at 12/30 Pm. "C" Coy continued work on Railway construction, 8 hours heavy digging.	
A 16. b. 2.4 Sheet 28	4/8/17		A. B & D Coys resting. "C" Coy completed 200 yds of Railway track and fitted 2 Bridges. Lieut A. PHILLIP proceeded on Lewis gun course.	

(A7092). Wt. W12839/M1293. 750,000. 1/17. D. D. & L., Ltd. Forms/C.2118/14.

Instructions regarding War Diaries and Intelligence Summaries are contained in F. S. Regs., Part II. and the Staff Manual respectively. Title pages will be prepared in manuscript.

WAR DIARY

~~or~~

~~INTELLIGENCE SUMMARY.~~

(Erase heading not required.)

Army Form C. 2118.

Continued.

Place	Date	Hour	Summary of Events and Information	Remarks and references to Appendices
A.16.b.2.4 Sheet 28.	5/8/17	6/30am	"B" & "D" Coys proceeded on Road Making at HUDDLESTON Rd, C.7.b.1.7 Sheet 28.	
		12/30pm	"A" Coy followed B & D Coys. HUDDLESTON Rd now passable up to CACTUS Trench, here there was an impassable swamp. "C" Coy 400 yds of grading made B.12.a.9.2 to B.12.b.7.9.	
A.16.b.2.4 Sheet 28	6/8/17	7am	Advance party and "B" Coy proceeded to Canal Bank and took over dugouts from Welsh Pioneers at C.19.a.0.3 "D" Coy followed at 8/30 am. "A" Coy proceeded to Bivouac at B.22.a.6.8 (Sheet 28). "C" Coy levelling and ballasting from B.12.C.7.0 to B.18.C.7.7. Sheet 28. 700 yds completed	
C.19.a.0.3 Sheet 28	7/8/17	5am	"D" Coy and half of "A" Coy proceeded to Repair and Make new Road from C.7.d.2.3 to C.14.a.8.8, St Julien map. "B" Coy and half "A" Coy went out on Relief at 11 am. "C" Coy grading at B.6.d.8.0. 3 O.R. Wounded.	
CANAL BANK C.19.a.0.3	8/8/17	5am	"D" Coy and half of "A" Coy continued work on Roads and Tracks. "B" Coy and half of "A" Coy relieved first 2 at 12 noon and continued the work. 2/Lieut. P. KEMP assumed duty as Trench Railway Officer. "C" Coy completed 240 yds grading, 120 yds of track raised and widened, 60 yds of track filled 1 foot.	
CANAL BANK C.19.a.0.3	9/8/17		"A" "B" & "D" Companies continued work on Roads. "C" Coy completed 350 yds of Railway Track	

(A7092). Wt. W12839/M1293. 750,000. 1/17. D. D. & L., Ltd. Forms/C.2118/14.

Army Form C. 2118.

Instructions regarding War Diaries and Intelligence Summaries are contained in F. S. Regs., Part II. and the Staff Manual respectively. Title pages will be prepared in manuscript.

WAR DIARY
or
~~INTELLIGENCE SUMMARY.~~
(Erase heading not required.)

Continued

Place	Date	Hour	Summary of Events and Information	Remarks and references to Appendices
CANAL BANK C 19. a. 0. 3 Sheet 28.	10/8/17	5/30 am	1½ Coys on Road making till 12 noon. 1½ Coys from noon till 6 Pm. "C" Coy, grading switch Railway line running South from C 7. a. 7. 6. 900 feet completed. 1 O.R. Wounded.	
Do	11/8/17		Repair of Roads by 3 Coys continued. New track commenced from C 13. b. 3. 2 to C. 14. a. 8. 8 "C" Coy completed 1400 feet of grading on Railway 1. O.R. wounded.	
Do	12/8/17		Repair of Roads continued. Battalion dump formed at C 14. a. 7. 5. 100 O.R. Carrying material. "C" Coy 120 yds grading on switch line C. 7. a. 9. 5. Lieut. F. HOPKINSON Wounded.	
Do	13/8/17		3 Coys working on Roads. "C" Coy resting. 2/Lieut BUSHELL Wounded on leave to U. K	
Do	14/8/17		Work on Roads and New track continued by 3 Companies. Gas shells sent over by the enemy about 11 Pm. "C" Coy, 300 yds Railway track worked C 7. b 0. 4 Sheet 28.	
Do	15/8/17	6 am	2 Companies worked 3 hours improving tracks and Carrying timber "C" Coy. 100 yards Railway track commenced, on BOESINGHE Rd & BRICK Spur 40 yds completed	
Do	16/8/17	4/45 a	Attack on LANGEMARCK commenced by 14th Corps. 9 am A. B & D Coys commenced work on new Road at PILCKEM. "C" Coy worked 750 feet Railway grading at C. 7. d. 1. 2 Captain J. TAYLOR, Wounded. 6 O.R. Killed. 1. O.R. died of wounds. 17. O.R. Wounded	

(A7092). Wt. W12839/M1293. 750,000. 1/17. D. D. & L., Ltd. Forms/C.2118/14.

Instructions regarding War Diaries and Intelligence Summaries are contained in F. S. Regs., Part II. and the Staff Manual respectively. Title pages will be prepared in manuscript.

WAR DIARY
or
~~INTELLIGENCE SUMMARY.~~ Continued

(Erase heading not required.)

Army Form C. 2118.

Place	Date	Hour	Summary of Events and Information	Remarks and references to Appendices
CANAL BANK	17/8/17	7 am	Work on plank road continued by 3 Coys. "C" Coy 1300 feet of grading worked on main line at C 7 b central. 7 O.R. wounded.	
MALAKOF FARM. AREA B23. C. Central SHEET 28.	18/8/17	2 Pm	"B" and "D" Coys moved from Canal Bank to LEIPZIG FARM on being relieved in Canal Bank by Welsh Divisional Pioneers. "C" Coy moved to bivouacs at B 23. b 5.5. "C" Coy completed 60 yds new track formation at GALLWITZ FARM.	
Do	19/8/17	8 Am	Camp shelled. 2/Lieut GARDINER wounded. 12.45 Pm "A", "B" and "D" Coys marched to ELVERDINGHE Station and there entrained for "S" Camps, arrived PROVEN at 3 Pm marched to Camp, 5 miles, and arrived at F5. C. 4. b at 4-30 Pm. "C" Coy resting.	
SEATON CAMP F5. C. 4. b Sheet 27	20/8/17	9 Am	Kit inspection, cleaning equipment, checking tools, "C" Coy Railway track repaired where damaged by shell fire. 3 O.R. wounded.	
Do	21/8/17	8/30 a	to 11-30 a Platoon drill for A. B & D Coys. "C" Coy no work. 2/Lieuts G. S. YOUDE and A. E. WILKINSON also 13 O.R. joined Bn. Captain A. W. DAWSON evacuated sick.	
Do	22/8/17	7 am to 4 P	3 Coys on bathing parade. "C" Coy ~~??~~ 900 yds of Railway track levelled and aligned.	
Do	23/8/17	8/30 A to 12/30 P	Platoon training. "C" Coy 2 Platoons prepared 170 yds formation. 2 Platoons levelled packed and straightened 500 yds of track.	
Do	24/8/17	8 am to 12/30 Pm	100 men on repair of roads in camp. 6 Lewis guns and teams proceeded on duty for Anti aircraft work. Platoon training. 9 Casuals arrived from Base. "C" Coy 180 yds formation completed, 750 yds levelled and straightened.	

Instructions regarding War Diaries and Intelligence Summaries are contained in F. S. Regs., Part II. and the Staff Manual respectively. Title pages will be prepared in manuscript.

WAR DIARY
or
~~INTELLIGENCE SUMMARY.~~
(Erase heading not required.) Continued.

Army Form C. 2118.

Place	Date	Hour	Summary of Events and Information	Remarks and references to Appendices
SEATON CAMP F5.C.4.6.	25/8/17	8/30am to 12/30pm	Platoon training. "C" Coy. 350 yds of track ballasted.	
"	26/8/17		Church Parade. C of E at 10/30 am. R.C. at 9/30 am. 4 Casuals joined from Base. "C" Coy, 500 yds formation dug. 3 sidings completed.	
"	27/8/17	8/30am	Platoon training. Bombing and Rifle range practice. "C" Coy 100 yds siding completed. 100 yds curve straightened.	
"	28/8/17	8/30am	Platoon training. Inspection of box respirators by Divisional Gas Officer. 3 Officers and 75 O.R. each, A. B & D Coy, under Capt Sear, proceeded by Motor Bus to B.23 Central. Sheet 28. for work under the 123rd F Coy R.E. "C" Coy. 1 Platoon loading rails. 3 Platoon laid 500 yds of track. Casualties. 1 O.R. wounded.	
"	29/8/17	8/30am	Platoon training. "C" Coy completed 700 yds formation.	
"	30/8/17	8/30am	Platoon training. Instruction of Signallers. "C" Coy 1,000 yds track laid & repaired.	
"	31/8/17	"	Platoon training. Instruction of Bombers & Signallers. 4 PM. Diary closed.	

	OFFICERS	O.R.
Battalion strength on 1-8-17	36	980
Joined during month.	2	38
Total.	38	1018
Struck off. Killed, Wounded & Sick.	4	61
Strength on 31st Aug 1917.	34	957

H. L. Lloyd Major
Comdg 11th D. L. I. (Pioneers)
31-8-1917.

(A7092). Wt. W12839/M1293. 750,000. 1/17. D. D. & L., Ltd. Forms/C.2118/14.

XI Durham L. I. (Pioneers)

OPERATION ORDER No 59

Aug 5th 17

The Battalion will take over quarters from the Welsh Pioneer Battn 38th Division tomorrow 6th July as follows -

1 Hd Qrs & B Coy will be at the CANAL BANK C.19 a 0.3 by 9 a.m. and will parade in marching order at 7 a.m. D Coy will be at the CANAL BANK by 10.30 a.m. Coy parade at 8.30 a.m.

A Coy will proceed to bivouacs at B.22 a 6.8 and will parade in marching order at 9 a.m.

2. An advanced party consisting of 1 officer, 4 N.C.O.s each B & D Coys and 2 N.C.O.s HQrs under the command of 2Lt. Moore will proceed to the CANAL BANK and take over the dugouts from the Welsh Divisional Pioneers. This party must arrive there by 8 a.m. They will parade at 6 a.m. in marching order.

3 The above officers from B & D Coys

will reconnoitre a new duck board track from East end of WINDSOR CASTLE tramway line running towards PILCKEM.

1 officer of A Coy will see the other work of the Welsh Divisional Pioneers on new trolley line & will proceed with the advance party.

4. The Battn Transport lines will remain in 'G' Camp.

5 A rear party consisting of 1 N.C.O and 9 men under Lieut Liddle will hand over the accommodation in G Camp to the advanced party of the Welsh Divisional Pioneers at 9 a.m.

6. The days rations will be carried on the man and water bottles filled.

7 Transport Officer will arrange for the removal of Officers kits & necessary tools to the new quarters in CANAL BANK

Water carts will proceed filled.

The route to be taken is as laid down in Traffic Map. if tracks are not fit to travel on

8. Acknowledge

Issued at - 7 pm. 2/8/17.

Copies to -
OC A. Coy
B
D
2nd in Command
T.O.
Office
Diary (2

[signature] Lieut & a/Adjt
XI D.L.I. (Pns)

Instructions regarding War Diaries and Intelligence Summaries are contained in F. S. Regs., Part II. and the Staff Manual respectively. Title pages will be prepared in manuscript.

WAR DIARY
or
~~INTELLIGENCE SUMMARY.~~
(Erase heading not required.) 17th Durham Light Infantry.

Army Form C. 2118. Vol 26

Place	Date	Hour	Summary of Events and Information	Remarks and references to Appendices
SEATON CAMP F.5.c.4.6	1-9-17	8/30 Am to 12/30 Pm.	3 Companies on Platoon Training. 5 to 8 Pm practice on Rifle Range. "C" Coy at BROAD St. C.8.a.8.5. Sheet 28. 300 yds track levelled and ballasted. 250 feet Siding at C.3 central completed. 200 O.R on detachment working on RE Dumps and BARD CAUSEWAY.	
"	2-9-17	10/30 A	Church Parade for A.B.&D Coys. "C" Coy repairing Railway line where broken by Shell fire also laying track. 200 O.R. working on RE Dumps and Trench Tramways.	
"	3-9-17	8/30 Am to 12/30 Pm	A.B.&D Coys on Platoon Training. "C" Coy Resting. 200 O.R. working on PILCKEM Rd Tram line and RE Dumps. 2/LIEUT M. COOPER and 3 O.R. Rejoined BN. from Base	
"	4-9-17	7/30 Am to 10 A	Rehersal parade for G.O.Cs inspection. 10/30 to 12 noon Platoon Training. "C" Coy Resting. 200 O.R. at work on R.E. Dumps and Trench Tram lines.	
"	5-9-17	9 am	Parade under 60th Brigade for G.O.Cs inspection and presentation of Medal Ribbons. "C" Coy Completed 340 yds Railway formation at C.2.a.2.1. 90 O.R. burying Cable for R.E. Signal Coy. 110 O.R. working on RE Dumps and Tram line.	
"	6-9-17	8/30 Am to 12/30 Pm.	A.B.&D Coys on Platoon Training. "C" Coy 200 yds Railway track ballasted. 200 O.R. working on Dumps and Tram lines.	
"	7-9-17	"	3 Coys on Platoon Training. "C" Coy laid 240 yds Railway track, 60 yds ballasted. 160 O.R. working on RE Dumps. 40 O.R. working on New baths. 1 O.R. Wounded.	

(A7092). Wt. W12839/M1293. 750,000. 1/17. D. D. & L., Ltd. Forms/C.2118/14.

Instructions regarding War Diaries and Intelligence Summaries are contained in F. S. Regs., Part II. and the Staff Manual respectively. Title pages will be prepared in manuscript.

WAR DIARY
~~or~~
~~INTELLIGENCE SUMMARY.~~
(Erase heading not required.)

Army Form C. 2118.

CONTINUED

Place	Date	Hour	Summary of Events and Information	Remarks and references to Appendices
SEATON CAMP F.5.C.4.6.-S27	8-9-17		All day sports held by 60th Brigade. "C" Coy 250 yds Railway line ballasted. 100 yds track made. 200 O.R. working under R.E.s on Dumps and Baths.	
C.19.a.0.2 Sheet 28. Canal bank	9/9/17	11 Am	A. B. D Coys & HQ paraded at 11 Am and proceeded by march route to INTERNATIONAL CORNER and then entrained for ELVERDINGHE, on arrival the Coys marched to CANAL BANK and relieved the Welsh Divisional Pioneers. "B" Coy proceeded to Bivouacs at B.23.b central. The detachment of 200 O.R. rejoined their respective Companies at 5 Pm. "C" Coy ballasted 100 yds Railway track. 6 Lewis Guns under 2/Lt F. ATLAY proceeded to the forward area and took over Anti Aircraft duties at LANGEMARCK and THE STEENBEEK.	
C.19.a.0.2 Sheet 28	10/9/17		"A" & "D" Coys improving accomodation at Canal bank. "B" Coy improving bivouacs. "C" Coy repaired and ballasted 200 yds Railway track. 2 O.R. arrived from Base.	
"	11/9/17		"A" "B" & "D" Coys working on dugouts and bivouacs. "C" Coy 300 yds Railway track ballasted.	
"	12/9/17		4 Platoons carrying material to forward dumps. 8 Platoons improving dugouts. "C" Coy moved back to rest at A.4.d.3.8. Lieut G.V. KEMP assumed duty as Officer i/c Trench Tramways. 2/Lieut V.E. TOWLSON Wounded	
"	13/9/17		2½ Companies carrying material to forward dumps. Casualties 1 O.R. Wounded.	

(A7092). Wt. W12839/M1293 750,000. 1/17. D. D. & L., Ltd. Forms/C.2118/14

Instructions regarding War Diaries and Intelligence Summaries are contained in F. S. Regs., Part II. and the Staff Manual respectively. Title pages will be prepared in manuscript.

WAR DIARY
or
INTELLIGENCE SUMMARY.
(Erase heading not required.)

Army Form C. 2118.

Place	Date	Hour	Summary of Events and Information	Remarks and references to Appendices
C.19.a.0.2 Sheet 28.	14/9/17		'A' & 'D' Coys wired about 700 yds of new line in forward area. 2 Platoon of 'B' Coy Carrying material. 'C' Coy resting and cleaning equipment.	
"	15/9/17		'A' 'B' & 'D' Coys wiring forward area. Casualties O.R. 1 Killed, 1 Wounded.	
"	16/9/17		'A' 'B' & 'D' Coys carrying material to forward area. 4 O.R. Wounded.	
"	17/9/17		'B' Coy completed wiring. 'A' & 'D' Coys at work on French Tramway. 'C' Coy resting. Casualties:- O.R. Killed 1. Wounded 5.	
"	18/9/17		'A' & 'D' Coys working on dry weather track C.14.a.5.9 to C.13.b.3.2 and C.8.a.8.8 to C.7.b.1.6 2 O.R. Wounded.	
"	19/9/17		2 Platoon of 'B' Coy at work on duckboard track. 'A' & 'D' Coys resting.	
"	20/9/17	7PM	'A' Company proceeded to new front line for work on strong points, the Company worked all night and constructed 4 strong points as per detailed instructions.	
		9PM	'D' Company proceeded to new front line to construct strong points. Owing to the Infantry guide loosing his way the whole Coy did not arrive on the work with the result that only one strong point was made before daybreak.	
			8 Lewis guns under 2/LIEUT F. ATLAY took part in the attack by the Division 4 guns being on Anti Aircraft duty and 4 guns in front line, 50 men with the 8 guns, 11 Casualties. Casualties:- 2/LIEUT. E. FLEMING Wounded O. Ranks. Killed 3. Wounded 11.	

Instructions regarding War Diaries and Intelligence Summaries are contained in F. S. Regs., Part II. and the Staff Manual respectively. Title pages will be prepared in manuscript.

WAR DIARY
or
~~INTELLIGENCE~~ SUMMARY.
(*Erase heading not required.*)

Army Form C. 2118.

Place	Date	Hour	Summary of Events and Information	Remarks and references to Appendices
C 19 a 0.2 Sheet 28	21/9/17		"A" "B" & "D" Coys repairing roads from U 27.c 3.1 to LANGEMARCK, Roads shelled throughout the night which made the work difficult. 2/LIEUT. B.H. Wounded. O. Rks. 6 Wounded	
"	22/9/17		3 Companies working on roads as for 21st. Casualties. O. Ranks. Killed 1. Wounded 6	
"	23/9/17		Work continued on roads till 2 a.m. 24th, a bombardment with gas shells compelled the work to cease, men returned to shelters.	
			2/LIEUTS R MORTON and J.R. BRANCH Wounded. O. Ranks. Killed 1. Wounded 2.	
"	24/9/17		210 Men dug a trench, about 600 yds, from U 23.b.17.20 to U 23.d.85.10, this trench was 3 feet wide by 3 feet 3" deep. 30 men wired at strong point at U 24.c 9.5. Casualties O.R. Wounded 2.	
"	25/9/17		Owing to hard work on night of 24th Companies rested.	
"	26/9/17		3 Companies worked on new trench at U 23.d 85.10 and generally improved same, a parapet giving head cover was made and bad parts in trench built up with sand bags. Casualties O.R. 3 Wounded.	
"	27/9/17		175 O. Ranks carried and laid duck boards to front line from LANGEMARCK. Shell fire over roads and tracks very heavy. Casualties 10 O.R. Wounded.	

Instructions regarding War Diaries and Intelligence Summaries are contained in F. S. Regs., Part II. and the Staff Manual respectively. Title pages will be prepared in manuscript.

WAR DIARY
or
INTELLIGENCE SUMMARY.
(Erase heading not required.)

Army Form C. 2118.

Place	Date	Hour	Summary of Events and Information	Remarks and references to Appendices
SEATON CAMP F5 C 4. b	28/9/17		'A' 'B' & 'D' Companies with Headquarters were relieved in the Canal Bank, C.19.a.0.2 by 3 Companies 21st West Yorkshire Regt. at 2/30 PM and marched to ELVERDINGHE Station and there entrained for INTERNATIONAL CORNER Station on detraining the Companies marched to SEATON CAMP arriving at 5-30 PM. "C" Company joined the Battalion during the morning on being relieved from Railway Construction work.	
"	29/9/17		Inspection of Clothing and equipment, sports in afternoon.	
"	30/9/17		Church Parades for C of E and Nonconformists.	
"	30/9/17		Diary closed at 6 PM.	

	Officers	O.R.
Battalion Strength on 1st Sept 1917.	31	957
Joined during Sept 1917.	1	5
	32	962
Struck off. Killed, Wounded and Sick	6	53
Battalion Strength 30th Sept 1917	26	909

G Hayes. Lieut Col
Comdg 11th D. L. I. (Pioneers)

(A7092). Wt. W12839/M1293. 750,000. 1/17. D. D. & L., Ltd. Forms/C.2118/14.

Instructions regarding War Diaries and Intelligence Summaries are contained in F. S. Regs., Part II. and the Staff Manual respectively. Title pages will be prepared in manuscript.

WAR DIARY
or
~~INTELLIGENCE SUMMARY.~~
(Erase heading not required.)

Army Form C. 2118.

Vol 27

11th Battalion Durham Light Infantry

Place	Date	Hour	Summary of Events and Information	Remarks and references to Appendices
Seaton Camp F5.C.4.6.	1/10/17	12 noon	'A' Coy marched to Hopoutre Station and there entrained for Bapaume, on transfer to III rd Army.	
"	2/10/17	12 noon	3 Coys, H.Q and Transport proceeded to Hopoutre and entrained for Bapaume, on transfer to III rd Army. The entrainment took one hour, and train left at 5 P.M	
Bapaume H.33b.	3/10/17	6 A.M.	3 Coys, H.Q & Transport arrived by rail, detrained and proceeded by march route to Barastre, arrived at 10.30 A.M. and there joined A. Coy who arrived on the previous day at 6 A.M.	
Barastre	4/10/17		Coys under Coy Commanders from 9 A.M to 12 noon. Struck off 23 O.R. Joined 1 O.R.	
"	5/10/17	3 P.M.	Batt with Transport paraded in marching order and proceeded by march route to Ytres	
Ytres P.20.d.0.	6/10/17	1 P.M.	Batt with Transport proceeded to Pioneer Camp at W.3.c arriving at 3.30 P.M. 'B' Coy marched to X18 d. and relieved a Coy of 12th Yorks Regt, Pioneers. 'D' Coy marched to W.34.d and relieved another Coy of 12th Yorks Regt. 2/Lt. D. J. Rees and 50 O.R proceeded to Fins for duty with III rd Corps Tramway Coy.	
Camp W3.C.5.7.	7/10/17		'B' & 'D' Coys at work in forward area, 'A' and 'C' at work in camp on huts	
"	8/10/17		'B' & 'D' Coys at work on trenches in forward area. MAC SUPPORT & DENNING AVENUE cleared, CIRCUS SWITCH dug to 6' deep. Two Coys on hutments. 2Lt A.C. Lynch with 220 O.R joined 2 O.R struck off	
"	9/10/17		B' C' D' Coys maintaining and improving trenches 'A' Coy working in Camp	
"	10/10/17		Work carried out as for 9th inst. 176 O.R. struck off strength	
"	11/10/17		'B' Coy working under orders of 61st Bgde. 'D' Coy under orders of 60th Bgde. One Coy on C.T's. 'A' Coy at work in Camp. LT & QMr H. Wilkinson and 39 O.R. joined 24 O.R struck off	

(A7092) Wt. W2289/M1293 750,000 1/17. D. D. & L., Ltd. Forms/C.2118/14.

Instructions regarding War Diaries and Intelligence Summaries are contained in F. S. Regs., Part II. and the Staff Manual respectively. Title pages will be prepared in manuscript.

WAR DIARY
or
~~INTELLIGENCE SUMMARY.~~
(Erase heading not required.)

Continued.

Army Form C. 2118.

Place	Date	Hour	Summary of Events and Information	Remarks and references to Appendices
Camp W3 C. 5. 7	12/10/17		'B' Coy continued work on MAC SUPPORT, CIRCUS SWITCH, & DENNING AVENUE. 'D' Coy deepened and boarded 150x of LOUGHBORO' LANE. 13 C.T's maintained. 'C' Coy deepened 360x of COALVILLE TRENCH & LOUGHBORO' POST. 11 C.T's maintained. 'A' Coy at work on hutments in Camp	
"	13/10/17		'B' Coy 220x of MAC SUPPORT trench boarded, work done on CIRCUS SWITCH & DENNING Av. 'C' Coy 360x of COALVILLE TRENCH deepened. 11 C.T's maintained. 'D' Coy 150x of LOUGHBORO' LANE deepened. 13 C.T's maintained. 'A' Coy at work on hutments in Camp	
"	14/10/17		'B' Coy Trench-boarding continued in MAC SUPPORT. 4 C.T's maintained. 'C' Coy work on trenches in central Bde area. 'D' Coy ASHBY LANE deepened. 13 C.T.S maintained. 'A' Coy at work on hutments	
"	15/10/17		'B' Coy Work continued on MAC SUPPORT & 4 C.T'S. 'C' Coy 30x front line revetted. 11 C.T's maintained. 'D' Coy LOUGHBORO' LANE & ASHBY LANE deepened, trench boards laid in former. 13 C.T's maintained. 'A' Coy Work on hutments in Camp	
"	16/10/17		'B' Coy Work continued on MAC SUPPORT. 4 C.T's maintained. 'C' Coy ~~[illegible]~~ SYMES AV. revetted. 11 trenches maintained. 'D' Coy LOUGHBORO' LANE completed. 100x ASHBY LANE deepened. 13 C.T'S maintained. 'A' Coy 220x of GRANTHAM ALLEY deepened and widened. 9. O.R. struck off	
"	17/10/17		'A' Coy Trench from Q12 b.6.6 to Q12 b.4.9. 150x deepened to 6'. 'B' Coy Fire-bays commenced in CIRCUS SWITCH facing N. Trenchboards complete in MAC SUPPORT. Work on 4 C.T's. 'C' Coy 8 fire-bays in FERN	

(A7092). Wt. W12539/M1293. 750,000. 1/17. D. D. & L., Ltd. Forms/C.2118/14.

Instructions regarding War Diaries and Intelligence Summaries are contained in F. S. Regs., Part II. and the Staff Manual respectively. Title pages will be prepared in manuscript.

WAR DIARY
or
INTELLIGENCE SUMMARY.
(Erase heading not required.)

Continued

Army Form C. 2118.

Place	Date	Hour	Summary of Events and Information	Remarks and references to Appendices
Camp W.3.C.5.7			TRENCH revetted 11 C.T's maintained. 'D' Coy 100x of ASHBY LANE deepened 14 C.T's maintained. 1 platoon of 'A' Coy at work repairing Ordnance Yard.	
"	18/10/17		'B' Coy 10 fire-bays excavated in CIRCUS SWITCH facing N. Work continued on MAC SUPPORT & C.T's in R. Bgde area. 'C' Coy 11 fire bays revetted in FERN TRENCH. 11 C.T's maintained. 'D' Coy 80x of PLOUGH SUPPORT cleared & drained. 14 C.T's maintained. 'A' Coy 1 Platoon repairing Ordnance Store. 12th Batt. Yorks Regt (Pioneers) marched out, accomodation taken over.	
"	19/10/17		'A' Coy Work on hutments in Camp. 'B' Coy fire-bays in CIRCUS SWITCH & MAC SUPPORT continued. 4 C.T's maintained. 'C' Coy Fire bays revetted in RHEY TR. 'D' Coy 115x deepened, 22x duckboards laid in RHONDA TR. 'C' Coy now all in GOUZEAUCOURT	
"	20/10/17		'A' Coy 50 men on shelters, 25 men at Ordnance Yard. Remainder at work in Camp. 'B' Coy. Work on 6 trenches in R Bgde area continued. 'C' Coy Fire-bays revetted & duckboards laid in RHEY TR. 'D' Coy 50x deepened 40x duckboarded in RHONDA TR. 14 C.T's maintained. 1. O.R struck off.	
"	21/10/17		'D' Coy RHONDA TR completed except 25x. 'A', 'B', 'C' Coys resting. C/E services in afternoon & evening.	

Instructions regarding War Diaries and Intelligence Summaries are contained in F. S. Regs., Part II. and the Staff Manual respectively. Title pages will be prepared in manuscript.

WAR DIARY
or
~~INTELLIGENCE SUMMARY.~~
(*Erase heading not required.*)

Continued

Army Form C. 2118.

Place	Date	Hour	Summary of Events and Information	Remarks and references to Appendices
W 3 C 5 7	22/10/17		'A' Coy 50 men on shelters. 25 men on Ordnance Yard. Remainder at work in Camp. 'B' Coy Revetting of fire steps & deepening of trenches in R. Bgde Area. 'C' Coy Work on fire bays in POPE AV. & RILEY TR. Drain from front line to S of RILEY AV. widened to 3'6". C.T.'s maintained. 'D' Coy. Deepening completed & 56^x duck boards laid in RHONDA TR 12^x of LEICESTER AV. revetted on both sides. 1 O R Struck off	
"	23/10/17		G.O.C Division visited the Camp. 'A' Coy 15 shelters completed at W.5.6. Work in Ordnance Yard. Wiring on A side of GRESHAM AV. 'B' Coy Work on fire bays in MAC SUPPORT & other trenches continued. 'C' Coy Work on fire bays & trench in RILEY TR & POPE AV. 90^x of wire put out on N side of GIN TR. 'D' Coy 36^x of duck boards laid in ASHBY ALLEY 24^x of duck boards laid & 1 fire bay completed in RHONDA TR	
"	24/10/17		'A' Coy. 17 shelters completed at W.5.6. 60^x of wire put out on S. side of GRESHAM AV 'B' coy. Fire-bays completed in CIRCUS SWITCH; GRESHAM AV. repaired & cleared. Trench from BROADHURST AV. to top of TURNER QUARRY deepened 'C' Coy 25^x revetted of LEICESTER AV, N of GIN AV. R27 a.7.5 200^x wired, double apron. 'D' Coy RHONDA TR 30^x widened, work on fire bays. ASHBY ALLEY 40^x duck boards laid. 5 O.R joined	
"	25/10/17		'A' Coy 19 shelters now complete at W.5.6. 150^x double apron wire completed. 'B' Coy Work on fire bays in MAC SUPPORT Trench from BROADHURST AV. to top of TURNER QUARRY deepened. 'C' Coy LEICESTER AV. 45^x one side revetted N side of GIN AV. 200^x wire 1st belt double apron put out. 'D' Coy RHONDA SUPPORT 13 firebays completed ASHBY ALLEY 32 trench boards laid on pickets. 3 O R joined	

(A7092). Wt. W12839/M1293. 750,000. 1/17. D. D. & L., Ltd. Forms/C.2118/14.

Army Form C. 2118.

Instructions regarding War Diaries and Intelligence Summaries are contained in F. S. Regs., Part II. and the Staff Manual respectively. Title pages will be prepared in manuscript.

WAR DIARY
or
~~INTELLIGENCE SUMMARY~~.
(Erase heading not required.)

Continued

Place	Date	Hour	Summary of Events and Information	Remarks and references to Appendices
F.S.C.4.6	26/10/17		'A' Coy 21 shelters now complete at W5.6. 85x wire fencing completed 200x commenced S side of GRESHAM AV 'B' Coy FIFE TR 150x widened. MAC SUPPORT work on fire bays continued. Trench from BROADHURST AV to top of TURNER QUARRY deepened. 'C' Coy LEICESTER AV. 35x of one side revetted. N of GIN AV. 250x 1st belt of double apron wire put out. 'D' Coy RHONDA TR work on fire-bays continued. PLOUGH SUPPORT 75x widened 2 Sump holes deepened 2'. ASHBY ALLEY 38x of trench boards laid on pickets. 2 O.R struck off.	
"	27/10/17		'A' Coy 2 more shelters completed. 8 camouflaged. 350x of wire completed double apron fence. S. side of GRESHAM AV 'B' Coy FIFE TR. 150x widened. MAC SUPPORT duckboards carried up & laid on fire steps; revetting of latter continued 'C' Coy LEICESTER AV. 20x prepared for revetting. LINCOLN AV. 30x pumped clear of water. N side of GIN AV. 300x 1st belt double apron wire put out. 'D' Coy. PLOUGH SUPPORT 120x widened. 30x trench boards laid; work on fire bays & sandbagging continued. ASHBY ALLEY 38x trench boards laid on pickets. The 5th Batt Northamptonshire Regt, 12th Div pioneers, moved into this camp.	
"	28/10/17		'C' Coy 100x of LINCOLN AV pumped clear of water. Only urgent work was carried out on this date, so three Coys rested. Church parades were held at 11 A.M. & 6.30 P.M. 2/Lts D. McGregor, C.A. Morris, C.H. Bonson, & R. Conacher joined with 4 O.R.	
"	29/10/17		'A' Coy 2 more shelters completed at W5.6. 250x double apron fence, 2nd belt, of wire put out. 'B' Coy. FIFE TR 150x completed. MAC SUPPORT Revetting of firebays continued; 3 new ones cut. 'C' Coy LEICESTER AV. 40x revetted (one side) 140x berm cleared. LINCOLN AV. 20x pumped clear of water. N. side of GIN. AV. 400x	

(A7092). Wt. W12839/M1293. 750,000. 1/17. D. D. & L., Ltd. Forms/C.2118/14.

Instructions regarding War Diaries and Intelligence Summaries are contained in F. S. Regs., Part II. and the Staff Manual respectively. Title pages will be prepared in manuscript.

WAR DIARY
or
~~INTELLIGENCE SUMMARY.~~

(Erase heading not required.)

Continued

Army Form C. 2118.

Place	Date	Hour	Summary of Events and Information	Remarks and references to Appendices
F.5.c.4.6	27/10/17		wired 1st belt double apron 'D' Coy ASHBY ALLEY 32x trench boards laid on pickets RHONDA SUPP 215x deepened & widened. Camp inspected by D.A.D.M.S who expressed satisfaction. 10 R joined	
"	30/10/17		'A' Coy 21 shelters complete at W.5.b. 3 camouflaged 250x double apron wire from FRONT LINE to MERSEY STREET 'B' Coy Road repaired & improved HEUDECOURT – GOUZEAUCOURT 'C' Coy LEICESTER AV 5x revetted 30x berm cleared N. of GIN AV 200x wired double apron W. of RESERVE LINE 20x wired 'D' Coy RAT & RHONDA TR 260x deepened widened & drained ASHBY ALLEY 23x duckboards laid on pickets	
"	31/10/17		'A' Coy 29 shelters now complete at W.5.b 1 platoon worked with C Coy 'B' Coy worked on road HEUDECOURT – GOUZEAUCOURT 'C' Coy LEICESTER AV 30x revetted 20x berm cleared GOUZEAUCOURT – VILLERS PLOUICH Rd Q.30.b.7.7 350x cleared of mud & repaired with metal R.19.d.1.9 300x cleared of mud. Crater cleared & street 400x of mud cleared 'D' Coy RHONDA SUPP 6 firebays completed 130x deepened between RAILWAY & RAT TR ASHBY ALLEY 30x duckboards laid	

	OFFICERS	O.R.
Batt. Strength on 1.10.17	26	909
Joined during Oct. 1917	6	280
	32	1189
Struck off Killed & Wounded etc	–	240
Batt Strength 31.10.17	32	949

[illegible] 2nd Lt.
Mc[illegible] 2nd Lt.

(A7092). Wt. W12839/M1293. 750,000. 1/17. D. D. & L., Ltd. Forms/C.2118/14.

24

Instructions regarding War Diaries and Intelligence Summaries are contained in F. S. Regs., Part II. and the Staff Manual respectively. Title pages will be prepared in manuscript.

WAR DIARY
or
~~INTELLIGENCE SUMMARY.~~
(*Erase heading not required.*)

R/20 Vol 28

Army Form C. 2118.

11th Bn. Durham Light Infantry (P.s)

Place	Date	Hour	Summary of Events and Information	Remarks and references to Appendices
W.3.c.5.7.	1/11/17		Three Companies working on roads, and communication trenches. One Company working on new accommodation at Q.30.d.	
W.3.c.5.7	2/11/17		Work on roads + communication trenches continued by 4 companies.	
W.3.c.5.7	3/11/17		Three and a half companies working on roads; half a Coy on C.T.s.	
W.3.c.5.7	4/11/17		Work on roads + C.T.s continued. 2/Lt H.S. Parkin took over duties as Officer i/c of Material + Transport. One other rank evacuated sick.	
W.3.c.5.7	5/11/17		Four Companies working on VILLERS PLOUICH — GOUZEAUCOURT Road and VILLERS PLOUICH — GONNELIEU Rd. A party of 50 under 2/Lt Atlay working on Railway.	
W.3.c.5.7	6/11/17.		Four Coys. working on craters + clearing roads.	
W.3.c.5.7	7/11/17.		Work continued on roads. Capt. C. Palmer transferred to Tank Corps and struck off. Capt. W.G.L. Sear assumed Command of "A" Coy vice Capt. Palmer.	
W.3.c.5.7.	8/11/17		Work on Roads + Craters continued. One O.R. joined, and 11 O.R.s struck off.	
W.3.c.5.7.	9/11/17.		Three Coys. work on roads. One Coy. working on Model ~~of~~ in connection with coming operations.	

A5834 Wt. W4973/M687 750,000 8/16 D. D. & L. Ltd. Forms/C.2118/13.

Instructions regarding War Diaries and Intelligence Summaries are contained in F. S. Regs., Part II. and the Staff Manual respectively. Title pages will be prepared in manuscript.

WAR DIARY
or
~~INTELLIGENCE SUMMARY.~~
(*Erase heading not required.*) (Continued)

Army Form C. 2118.

Place	Date	Hour	Summary of Events and Information	Remarks and references to Appendices
W.3.c.5.7	10/11/17		Work on Model at W.19.a.4.1 continued. Three Coys working on roads + C.T.s	
W.3.c.5.7	11/11/17		Work on Roads, C.T.s, + Model continued. 1 OR. killed.	
W.3.c.5.7	12/11/17		Work carried out as for the 11th. Three OR. struck off sick.	
W.3.c.5.7	13/11/17		Work on Model, Roads + C.T.s Continued. Capts. W.G.L. Sear + R. Jee proceeded with C.E. III Corps to ALBERT to take part in a Conference.	
W.3.c.5.7	14/11/17		Work on Model finished and work on Roads continued	
W.3.c.5.7	15/11/17		Three Coys working on roads + C.T.s; one Coy making shelters at R.13.d.7.4.	
W.3.c.5.7	16/11/17		Work on roads + shelters continued. A Coy moved to shelters at W.5.b. 13 OR joined; 5 OR. struck (one O.R wounded)	
W.5.b.	17/11/17		HeadQuarters moved from W.3.c.5.7 to W.5.b. Work on roads continued	
W.5.b.	18/11/17		A + B Coys moved to shelters at R.13.d.7.4. D Coy moved from GOUZEAUCOURT WOOD into GOUZEAUCOURT. 1 OR died of wounds.	
W.5.b.	19/11/17		Headquarters moved into shelters at Q.36.a.8.2. Work on roads completed	
Q.36.a.8.2	20/11/17		At 6.20 a.m. attack by 20th Division commenced on enemy trenches. A + B Coys proceeded at 6 a.m for special work on roads + tracks for Cavalry, assisted by tanks. At 6.40 a.m. C + D Coys proceeded to dig a new C.T. from British Front Line to the enemy Front Line. In the afternoon these 2 Coys worked on VILLERS PLOUICH — LA VACQUERIE Rd. Two platoons remained on the work all night	

A5834 Wt. W4973/M687 750,000 8/16 D. D. & L. Ltd. Forms/C.2118/13.

Instructions regarding War Diaries and Intelligence Summaries are contained in F. S. Regs., Part II. and the Staff Manual respectively. Title pages will be prepared in manuscript.

WAR DIARY
or
~~INTELLIGENCE SUMMARY~~.
(*Erase heading not required.*)

Army Form C. 2118.

Continued

Place	Date	Hour	Summary of Events and Information	Remarks and references to Appendices
Q.36.a.8.2	20/11/17		8 Lewis Guns under Charge of 2/Lt D. Ellwood proceeded at 6.40 a.m. for anti-aircraft duty in connection with the Operations. These guns later on joined the Brigades + remained in the Forward Area throughout the day.	
			Casualties :- Lieut W. W. INGLIS, killed, 2/Lt. D. MacGregor + 3 O.R. wounded	
Q.36.a.8.2	21/11/17		Two Coys working on roads under orders of C.E. III Corps. Two Coys. working on VILLERS PLOUICH — LA VACQUERIE Rd. Eight Lewis Guns still on anti-aircraft duty with troops in Forward Area	
Q.36.a.8.2	22/11/17		Work on roads continued by 4 Coys Lewis Guns still in forward Area	
Q.36.a.8.2	23/11/17		Four Coys working on roads	
Q.36.a.8.2.	24/11/17		Four Coys working on roads. Two for III Corps + Two on VILLAGE Road.	
Q.36.a.8.2	25/11/17.		Work on roads continued as for 24th	
—"—	26/11/17		As 25th	
—"—	27/11/17.		Work on roads continued. Transport moved back to Lines at W.13.a.9.9.	
—"—	28/11/17		'B' Coy move forward to trenches at about R.4.a+C. 'D' Coy move to trenches at R.3.b+d.	
—"—			A+C Coys working on roads	
—"—	29/11/17		A+C Coys working on roads, B+D Coys working on new C.T in forward area.	

A5834 Wt. W4973/M687 750,000 8/16 D. D. & L. Ltd. Forms/C.2118/13.

Army Form C. 2118.

Instructions regarding War Diaries and Intelligence Summaries are contained in F. S. Regs., Part II. and the Staff Manual respectively. Title pages will be prepared in manuscript.

WAR DIARY
or
INTELLIGENCE SUMMARY.
(Erase heading not required.)

Place	Date	Hour	Summary of Events and Information	Remarks and references to Appendices
	30/10/17		The Battalion was situated as follows:- B and D Coys in the Hindenburg support line near R4 a 25. A Coy in shelters in the Railway Cutting at VILLERS PLOUICH. H.Q. and C Coy in shelters in sunken road in GOUZEAUCOURT in Q16 a. B Coy went out on the night 29/30th digging trenches at Cemetery strong point N.W. of [illegible] VINES. Whilst returning to trenches in R4 a heavy hostile barrage [illegible] about [illegible]. After [illegible] to the [illegible] commander, Captain Lee that large bodies of men were massing in a [illegible]. Capt Lee stood to at once and [illegible] platoons took up a defensive position at R4 a 3.5 in the sunken road two platoons at R3 a 6.0 in support to [illegible] the platoons and to stop the enemy from working up MARCOING VALLEY. Capt Lee reported to [illegible] Gen Banbury 61st I.B. who [illegible] him to hold the [illegible] trench (leaving sunken road at R4 a 3.0) with two platoons.	

II

Instructions regarding War Diaries and Intelligence Summaries are contained in F. S. Regs., Part II. and the Staff Manual respectively. Title pages will be prepared in manuscript.

WAR DIARY
or
INTELLIGENCE SUMMARY.
(Erase heading not required.)

Army Form C. 2118.

Place	Date	Hour	Summary of Events and Information	Remarks and references to Appendices
			The remaining [illegible] were to stay where they were. This position lasted till 5.30 PM during which time fire was opened on several occasions on the enemy. [illegible] were very harassing during this period. At 5.30 PM the company [illegible] in the [illegible]. Casualties - 1 officer wounded (severely) 3 OR killed [illegible] O.R. wounded.	

Army Form C. 2118.

WAR DIARY
or
INTELLIGENCE SUMMARY.
(Erase heading not required.)

Instructions regarding War Diaries and Intelligence Summaries are contained in F. S. Regs., Part II. and the Staff Manual respectively. Title pages will be prepared in manuscript.

Place	Date	Hour	Summary of Events and Information	Remarks and references to Appendices
			[illegible] were in trench at R9.b.5.8. After the hostile bombardment had been on for some time Capt. Pemberton observed men coming back from the front line who said that the Germans had broken through. The company stood to and took up a position in the [illegible] line about R9 b facing NE. The company commander then received a message from Major Morgan [illegible] 11th R.B. addressed to 7th D.C.L.I. asking for reinforcements on his left. Capt. Pemberton at once advanced to the trench running from R3 b 9.1 to R10.a.3.5 and [illegible] touch with the 11th R.B. on his right. He then reported personally to Brigadier Gen. Banbury [illegible] to get touch with 7th K.O.Y.L.I. [illegible] remainder of his company in support. Capt. Pemberton went along the front line from the 11th R.B. to the 7th K.O.Y.L.I. and established touch and gradually withdrew [illegible] [illegible] more line. This was completed by 5.30 PM	

Instructions regarding War Diaries and Intelligence Summaries are contained in F. S. Regs., Part II. and the Staff Manual respectively. Title pages will be prepared in manuscript.

WAR DIARY
or
INTELLIGENCE SUMMARY.
(Erase heading not required.)

Army Form C. 2118.

Place	Date	Hour	Summary of Events and Information	Remarks and references to Appendices
			A Coy under Capt [illegible] M.C. which was working [illegible]	
			on the VILLERS PLOUICH – MARCOING road when they were [illegible]	
			that the enemy had broken through. The [illegible]	
			of VILLERS PLOUICH and Capt [illegible] reported to Div H.Q. from whom	
			he received instructions to take up a position on [illegible]	
			RIDGE [illegible] enemy approaching VILLERS PLOUICH from	
			the direction of GOUZEAUCOURT [illegible]	
			[illegible]	
			with 183 H.Q. [illegible]	
			[illegible]	
			[illegible]	
			[illegible]	
			Div H.Q. [illegible] VILLERS PLOUICH	
			Casualties [illegible] O.R. wounded	

(A7092). Wt. W12839/M1293. 750,000. 1/17. D. D. & L., Ltd. Forms/C.2118/14.

Instructions regarding War Diaries and Intelligence Summaries are contained in F. S. Regs., Part II. and the Staff Manual respectively. Title pages will be prepared in manuscript.

WAR DIARY
or
INTELLIGENCE SUMMARY.
(Erase heading not required.)

Army Form C. 2118.

Place	Date	Hour	Summary of Events and Information	Remarks and references to Appendices
			H.Q. and A Coy were in Gouzeaucourt. Nothing very unusual	
			was noticed except fairly heavy gun fire [illegible]	
			towards [illegible] 8 am Gouzeaucourt was [illegible] shelled [illegible]	
			[illegible] but it did not seem heavy enough [illegible]	
			uneasiness. About 9.15 am the C.O. [illegible]	
			[illegible]	
			[illegible] in the direction of [illegible] rumour [illegible]	
			that the Germans had [illegible]	
			[illegible]	
			[illegible]	
			[illegible]	
			[illegible]	
			[illegible]	
			from the direction of Villers Guislain [illegible]	
			at once [illegible] the H.Q. [illegible]	
			Hill 135 [illegible] Gouzeaucourt [illegible]	
			[illegible] Hill [illegible] the Germans [illegible]	

(A7092). Wt. W12839/M1293. 750,000. 1/17. D. D. & L., Ltd. Forms/C.2118/14.

Instructions regarding War Diaries and Intelligence Summaries are contained in F. S. Regs., Part II. and the Staff Manual respectively. Title pages will be prepared in manuscript.

WAR DIARY
or
INTELLIGENCE SUMMARY.
(Erase heading not required.)

Army Form C. 2118.

Place	Date	Hour	Summary of Events and Information	Remarks and references to Appendices
			the most perfect [illegible]	
			They were also [illegible]	
			[illegible] QUENTIN RIDGE [illegible]	
			[illegible]	
			QUENTIN RIDGE [illegible]	
			[illegible] CHAPEL HILL [illegible]	
			[illegible]	
			[illegible]	
			[illegible]	
			[illegible]	
			[illegible]	
			[illegible]	
			[illegible]	
			about three [illegible]	
			[illegible]	
			[illegible]	
			[illegible]	

(A7092). Wt. W12839/M1293. 750,000. 1/17. D. D. & L., Ltd. Forms/C.2118/14.

Instructions regarding War Diaries and Intelligence Summaries are contained in F. S. Regs., Part II. and the Staff Manual respectively. Title pages will be prepared in manuscript.

WAR DIARY
or
INTELLIGENCE SUMMARY.
(Erase heading not required.)

Army Form C. 2118.

Place	Date	Hour	Summary of Events and Information	Remarks and references to Appendices
			all kinds coming down the Fins Road in a [illegible] panic, also many stragglers about doing nothing. Major Robinson, whose men were ignorant of open warfare training, handled his men with great coolness and courage. The machine gun fire was by now very heavy indeed, and hostile machine guns were also enfilading from the south. The enemy's infantry had broken through on the left of GOUZEAUCOURT and were also firing down the [illegible]. The battery sent there had been unable to hold up the hostile advance as the German infantry were already in the houses when they got there, and there was considerable confusion. The C.O. [illegible] Major McEntee to take 20 men at once and place them in the old BROWN LINE south of the GOUZEAUCOURT–FINS road at about W4 b 7.5 and to hold fast to the last man. The [illegible] was also [illegible] [illegible] of others. The remainder of the [illegible] and the R.E. then got back to the BROWN LINE under heavy machine gun fire from GOUZEAUCOURT and Hill 126 [illegible] from the ridge south of this.	

Army Form C. 2118.

WAR DIARY
or
INTELLIGENCE SUMMARY.
(Erase heading not required.)

VIII

Instructions regarding War Diaries and Intelligence Summaries are contained in F. S. Regs., Part II. and the Staff Manual respectively. Title pages will be prepared in manuscript.

Place	Date	Hour	Summary of Events and Information	Remarks and references to Appendices
			There was a certain amount of confusion due to the surprise, heavy fire and lack of training, but the party reached the BROWN LINE and was rallied there astride the main road. Here every man was collected and put into the trench. Capt. Symons of the 27th Siege Battery R.G.A. rendered splendid service in rallying men and in organising a defence. He had fought his howitzers till the enemy was almost on him and then after rendering his guns useless joined the mixed party of C Coy and R.E. He was extremely cool throughout. The casualties, under the circumstances, were very light due to the bad shooting of the Germans.	
			When the party formed up in the BROWN LINE the enemy seemed to come on very cautiously and pushed patrols out which when fired on returned. He made a slight effort to reach the BROWN LINE south of the road but this was easily repulsed. The C.O. sent an urgent message to SOREL for machine guns and ammunition. The Adjutant, Capt Tollit also went down	

(A7092). Wt. W12839/M1293. 750,000. 1/17. D. D. & L., Ltd. Forms/C.2118/14.

Instructions regarding War Diaries and Intelligence Summaries are contained in F. S. Regs., Part II. and the Staff Manual respectively. Title pages will be prepared in manuscript.

WAR DIARY
or
INTELLIGENCE SUMMARY.
(Erase heading not required.)

Army Form C. 2118.

Place	Date	Hour	Summary of Events and Information	Remarks and references to Appendices
			[illegible] At ~~Noon~~ 11.30 AM. the C.O. [illegible] Capt [illegible] along the Brown Line in the direction of [illegible] Cross [illegible] Major [illegible] (who had [illegible]) in temporary command near the main road. Capt [illegible] collected stragglers and placed them [illegible] astride the Metz – Gouzeaucourt road. [illegible] time the [illegible] signs of [illegible]. The 20th Hussars [illegible] the Brown Line [illegible] of the [illegible] line. The [illegible] the Brown Line [illegible] The C.O. of the 20th Hussars [illegible] offered assistance [illegible] The 2nd [illegible] the most [illegible] [illegible]	

(A7092). Wt. W12839/M1293. 750,000. 1/17. D. D. & L., Ltd. Forms/C.2118/14.

Instructions regarding War Diaries and Intelligence Summaries are contained in F. S. Regs., Part II. and the Staff Manual respectively. Title pages will be prepared in manuscript.

WAR DIARY
or
INTELLIGENCE SUMMARY.
(Erase heading not required.)

Army Form C. 2118.

Place	Date	Hour	Summary of Events and Information	Remarks and references to Appendices
			dismounted cavalry and advanced with them	
			The lack of training was very noticeable though on the whole	
			the men were willing and steady when [illegible] by [illegible]	
			[illegible]. The shooting was wild in the extreme. If [illegible]	
			had not [illegible] [illegible] the [illegible] casualties would have	
			been extremely heavy. [illegible] [illegible] [illegible] Coy showed	
			conspicuous coolness and courage [illegible] [illegible] [illegible] [illegible] man	
			who was killed early on also showed [illegible] [illegible]	
			Casualties [illegible] [illegible] [illegible]	
			[illegible] killed	
			[illegible] [illegible] [illegible]	
			6 O.R. killed	
			21 O.R. wounded	
			[illegible] [illegible] Helieve [illegible] [illegible] [illegible] [illegible] [illegible] [illegible]	

(A7092). Wt. W12839/M1293. 750,000. 1/17. D. D. & L., Ltd. Forms/C.2118/14.

WAR DIARY
or
INTELLIGENCE SUMMARY.
(Erase heading not required.)

Army Form C. 2118.

Place	Date	Hour	Summary of Events and Information	Remarks and references to Appendices
			The Chaplain, the Rev. H.P. Walton, went out with B Coy and rendered excellent services to the wounded under heavy rifle and machine gun fire and rifle fire. He also collected stragglers and brought them back to the BROWN LINE.	
			The Adjutant, who had returned to the Orderly Room after having been out on the hill with the C.O. managed to get the Confidential papers and maps his [illegible]. He was sent to SOREL for machine guns and reinforcements for the BROWN LINE and then returned.	
			Strength.	
			Battalion Strength 1-11-17 Officers 32 ORs 949	
			Joined during Nov " " 21	
			Total 32 970	
			Struck off during Nov } Killed. Wounded & Sick etc } Officers 3 OR's. 54	
			Battalion Strength 1/12/17 Officers 29. OR's 916	G. Hayes. Lieut Col Comdg 11th E L Infantry.

A5834 Wt. W4973/M687 750,000 8/16 D. D. & L. Ltd. Forms/C.2118/13.

<u>20th Division</u>

11th D.L.I.
<u>Pioneers.</u>

No 7

II. Pt. I.

(Princess)

30/11/1917

On the 30th the Bn was situated as follows:-
B and D. Coys in the Hindenburgh support line
near R4 a.25. A Coy in shelters in the
Railway Cutting at VILLERS PLOICH.
HQ and C Coy in shelters in sunken road
in GOUZEAUCOURT in Q16a. B. Coy were out
on the night 29/30th digging trench at
cemetary strong point N.W. of RUE des VIGNES.
Whilst returning to trenches in R4 a heavy
hostile barrage dropped about. AM. About
6.45 AM it was reported to the company
commander Capt Lee that large bodies of
men were retiring in a disorderly manner.
Capt Lee stood to at once, and 2 platoons
took up a defensive position at R4 a 8c in
the sunken road. Two platoons at R3 a 6.c
in support to front two platoons, and to
bar the enemy from working up MARCOING
VALLEY. Capt Lee reported to Brigadier Gen.
Banbury 61st I.B. who ordered him to hold
the trench leaving sunken road at R4.a.3.6.
with two platoons. The remaining two were
to stay where they were. This position
lasted till 6.30 PM during which time fire was
opened on several occasions on the enemy.
Hostile aeroplanes were very harassing
during this period. At 6.30 PM the company
then joined D coy in the trench at R9.b.5.8.
Casualties 1 officer wounded (severely) 3 OR
killed and 6 OR wounded.

II

D Coy under Captain Pemberton was in trench at R9 b 55. After the battle bombardment had been on for some time, Captain Pemberton observed men coming back from the front line who said that the Germans had broken through. The company stood to, and took up a position on the Hindenburg Line about R9 b facing N.E. The company commander then received a message from Major Norman Orr 11th R.B. addressed to 7th D.C.L.I asking for reinforcements on his left, so Captain Pemberton at once advanced to the trench running from R3 d.9.1 to R10 a 35 and established touch with the 11th R.B. on his right. He then reported personally to Brigadier Gen. Banbury who ordered him to get touch with 7th K.O.Y.L.I in front and to withdraw the remainder of his company in support. Captain Pemberton went along the front line from the 11th R.B. to the 7th K.O.Y.L.I and established touch and gradually withdrew D Coy as 7th K.O.Y.L.I took over more line. This was complete by 5.30 PM.

[illegible] was nil.

[illegible]

A. Coy under Capt Sear M.C. which was working on roads, was on the VILLERS-PLOUICH – METZ road when they learned that the enemy had broken through. The company returned to VILLERS PLOUICH and Capt Sear reported to Div. H.Q. from whom he received instructions to take up a position on [illegible] ridge to prevent enemy approaching VILLERS PLOUICH from the direction of GOUZEAUCOURT. The company dug in under light shell and machine gun fire. The O.C. got in touch with 18N H.Q. during the course of the afternoon. The company remained here the night of the 30th Nov/1st Dec. Touch was obtained with A Coy and [illegible] about 3 PM. The C.O. was then informed by Capt Sear that Div. H.Q. had remained at [illegible] near VILLERS PLOUICH. Casualties 2 O.R. wounded.

H.Q. and C Coy were in GOUZEAUCOURT. Nothing very unusual was noticed except fairly heavy gun fire from about 6 AM onwards. About 8 AM GOUZEAUCOURT was being shelled a certain amount but it did not seem heavy enough to cause uneasiness. About 9.15 AM the C.O. noticed garrison artillery men and civil people rushing about wildly and horses galloping in the direction of Fins. a rumour came down that the Germans had broken through. The [illegible] [illegible] telephoned to Divl. H.Q. who reported everything O.K. Just then heavy machine gun fire was heard close to VILLAGE and bullets were coming through. The C.O. then asked a Sergt. Major of the R.A. what was the matter and he reported that the enemy was coming over in masses from the direction of VILLERS-GUISLAIN. Every man fell in at once and the C.O. led them out in the direction of Hill 135 about 500x S.W. of GOUZEAUCOURT. The C.O. who went up on to the hill then saw the Germans advancing in the most perfect order with absolutely no opposition of any kind. They were also sweeping the crest of Hill 135 with machine gun fire from QUENTIN RIDGE. The first waves of Hostile infantry were then across the railway, and the others were in force on the QUENTIN RIDGE. There was a line of our infantry retiring South Westward on Chapel Hill being followed up by the German Infantry. The C.O. ordered 1 platoon to fight the houses in the southern end of GOUZEAUCOURT to cover his left flank. Two platoons were placed along HEUDICOURT-GOUZEAUCOURT road in W.6.a to check the hostile advance from QUENTIN RIDGE, and the remaining platoon was sent over front or to the right to about W5 d central to protect the right flank which was open. The men were well led by Lt. Bushell. About 3 sections of T.E. under Major Robinson then came up and were ordered 2 sections to reinforce the left flank and one section to fill in the gap between Hill 135 and the platoon on the right. There was great confusion, troops of all kind pouring down the Fins road in a blind panic, also many standing about doing nothing. Major Robinson whose men were ignorant of open warfare training handled his men with great coolness and courage. The machine gun fire was by now very heavy indeed and hostile machine guns were now enfilading from the south. The enemy's infantry had broken through the village of GOUZEAUCOURT and were also firing from the houses. The platoon sent there had been unable to hold up the hostile advance, as the German infantry were already in the houses when they got there and there was indescribable confusion. The C.O. ordered 2nd Lt. Major Mc[illegible] to take the 20 men at HQ and place them in the old trench line south of the GOUZEAUCOURT–FINS road at about W4 d 8.6 and to hold this to the last man. This party would also cover retirement of others. The remainder of the company and the T.E. then got back to the BROWN LINE under heavy machine gun fire from GOUZEAUCOURT and Hill 135 and from the ridge south of this.

VI

There was a certain amount of confusion due to the surprise, heavy fire and lack of warning but the party reached the Brown Line. This was rallied here astride the main road. Here every man was collected and put into the trench. Lt Symons of the 27th Siege Battery rendered splendid service in rallying men and in organising a defence. He had fought his howitzers till the enemy was almost on him and then after rendering his guns useless joined the mixed party of C Company and R.E. He was extremely cool throughout. The casualties, under the circumstances were very light due to the bad shooting of the Germans. When the party formed up on the Brown Line the enemy seemed to come on very cautiously and pushed patrols out which when fired on returned. He made a slight effort to reach the Brown Line south of the road but this was easily repulsed. The C.O. sent an urgent message to Bde for machine guns and ammunition, the Adjutant, Capt. Tollet also went down to explain situation. At 12.10 PM the C.O and Lt Symons went along the Brown Line in the direction of Queen's Cross, leaving Major Lloyd (who had sprained his ankle, in temporary charge near the main road). Lt Symons collected stragglers and placed them astride the METZ - GOUZEAUCOURT road. By this time the local rout began to show signs of checking.

VII

The 20th Hussars reinforced and occupied the Brown Line on the south of the existing line. The body in the Brown Line was a mixed party of about 200 rifles. The C.O of the 20th Hussars then came over and conferred with the C.O of the Battalion and offered assistance with Hotchkiss guns. As the 2nd Coldstreams were now coming up in support these were not needed. The 2nd Coldstreams in the early afternoon came through in the most perfect order and counter attacked. The C.O did not push the mixed party forward with the Guards as they would have hindered them more than helped them. About 12 men of C. Coy on the right of the road attached themselves to the dismounted cavalry and advanced with them.

The lack of training [illegible] though on the whole the men were willing and steady when directed by an officer. The shooting was wild in the extreme. If C. Coy had had Lewis guns the German casualties would have been extremely heavy. Lt Bushell comdg C. Coy showed conspicuous coolness and courage throughout. Lt Greenman, who was killed early on also showed great gallantry.

VIII

Casualties C Coy and H.Q.

1 Officer killed
1 " wounded (slightly)
6 O.R. killed
34 " wounded

The T.E. had more heavy [illegible] in number engaged.

The Chaplain the Rev. H. R. [illegible] went over with C Coy and rendered excellent service to the wounded under heavy direct machine gun and rifle fire. He also collected stragglers and brought them back to the Brown Line.

The Adjutant who had returned to the Brickfly Farm after having been out on the Hill with the C.O. managed to get the confidential papers and made his own escape. He was sent to SOREL for machine guns and reinforcements for the Brown Line and then returned.

COMMANDS ETC.   11th (S) Durham L. I. (Pns)

Aug 1914 to date

Date	Commanding	2nd in Command	Adjutant
Aug 14 to 1.8.15	Bt. Col J. N. Davison	Maj. A. E. Collins, D.S.O	Capt G. Hayes
2.8.15 to 15.10.15	" "	" "	Capt A. W. Dawson
16.10.15 to 31.7.16	Lieut-Col A. E. Collins, D.S.O	Major G. Hayes	
1.8.16 to 30.10.16	Major G. Hayes	Major H. P. Lloyd	Lieut G. H. Tollit
1.11.16 to 15.12.16	Lieut-Col A. E. Collins, D.S.O.	Major G. Hayes	" "
16.12.16 to 20.1.17	Maj. G. Hayes	Major H. P. Lloyd	" "
21.1.17 to 15.7.17	" "	" "	Capt A. W. Dawson
16.7.17 to 10.10.17	" "	" "	Lieut G. H. Tollit
11.10.17 to 28.11.17	Lieut-Col G. Hayes, D.S.O.	" "	Capt G. H. Tollit
29.11.17 to 16.4.18	" "	Major R. L. S. Pemberton M.C	" "
17.4.18 to 11.5.18	Lieut-Col R. E. Boulton	" "	" "
12.5.18 to 13.8.18	" "	a/Maj. H. F. Ling, M.C	" "
14.8.18 to 8.11.18	Lt-Col. J. H. Carlisle, D.S.O, M.C, R.E.	" "	" "
9.11.18 to 18.1.19	" "	Major R. L. S. Pemberton. M.C	" "
19.1.19 to 4.2.19	" "	Major. H. C. Boocer	" "
5.2.19 to date	" "	—	" "

07

Major J. G. Taylor. awarded M.C. (Supp L.G. 1.1.17)

<u>mentioned in Despatches</u>

2nd Lieut W. Cooper } (L.G. 4.1.17)
" " A.T. Ward. }

Lt. Col. G. Hayes }
Capt. C. Palmer } (L.G. 15.5.17)
2nd Lieut C. Phillips }

21503 Sgt. H. Hodge (L.G. 4.1.17)

13308 Sgt. J. Dawson }
21508 Cpl. J.A. Payne }
16814 " A. Siggar } (L.G. 15.5.17)
16009 Cpl. H. Johnstone }

Miscellaneous.

1st Draft joined Battalion – 16 Durham L. I.
on August 3rd 1915.

12056 R.Q.M.S. R. Spalding – To England for Commission 24.10.15.

15825 Sergt. R. P. Paynter – To England for Commission 5.11.15.

28026 L/Cpl. J. D. Marren – To England for Commission 3.12.16.

15180 C.S.M. T. Williams – To England for Commission 16.4.17

3308 Sergt J Dawson – To England for Commission 16.4.17.

53564 Cpl A W Wallington – To England for Commission 11.8.17

53568 Cpl. L. G. Waine – Posted to R.A.F. Depot. Farnborough. 12.12.17.

4/8891 Sergt Aldridge – For Commission 8.6.18.

53705 Sergt S. Shepherd. – To England for Commission 13.7.18.

Honours and Rewards. 11.D.L.I

T/Capt. W. G. L. Sear – Awarded the Military Cross (Auth. Supp. to London Gazette dated 27.10.17.)
– Awarded Bar to M.C. (Supp. to London Gazette d/ 18.3.18)

Lieut-Col. G. Hayes awarded D.S.O. (Auth. London Gazette d/ 1.1.18.)

Major R. L. S. Pemberton awarded M.C. (London Gazette d/ 1.1.18
awarded Bar (Auth. London Gazette d/ 16.9.18)

Lieut D. C. Cooke
" W. J. C. Endean
2nd Lieut. R. H. King.
} Awarded M.C. Auth. London Gazette d/ 16.9.18)

Lieut-Col. G. Hayes
Lieut P. V. Kemp.
Capt. J. Liddle
Major H. P. Lloyd.
Capt. G. H. Tollit.
} Mentioned in Despatches. (Auth. Supp. to London Gazette. 21.12.17.)

Other Ranks.

18754 Sergt J. Hook Awarded D.C.M. (Supp. to London Gazette d/ 1.1.18.
15055 Pte F. Ingram — " — "
19457 Sgt J. Basham Awarded M.M. (L.G. d/ 13.3.18)
21508 " J. A. Boyne — " — "
17982 Pte F. Smith. — " — (L.G. d/ 2.11.18.)
16871 " J. W. Waites. — " — (Supp. L.G. 19.3.18)
25732 Sgt W. Cowie — " — (L.G. d/ 6.8.18)
53711 " G. E. Barritt. — " — (L.G. d/ 6.8.18)
25281 " H. Doskett — " — (1st Army No 21/2300/AMS d/ 2.11.18)
18106 L/Cpl Pennington — " — (L.G. d/ 6.8.18.)
53242 Cpl W. Dale. Awarded M.S.M (L.G. 17.6.18.)
24139 Sgt T. Armstrong — " — (L.G. 18.1.19.)
15045 Pte R. Horsburgh. Awarded "Croix de Guerre"
17970 " F. Irving
Auth. 4th French Cavalry Order 477 d/ 5.4.18)
15180 Pte L. Williams Medaille Militaire conferred by President, French Republic (L.G. Supp. d/ 24.2.16

20

Vol 29

Army Form C. 2118.

WAR DIARY
or
INTELLIGENCE SUMMARY.
(Erase heading not required.)

Instructions regarding War Diaries and Intelligence Summaries are contained in F. S. Regs., Part II. and the Staff Manual respectively. Title pages will be prepared in manuscript.

11th Durham Light Infantry

Place	Date	Hour	Summary of Events and Information	Remarks and references to Appendices
BORDER RIDGE	1/12/17	7 AM	"A" Company moved from BORDERER RIDGE to LINCOLN AVENUE. Shelling very heavy. 6 PM moved to RAILWAY CUTTING, VILLERS PLOUICH. 10 PM moved into Support line running from R 9 d. 9.5 to R.15.b.1.8. in front of LA VACQUERIE. "B" Company holding trench in R.3.c. in support to 7th K.O.Y.L.I. Carried up rations to front line.	
		7 AM	"C" Company moved from BROWN LINE to a trench near VILLERS PLOUICH and covered the Valley. 6 PM Company moved into RAILWAY CUTTING. 7 PM moved again into Hindenburgh Communication trench and converted it into a fire trench. "D" Company in Hindenburgh at R.3.c. 5 AM stand to, 7 AM stand down, all quiet. Rations delivered to 7th KOYLI & 7th DCLI. Shelling very heavy all day by our own guns captured by the enemy. 4-30 PM stand to, 6 PM stand down. 9 PM Rations collected from Brigade H.Q. 7 AM BN H.Q. moved from BROWN LINE to VILLERS PLOUICH and remained there throughout the day. The C.O. proceeded at visit Companies in front line, he returned to BROWN LINE at night and there established BN H.Q. The Companies were exposed to heavy shelling throughout the day.	
			Casualties. O.Rs. Killed 1. Wounded 32.	

A5834 Wt. W4973/M687 750,000 8/16 D. D. & L. Ltd. Forms/C.2118/13.

Instructions regarding War Diaries and Intelligence Summaries are contained in F. S. Regs., Part II. and the Staff Manual respectively. Title pages will be prepared in manuscript.

WAR DIARY
or
~~INTELLIGENCE SUMMARY.~~
(Erase heading not required.)

P/20

CONTINUED.

Army Form C. 2118.

Place	Date	Hour	Summary of Events and Information	Remarks and references to Appendices
LA VACQUERIE	2/12/17	1 AM	'A' Company holding trench at R9. d 8.5. 10 PM Relieved by 2/6th WARWICKS. During the day a party of men under 2/Lt H. S. PARKIN proceeded to clear a trench occupied by the enemy the trench was cleared for 40 yds then the bombs gave out, the men held the trench until the 11th R. Bs occupied a new position and saved the position which had been occupied by the enemy. The Company then held part of the front line till relieved at 10 Pm. "B" Company holding trench at R. 3. c until 4-30 pm Company then sent to occupy front line at R. 10. d and close a gap that existed between the 11th R. B and 2/6th WARWICKS. "C" Company holding Hindenburgh C. T. where they remained all day, at 10 PM this Company was relieved, the Company then marched back to BROWN LINE at W. 4 B. 8. 5. 'D' Company still holding trench about R 3. C, about 8 am Enemy seen massing in PAM PAM Farm. 10 PM Company relieved. Shelling continued heavy all day.	
			Evacuations — H. Q Company moved from VILLERS PLOUICH to BROWN LINE at about Q 34 C. 8. 5	
			Casualties — O. Rs. Killed 1 Wounded 3.	

Instructions regarding War Diaries and Intelligence Summaries are contained in F. S. Regs., Part II. and the Staff Manual respectively. Title pages will be prepared in manuscript.

WAR DIARY
or
~~INTELLIGENCE SUMMARY~~.

(Erase heading not required.)

CONTINUED

Army Form C. 2118.

Place	Date	Hour	Summary of Events and Information	Remarks and references to Appendices
	3/12/17	6am	Battalion now concentrated in old BROWN LINE. "A" and "B" Companies at about Q 34 b. and d. "C" and "D" Companies at about W. 4. b. and D. H.Q. Company at Q 34. c. 8. 5. Companies marched from positions held on 2nd December to present position, during the night of 2nd/3rd Dec.	
Q 34. c. 8. 5	3/12/17	10 PM	The 4 Companies and H.Q. marched out to FINS and occupied billets for the night.	
			Casualties night of 2nd/3rd December O.R.s Killed 2. Wounded 7.	
Q 34 c 8.5	3/12/17	11/30 PM	BN now at FINS.	

Instructions regarding War Diaries and Intelligence Summaries are contained in F. S. Regs., Part II. and the Staff Manual respectively. Title pages will be prepared in manuscript.

WAR DIARY
or
~~INTELLIGENCE SUMMARY.~~

(Erase heading not required.)

Army Form C. 2118.

11th Bn Durham Light Infantry

Place	Date	Hour	Summary of Events and Information	Remarks and references to Appendices
FINS	4/12/17	9 Am	Battalion marched from billets to hutments at SOREL.	
SOREL	5/12/17	3 Pm	4 Companies under Captain W.G.L. SEAR proceeded to work on Trenches at Q.29. Central	
"	6/12/17	3 Pm	4 " " " R L S PEMBERTON Working under orders of C E III Corps. Trench deepened and fire steps excavated at Q 29 Central.	
"	7/12/17		Work on Trench. Q 29. Central Continued.	
"	8/12/17	2 Pm.	Battalion with transport entrained at FINS and proceeded to HESDEN.	
HESDEN	9/12/17	3 AM	BN arrived at HESDEN and marched to billets at BOUIN - AUBYN St VAST and ECQUEMICOURT. H.Q established at latter place	
ECQUEMICOURT	10/12/17		Inspection of Kits and equipment. Half holiday for all Ranks.	
"	11/12/17	9 Am	Battalion proceeded by Motor Bus to WARDRECQUES arriving 2-30 Pm.	
		11 Am	Transport moved by Road to LE LOQUIN and halted there for the night.	
			2/Lieuts W. ALEXANDER - O.G. DAY - R.R GALLEY - E.W. ENGLISH - N.F GIBSON & H.J.E WHITFIELD joined the BN.	
WARDRECQUES.	12/12/17		Drill and instruction till 12-30 Pm and again from 2-30 to 3-30 Pm	
"	13/12/17	9.30 Am to 12.30 Pm	Training of Lewis Gunners - Bombers and Rifle Bombers; drill for Riflemen	
"	14/12/17		" " " " " " " " " " "	
"	15/12/17		Bathing for Battalion from 9 am till 2 Pm.	

Instructions regarding War Diaries and Intelligence Summaries are contained in F. S. Regs., Part II. and the Staff Manual respectively. Title pages will be prepared in manuscript.

WAR DIARY
or
INTELLIGENCE ~~SUMMARY~~.

(*Erase heading not required.*)

CONTINUED

Army Form C. 2118.

Place	Date	Hour	Summary of Events and Information	Remarks and references to Appendices
WARDRECQUES	15/12/17	2 Pm	Battalion Transport proceeded by Road to STRAZEELE enroute to DICKIEBUSH	
"	16/12/17	8 Am	BN marched to EBBLINGHEM and entrained for DICKIEBUSH arriving at 2-30 Pm	
DICKIEBUSH	16/12/17	3 Pm	Transport arrived from STRAZEELE at 3 PM	
DICKEBUSH	17/12/17		Improving billets and inspection of Arms.	
"	18/12/17		4 Companies on drill for 4 hours. Training of Lewis gunners	
"	19/12/17		200 O.R from 4 Companies working under C.R.E carrying Wiring material.	
"	20/12/17		" " " " " " " " " "	
"	21/12/17		4 Companies carrying material for dumps being made forward.	
"	22/12/17		Companies carrying and Wiring. 3 O.R. Wounded.	
"	24/12/17		Wiring of Corps front continued.	
"	25/12/17		Church Parades during the morning. No work at night.	
"	26/12/17		Wiring Continued by 4 Companies. 2 O.R Wounded. 100 O.R joined	
"	27/12/17		Wiring continued. Lewis gunners on Rifle Range. 1 O.R Wounded.	
"	28/12/17		" " " " " " "	
"	29/12/17		" " " " " " " " " 1 N.C.O Proceeded on Snipers Course	
"	30/12/17		Wiring Continued. 2/Lt J.H.E WHITFIELD proceeded to Corps School of Signalling. 2/Lt F.G ANDREW and 2 N.C.O's Proceeded to PIONEER SCHOOL. ROUEN. 100 O.R's under 2/Lt J.B FITZSIMMONS Proceeded on transfer to 2nd & 14th D.L.I. 50 men each.	

A5834 Wt. W4973/M687 750,000 8/16 D. D. & L. Ltd. Forms/C.2118/13.

Instructions regarding War Diaries and Intelligence Summaries are contained in F. S. Regs., Part II. and the Staff Manual respectively. Title pages will be prepared in manuscript.

WAR DIARY
or
~~INTELLIGENCE SUMMARY.~~
(Erase heading not required.)

Army Form C. 2118.

CONTINUED

Place	Date	Hour	Summary of Events and Information	Remarks and references to Appendices
DICHEBUSCH	31/12/17		'A'-'B'-'C' and 18 men 'D' Company proceeded at 2 pm to continue wiring on Corps front. Lewis gunners on range firing and general instruction.	
"	31/12/17	6 pm	Diary closed.	

"STRENGTH"

	OFFICERS	OTHER RANKS
Battalion strength on December 1st 1917	29	916
Joined Bn during December 1917	6	131
TOTAL.	35	1047
Struck off Killed - Wounded - Sick etc.	-	280
Bn strength 31st December 1917	35	767

[illegible] Captain

Comdg 11th D. L. I.

31/12/1917

A5834 Wt. W4973/M687 750,000 8/16 D. D. & L. Ltd. Forms/C.2118/13.

Instructions regarding War Diaries and Intelligence Summaries are contained in F. S. Regs., Part II. and the Staff Manual respectively. Title pages will be prepared in manuscript.

WAR DIARY
or
~~INTELLIGENCE SUMMARY.~~ 11th Durham Light Infantry

(*Erase heading not required.*)

Army Form C. 2118.

Vol 3

Place	Date	Hour	Summary of Events and Information	Remarks and references to Appendices
DICKEBUSCH	1/1/18		A, B, C + D Coys. wiring the front held by the IXth Corps. Lewis Gunners on Rifle Range. 2 O.R.s wounded	
DICKEBUSCH	2/1/18		4 Coys. carrying material to work in the forward area.	
— " —	3/1/18		Wiring on Corps Front continued by 4 Coys.	
— " —	4/1/18		Wiring on Corps Front Continued by 4 Coys.	
— " —	5/1/18		Battalion relieved 11th South Lancashire Regt. (Pioneers) at ZILLEBEKE BUND I. 15. d. 1. 3. 2 Coys. proceeding by road, and 2 Coys. by rail. 2/Lt. T. A. Atlay and 25 O.R.s proceeded to VOORMEEZELE for duty with IXth Corps Tramway Coy.	
I. 15. d. 1. 3.	6/1/18		Inspection of kit + equipment. 1 Lewis Gun placed at I. 21. b. 05. 35. for Anti-Aircraft duty.	
— " —	7/1/18		4 Coys. working on mule tracks in forward area	
— " —	8/1/18		Coys. at work as for 7th. 74 O.R. proceeded to ROUEN on transfer to R.E. Base Depot. 3 O.R. joined. 2/Lt. J.K. Fitzsimmons wounded.	

Instructions regarding War Diaries and Intelligence Summaries are contained in F. S. Regs., Part II. and the Staff Manual respectively. Title pages will be prepared in manuscript.

WAR DIARY

or

~~INTELLIGENCE SUMMARY~~. 11th Bn. Durham L.I. (Pioneers).

(Erase heading not required.)

Army Form C. 2118.

Place	Date	Hour	Summary of Events and Information	Remarks and references to Appendices
I.15.d.1.3	9/1/18		'A' Coy. maintenance of tracks; 'B' Coy. wiring; 'C' Coy working on PERTH AVENUE; 'D' Coy working on new Track at J.19.b.4.7.	
"	10/1/18		Work Continued as for the 9th. 2/Lt. H.J.C. Whitfield returned from Intelligence Course	
"	11/1/18		A+D Coys. working on new track: 'C' Coy on PERTH AVE. + 'B' Coy. on wiring.	
"	12/1/19		Work Continued as for the 11th. Lt. P.V. Kemp assumed Command of 'C' Coy.	
"	13/1/18		Work on tracks etc Continued; 46 O.R. inspected by A.D.M.S.	
"	14/1/18.		A+D Coy working on new track (CULLEY'S TRAIL) B+C Coy, working on PERTH AVENUE	
"	15/1/18.		A,B+D Coys. working on CULLEY'S TRAIL; 'C' Coy working on PERTH AVE; 2 Lewis Guns posted at RUDKIN HOUSE ~~[illegible]~~ (I.24.c.2.1) for anti-aircraft duties; also 2 guns at Yeomanry Post (I.17.d.6.0.) 2 O.R. accidentally wounded.	
"	16/1/18.		4 Coys. at work as for 15th.	
"	17/1/18		Work Continued on tracks etc. in forward area.	
"	18/1/18.		A,B+D Coys. at work on CULLEY'S TRAIL; 'C' Coy at work on PERTH AVENUE. 2/Lt. A.C. Wilkinson took over duties of Officer i/c Woodcutting	
"	19/1/18.		Work on tracks Continued; 1 O.R. wounded.	
"	20/1/18		Work on tracks continued; 12 O.R. proceeded to Base medically unfit for duty in the forward area	

A5834 Wt. W4973/M687 750,000 8/16 D. D. & L. Ltd. Forms/C.2118/13.

Instructions regarding War Diaries and Intelligence Summaries are contained in F. S. Regs., Part II. and the Staff Manual respectively. Title pages will be prepared in manuscript.

WAR DIARY (Continued)
or
~~INTELLIGENCE SUMMARY.~~ XIth Bn. Durham L I. (Pioneers)

(Erase heading not required.)

Army Form C. 2118.

Place	Date	Hour	Summary of Events and Information	Remarks and references to Appendices
I.15.d.1.3.	21/1/18		4 Coys. at work on tracks. The following officers joined the Battn. 2/Lts. H. RUTHERFORD, J. MARTIN, J.H. DODDS, R.H. KING, F. ARNOTT, F. NAYLOR, F.G. McGREEHIN, R. HARBRON. 2/Lt. W.J. Alexander admitted to hospital sick.	
— " —	22/1/18		Coys. at work as follows - 'A' Coy - Tracks, 'B' 'C' Coys. PERTH AVE., 'D' Coy. CULLEY'S TRAIL. Transport moved from DICKEBUSCH to new lines at H.30.C.2.0. 14 OR. joined.	
— " —	23/1/18		'A' Coy, working on tracks. B, C, + D Coys, improving + extending PERTH AVENUE	
— " —	24/1/18		Work continued as for 23rd. 5 O.R. Category B(1) joined.	
— " —	25/1/18		A Coy working on maintenance of tracks. B, C, D Coys working on PERTH AVENUE. Lieut. R. Bushell and 2 OR proceeded to Pioneer School ROUEN; 1 OR to Base medically unfit.	
— " —	26/1/18		Work continued as for the 25th.	
— " —	27/1/18		Four Coys. working on tracks + PERTH AVENUE Trench. 2/Lt. H. Andrews + 2 O.R. rejoined from Pioneer School.	
— " —	28/1/18		'A' Coy working on maintenance of tracks: B, C, D Coys working on PERTH AVENUE: 5 OR. joined.	
— " —	29/1/18		Work continued as for 28th. a/Capt. A. Philip joined from hospital.	
— " —	30/1/18		Four Coys working as for 29th. a/Capt. A. Philip assumed temporary Command of 'A' Coy.	
— " —	31/1/18		A Coy working on maintenance of tracks. B, C + D Coys. working on PERTH AVENUE. Lt. J. Liddell proceeded to U.K. for 6 months tour of duty.	

(A7092). Wt. W12839/M1293. 750,000. 1/17. D. D. & L., Ltd. Forms/C.2118/14.

Instructions regard[illegible] War Diaries and Intelligence Summaries are [illegible]ned in F. S. Regs., Part II. and the Staff Ma[illegible]al respectively. Title pages will be prepared in manuscript.

WAR DIARY
or
~~INTELLIGENCE SUMMARY.~~
(Erase heading not required.)

CONTINUED

Army Form C. 2118.

Place	Date	Hour	Summary of Events and Information	Remarks and references to Appendices
			"STRENGTH"	

	OFFICERS	O.R^s
Battalion strength 31.12.1917	34	765
Joined during January 1918.	8	21
Total - - - - - - - - - - - -	42	786
Struck off during January 1918.	1	114
Battalion strength 31-1-1918.	41	672

The Field
1st Feby 1918

G Hayes Lieut Col
Comdg 11th D.L.I.

(A7092). Wt. W12839/M1293. 750,000. 1/17. D. D. & L., Ltd. Forms/C.2118/14.

Instructions regarding War Diaries and Intelligence Summaries are contained in F. S. Regs., Part II. and the Staff Manual respectively. Title pages will be prepared in manuscript.

February 1918

WAR DIARY
or
~~INTELLIGENCE SUMMARY.~~
(Erase heading not required.)

11th Bn. Durham L. Infantry.

Army Form C. 2118.

Vol 31

Place	Date	Hour	Summary of Events and Information	Remarks and references to Appendices
ZILLEBEKE BUND	1/2/18		4 Coys working on mule tracks. Three other ranks proceeded to Lewis Gun School.	
— " —	2/2/18		Work continued on tracks.	
— " —	3/2/18		One Coy. on maintenance work; three Coys. working on tracks. R.C. Church Parade	
— " —	4/2/18		Work continued as for 3rd.	
— " —	5/2/18		Work continued on tracks etc.	
— " —	6/2/18		Four Coys working on tracks; 2/Lt. A.S. Parkin proceeded to England for six months tour of duty. 2/Lt. F.J. McGrechin admitted to hospital.	
— " —	7/2/18		Work on tracks and C.T.s continued.	
— " —	8/2/18		Work continued as for 7th. 118 O.R.s joined from 14th D.L.I., also the following officers:- Capt W.J. Endean, 2/Lts. G.F. Martin, V.G. Duckett, W. Banks, B.C. Barrans, G.V. Tottle;	
— " —	9/2/18		Four Coys. working on tracks and C.T.s. 2/Lt. J.H. Dodds and 1 N.C.O. to Corps School.	
— " —	10/2/18		Work continued as for 9th.	
— " —	11/2/18		Work continued	
— " —	12/2/18		Work on tracks and C.T.s. continued.	
— " —	13/2/18		Work in forward area continued as for the 12th.	

D. D. & L., London, E.C.
(A7883) Wt. W803/M1672 350,000 4/17 Sch. 52a Forms/C/2118/14

Instructions regarding War Diaries and Intelligence Summaries are contained in F. S. Regs., Part II, and the Staff Manual respectively. Title pages will be prepared in manuscript.

WAR DIARY (Continued)
or
~~INTELLIGENCE SUMMARY.~~
(Erase heading not required.)

XIth Durham L. I.

Army Form C. 2118.

Place	Date	Hour	Summary of Events and Information	Remarks and references to Appendices
LILLEBEKE BUND	14/2/18		Four Coys at work on tracks etc. in the forward area.	
— " —	15/2/18		Four Coys working on tracks in the forward area.	
— " —	16/2/18		Lieut & Q.Mr H. Wilkinson and advance party proceeded by rail to RACQUINGHEM. Transport proceeded by road to STRAZEELE.	
— " —	17/2/18		Battn. relieved by 9th Bn. North Staffordshire Regt. 12.30pm. Battn. marched to DICKEBUSCH and entrained for EBBLINGHEM, arriving at 5pm. 6.30pm. Battn. arrived at RACQUINGHEM and went into billets. Transport arrived at 2pm.	
RACQUINGHEM	18/2/18		Drill, Inspection of Arms etc. from 8.30 a.m. to 12.45 pm. 2/Lt. T.W. Applegarth joined.	
— " —	19/2/18		Four Coys. on drill & musketry from 8.30 am to 12.45 pm. 28 OR.s arrived	
— " —	20/2/18		Parades and musketry from 8.30 am to 12.45 pm.	
— " —	21/2/18		Four Coys. on drill and musketry. 2/Lt. W.G. Craig with advance party proceeded to STEENBECQUE and entrained for NESLE. 6.30pm. A & B Coys. under Capt. W.J. Endean proceeded to STEENBECQUE Station and entrained for NESLE. HdQrs. C & D Coys & Bn Transport under Capt. W.G.L. Sear M.C., proceeded at 11pm to STEENBECQUE Station & entrained for NESLE.	

Instructions regarding War Diaries and Intelligence Summaries are contained in F. S. Regs., Part II. and the Staff Manual respectively. Title pages will be prepared in manuscript.

WAR DIARY (Continued) or ~~INTELLIGENCE SUMMARY.~~

(Erase heading not required.)

Army Form C. 2118.

11th Bn. Durham L. I.

Place	Date	Hour	Summary of Events and Information	Remarks and references to Appendices
NESLE	22/2/18	10.30 a.m.	A & B Coys. arrived by train. 5.30 pm. HQ C & D Coys. with Bn. Transport arrived. After detraining Coys. proceeded to billets in MUILLE VILLETTE and GOLANCOURT.	
GOLANCOURT	23/2/18		Coys. at training under Coy Commanders.	
"	24/2/18		Billets at MUILLE VILLETTE vacated. 'C' Coy. broken up and men posted to the three other Coys. Battn. reorganized as a 3 Coy. Battn. Lieut R.H. Bushell returned from Pioneer Course at ROUEN. 4 ORs. joined.	
"	25/2/18		Coy. Training, Musketry and Training of Signallers. Lieut. D.E. Cooke joined.	
"	26/2/18		Platoon & Coy Training: Rifle practice: Inspection of Box Respirators by D.G.O.	
"	27/2/18		A, B & D Coys. Commenced work on the HAM – NOYENS Railway.	
"	28/2/18		Three Coys. at work on the HAM – NOYENS Railway.	

STRENGTH

	Officers	ORs.
Battn. Strength on 1st Feb.	41	672
Joined during month Feb.	9	164
Total	50	836
Struck off Strength	2	6
Battalion Strength :-	48	830

W. Clear Capt
Comdg. XIth Durham L. I.

D. D. & L., London, E.C. (A7883) Wt. W803/M1672 350,000 4/17 Sch. 52a Forms/C/2118/14

20th Divisional Pioneers

PIONEERS

11th BATTALION

DURHAM LIGHT INFANTRY

MARCH 1 9 1 8

1

Instructions regarding War Diaries and Intelligence Summaries are contained in F. S. Regs., Part II. and the Staff Manual respectively. Title pages will be prepared in manuscript.

Pioneers / 20

WAR DIARY
or
~~INTELLIGENCE SUMMARY.~~
(Erase heading not required.)

Army Form C. 2118.

11th Bn Durham L. Infantry

VR 32

Place	Date	Hour	Summary of Events and Information	Remarks and references to Appendices
GOLANCOURT	1/3/18		3 Companies at Work on HAM - NOYAN Railway	
"	2/3/18		Work on Railway continued. Musketry and training of Lewis Gunners.	
"	3/3/18		" " " " " " " " "	
"	4/3/18		" " " " 10% of strength on musketry.	
"	5/3/18		" " " " " " " "	
"	6/3/18		" " " " Training of Lewis Gunners.	
"	7/3/18		3 Companies unloading Railway Material and making new formation.	
"	8/3/18		3 " " " " " " " " "	
"	9/3/18		Companies at work on Railway. 28 O.R. joined.	
"	10/3/18		C.O. inspected Bn also kits.	
"	11/3/18		3 Companies laying new Railway line from HAM	
"	12/3/18		All available men laying new Railway line.	
"	13/3/18		" " " " "	
"	14/3/18		"A" Company moved to VOYENNES. "B.D" Companies at Work on Railway	
"	15/3/18		Work on Railway continued.	
"	16/3/18		" " " "	

D. D. & L., London, E.C.
(A7883) Wt. W803/M1672 350,000 4/17 Sch. 52a Forms/C/2118/14

Instructions regarding War Diaries and Intelligence Summaries are contained in F. S. Regs., Part II. and the Staff Manual respectively. Title pages will be prepared in manuscript.

WAR DIARY
or
~~INTELLIGENCE SUMMARY.~~
(Erase heading not required.)

CONTINUED

Army Form C. 2118.

Place	Date	Hour	Summary of Events and Information	Remarks and references to Appendices
GOLANCOURT	17/3/18	.	Lectures and gas demonstration.	
"	18/3/18	.	Work on HAM - NEYAN Railway Continued.	
"	19/3/18	.	'B' Company moved to Camp at J. 35 c Sheet 66d. Working on Railway	
"	20/3/18	.	Two Companies on detachment. 'D' Company at work on Railway	
"	21/3/18		The Battalion was billetted as follows:- HQ + 'D' Coy at GOLANCOURT, 'A' Coy at VOYENNES,	
"	"		'B' Coy in Quarries in J.35.c (Sheet 66 D. N.E. At 6·20 am a message was received	
"	"		"XVIII Corps manning Battle Stations". Orders were received to concentrate at GOLANCOURT	
"	"		about 9·30 a.m The Concentration was completed by 1·20pm. At 2·5pm. orders were	
	"		received to move to VILLERS St CHRISTOPHE at 4pm. Marched off carrying packs etc. +	
	"		arrived at VILLERS St CHRISTOPHE about 6·50pm. Capt. Jee with 6 officers + 133 OR	
	"		were detached as details + reported to MATIGNY	
	"		At about 8pm. orders were received for one Coy. to report to 61st Inf. Bde	
	"		at DURY. "D" Coy was sent.	
	"		A party of 130 OR with Capt R Jee, 2/Lts Whitfield, King, McGreekin, Arnott,	
	"		Applegarth and Dodds, under the command of Major Storr, 12th Kings	
	"		marched from GOLANCOURT to MATIGNY.	

D. D. & L., London, E.C.
(A7883) Wt. W803/M1672 350,000 4/17 Sch. 52a Forms/C/2118/14

Instructions regarding War Diaries and Intelligence Summaries are contained in F. S. Regs., Part II. and the Staff Manual respectively. Title pages will be prepared in manuscript.

Army Form C. 2118.

WAR DIARY of 11th Bn. DURHAM LIGHT INFANTRY
or
~~INTELLIGENCE SUMMARY.~~

(Erase heading not required.)

Place	Date	Hour	Summary of Events and Information	Remarks and references to Appendices
			[to MATIGNY]	
	22/3/18		This party dug a line N. of MATIGNY - DOUILLY Road facing N.E., and retired from	
	"		this line to VOYENNES at midnight.	
	23/3/18		Covered the retirement of the Scottish Rifles across the canal bridge. This Battn.	
	"		relieved the party of D.L.I. + details but retained 2/Lt. King + 20 OR to hold a front	
	"		post on their left flank until mid-day. 2/Lt King rejoined later. At 9 a.m.	
	"		the party moved to behind the NOYON Canal and dug a line facing N.E.	
	"		near LANGEVOISIN. At 2 pm orders were received to support the 59th Bde. A	
	"		position was taken up at 5 pm, 1 mile N. of ROUY-LE-PETIT facing north.	

D. D. & L., London, E.C.
(A7883) Wt. W803/M1672 350,000 4/17 Sch. 52a Forms/C/2118/14

Army Form C. 2118.

Instructions regarding War Diaries and Intelligence Summaries are contained in F. S. Regs., Part II. and the Staff Manual respectively. Title pages will be prepared in manuscript.

WAR DIARY of 11th Bn Durham Light Infantry
or
~~INTELLIGENCE SUMMARY.~~
(Erase heading not required.)

Place	Date	Hour	Summary of Events and Information	Remarks and references to Appendices
	22/3/18		Gunfire heard from direction of ST. QUENTIN + HOLNON Wood. At about 10.30 am. C.O. arranged with 59th Inf Bde. to attach Bn. Transport to 59th Bde Group; at about 12 noon gunfire became very intense, and at about 12.30 the battle appeared to be getting nearer + transport etc. was observed retiring. C.O. reported to G.O.C 59th Inf Bde. + asked if Battn was under his orders as it was in the group: offered to cooperate and was informed that the best thing that could be done to assist the 59th Bde. was to occupy a trench system covering GERMAINE and supporting VAUX – BEAUVAIS.	
			HQ + A + B Coys. marched out to GERMAINE at 3pm. Arrived there when orders arrived from Division to report to 60th Bde – Moved back. The C.O went + reported to G.O.C. 60th Bde. + received orders from the latter to join up with the left of the 61st Inf Bde. + the right of the 60th Bde., the K.S.L.I on the line TUGNY – LAVESNE. Posts etc. had been sited by someone + marked on the map but were not dug. Lieut Col Hayes + Lieut Buchell with Capt. Endean (A Coy) + Capt Kemp (B Coy) found the supporting Coy. of the 12th Kings + D Coy of this Battalion dug in astride the TUGNY – DURY Road in L.19.d. and stretching towards the Canal. Hd. Qrs. and A + B Coys. came on afterwards + arrived at about 8pm.	

D. D. & L., London, E.C.
(A7883) Wt. W609/M1672 350,000 4/17 Sch. 52a Forms/C/2118/14

Instructions regarding War Diaries and Intelligence Summaries are contained in F. S. Regs., Part II. and the Staff Manual respectively. Title pages will be prepared in manuscript.

WAR DIARY of 11th Bn. Durham Light Infantry.
or
~~INTELLIGENCE SUMMARY.~~
(Erase heading not required.)

Army Form C. 2118.

Place	Date	Hour	Summary of Events and Information	Remarks and references to Appendices
			[arrived at about 8/pm]	
			The Coy of the 12th Kings which was in TUGNY had been driven out + the supporting Coy became the front line. Lieut Cooper Cmdg. 'D' Coy. 11th D.L.I. + the officer with the Kings' Coy informed Col. Hayes that they were expecting to retire to L.31 central very shortly. The C.O. told them not to evacuate the position without informing him, + the Coy Commander of the Kings' informed his C.O. Lt. Col. Vince D.S.O. of the arrival of the remainder of the D.L.I. Touch was established with the K.S.L.I on the left at the junction of the tracks in K.18.d 'A' Coy was on the Right + 'B' Coy on the Left. At about 8.30 pm or 9 oclock Capt. Endean reported that 'D' Coy + the Coy of the 12th Kings had retired + left his flank in the air. Lt. Col. Hayes who had found Lt. Col Welch of the 6th K.S.L.I sent a message to the 60th Bde HQ. informing the Bde. of what was happening. The message was received by the O.C. Dvl. M.G. Battn. at AUBIGNY as Bde. HQ had moved. The Coys could not retire without uncovering the K.S.L.I + there were no orders to that effect. Two posts were dug in echelon on the right flank. A thick fog had set in. The enemy could be heard in TUGNY shouting in English + making a lot of noise. Patrols were sent out towards TUGNY, but the enemy had worked round after the party which had retired and at	

Instructions regarding War Diaries and Intelligence Summaries are contained in F. S. Regs., Part II. and the Staff Manual respectively. Title pages will be prepared in manuscript.

WAR DIARY of 11th Bn. DURHAM LIGHT INFANTRY
or
~~INTELLIGENCE SUMMARY.~~

(Erase heading not required.)

Army Form C. 2118.

Place	Date	Hour	Summary of Events and Information	Remarks and references to Appendices
			[and at]	
			about midnight or 12.15 a.m. 'B' Coy was rushed from the right rear. The posts then became mixed up + there was confusion. Some men fired, but in the fog it was difficult to tell which were enemy. The Right of the K.S.L.I. was also thrown into some confusion + became mixed with part of 'B' Coy. Capt Endean with a strong party of 'A' Coy held out in a post in L.19.d. central which was the right of his line. Hostile machine guns were also firing into AUBIGNY Village from between AUBIGNY + DURY. Bn. HQ was preparing to dig in in the open near that of the K.S.L.I near the AUBIGNY DURY ROAD. There was confused firing in the fog. About 70 men of the D.L.I and 30 of the K.S.L.I + a few of the M.G.C. were collected just S.W. of AUBIGNY. This party was disorganised + also owing to the fog + uncertainty the C.O decided that it was no use attempting a vague counter attack. Capt Kemp of 'B' Coy had reported that the Coy had been surprised + many men had broken through + that 'A' Coy was surrounded. The party then proceeded down the HAM Main Road, leaving a rearguard of 20 men under 2/Lt. English to support 2 Vickers Guns of the M.G.C. which had been placed in position in the main road. Instead of retiring on the trench line N.E. of HAM, a message	

D. D. & L., London, E.C.
(A7883) Wt. W803/M1672 350,000 4/17 Sch. 52a Forms/C/2118/14

Instructions regarding War Diaries and Intelligence Summaries are contained in F. S. Regs., Part II. and the Staff Manual respectively. Title pages will be prepared in manuscript.

WAR DIARY of 11th Bn Durham Light Infantry
or
~~INTELLIGENCE SUMMARY.~~
(Erase heading not required.)

Army Form C. 2118.

Place	Date	Hour	Summary of Events and Information	Remarks and references to Appendices
			[a message]	
	22/3/18		was received for the DLI to report to the 60th Bde in HAM. They were ordered by the	
	"		G.O.C. 60th Bde. to proceed to OFFOY to hold the bridge head there.	
	"		Capt. Endean with 2/Lts Galley + Craig and about 40 men made their way back in the	
	"		fog through DURY to HAM where they joined some mixed troops holding the HAM	
	"		defences. C.S.M. Craggs + a small party of 'B' Coy did the same, fighting their way	
	"		back in a rearguard action with some of the 12th R.B.	
	"		There were previous to this action, HQrs Lieut Col Hayes D.S.O: Acting Adjt Lieut. Cooke	
	"		L.G.O. 2/Lt Ellwood: Scouting + Intelligence Officer Lieut Bushell + the M.O Capt Turnbull R.A.M.C.	
	"		'A' Coy, Capt Endean, 2/Lts Craig, Galley, Rutherford + Alexander.	
	"		'B' Coy Capt Kemp, 2/Lts Martin, Morris, Naylor + English.	

D. D. & L., London, E.C.
(A7883) Wt. W803/M1672 350,000 4/17 Sch. 52a Forms/C/2118/14

Army Form C. 2118.

*Instructions regarding War Diaries and Intelligence Summaries are contained in F. S. Regs., Part II. and the Staff Manual respectively. Title pages will be prepared in manuscript.

WAR DIARY of 11th Bn DURHAM LIGHT INFANTRY
or
~~INTELLIGENCE SUMMARY.~~
(Erase heading not required.)

Place	Date	Hour	Summary of Events and Information	Remarks and references to Appendices
	23/3/18		At about 4 am 97 men of 'A' + 'B' Coys, mostly B Coy, were formed into one Coy under	
	"		Lieut Bushell; with him 2/Lts Martin, Naylor, + English + C.S.M. Craggs	
	"		The 12th K.R.R.C under Lieut Col Moore D.S.O had arrived, + took over the defence of	
	"		the Canal at OFFOY. The D.L.I as above with 26 of the K.S.L.I who were then	
	"		attached to them prolonged the line to the right + took over part of the sector	
	"		from about J.21.c 8.0 to J.22.c.1.0. A pioneer Battn of the D.C.L.I which	
	"		had been digging in here was moved away shortly after daylight, + the	
	"		party of DLI and one platoon of the K.R.R. prolonged the line up to the outskirts of	
	"		the village of CANIZY at about J.22.c.5.2. Touch was obtained with the	
	"		30th Entrenching Battalion who were holding the line of the Canal + village.	
	"		Bn. HQ was then dug in at about J.27.a.8.7 about 200yds behind the	
	"		trench line held by 'B' Coy. This afterwards moved to the railway cutting about	
	"		J.27.c 3.5. Lt Col Moore was in railway cutting at J.26.d.4.6. Telephone	
	"		Communication was established with 60th Bde HQ. in HOMBLEUX. The 23rd was a	
	"		quiet day. There was intermittent sniping over the CANAL. On the evening of the 23rd	
	"		after dark there were slight bursts of hostile machine guns + trench mortar fire.	

D. D. & L., London, E.C. (A7883) Wt. W803/M1672 350,000 4/17 Sch. 52a Forms/C/2118/14

Instructions regarding War Diaries and Intelligence Summaries are contained in F. S. Regs., Part II. and the Staff Manual respectively. Title pages will be prepared in manuscript.

WAR DIARY of 11th Bn. DURHAM LIGHT INFANTRY
or
~~INTELLIGENCE SUMMARY.~~
(Erase heading not required.)

Army Form C. 2118.

Place	Date	Hour	Summary of Events and Information	Remarks and references to Appendices
			[+ trench mortar fire]	
	24/3/18		The Battalion on the right had been retiring from the posts & returning again, & as their movements were uncertain Lt Col Moore obtained the assistance of two platoons of the 2nd/7th Warwicks of the 61st Division to assist the right flank at CANIZY. Lt Col Moore instructed them to dig in South east of CANIZY & to have a standing patrol at the broken foot bridge in J.29.a. Capt Endean, 2/Lieut Galley & about 34 men of 'A' Coy. arrived at about 4 a.m. At about 6 a.m a hostile artillery & trench mortar bombardment of CANIZY Commenced. Artillery support was asked for but was not received. 2/Lt Galley and 30 men were sent up to the cutting at J.34.a.1.7. with a Lewis & a Vickers gun to make a strong point & cover the valley to the CANAL & also to cover the exits to CANIZY. This party also protected the right flank along the railway. The South Lancashire Pioneers who had been there had vacated this position previously.	
			A Coy of the 2nd/7th Warwicks arrived about 7 a.m. to support the right & to connect up with the Entrenching Battalion on the right. This Battalion had a line along the railway. Capt. Parker of the Bedfordshire Regt with about 20 men joined 2/Lt Galley's party & took Command of the post at the cutting.	

D. D. & L., London, E.C.
(A7883) Wt. W809/M1672 350,000 4/17 Sch. 52a Forms/C/2118/14

Instructions regarding War Diaries and Intelligence Summaries are contained in F. S. Regs., Part II. and the Staff Manual respectively. Title pages will be prepared in manuscript.

Army Form C. 2118.

WAR DIARY of 11th BN DURHAM LIGHT INFANTRY
~~or INTELLIGENCE SUMMARY.~~

(Erase heading not required.)

Place	Date	Hour	Summary of Events and Information	Remarks and references to Appendices
			[at the cutting]	
	24/3/18		Lt Col Hayes sent him to see the O.C. Entrenching Battn to ask him to push his left	
	"		forward through J.35. Central to hold copse in J.34.b. + join up with the 2 platoons	
	"		of the Warwicks. A reply was received later that this had been done. At the same	
	"		time as the situation on the right seemed uncertain, a platoon of the 2nd/7th Warwicks	
	"		was sent to dig in S.E. of cutting at J.34.a.1.7. to connect up with troops on the	
	"		right, + to cover the right flank. Another platoon of the Warwicks was aligned	
	"		along the cutting from J.34.a.1.7 westwards covering the ground down to	
	"		CANIZY. When daylight came there was a thick fog. The remaining 2 platoons	
	"		of the Warwicks were kept in the cutting as a local reserve at about J.27.c.8.2.	
	"		No reports came through from the 2 platoons of Warwicks at CANIZY + a patrol	
	"		which went out to get in touch with them did not return.	
	"		At about 8 a.m machine gun + rifle fire was directed towards the railway	
	"		from CANIZY + some men of 'B' Coy and the K.S.L.I. were ~~sent~~ seen retiring	
	"		westwards in J.27.b. This party afterwards reformed in J.27.a + c + counter-	
	"		attacked with a Coy of K.R.R. The enemy were then seen approaching as the	
	"		fog lifted. Fire was opened on them from the railway + they were driven back	

D. D. & L., London, E.C.
(A7883) Wt. W809/M1672 350,000 4/17 Sch. 52a Forms/C/2118/14

Army Form C. 2118.

Instructions regarding War Diaries and Intelligence Summaries are contained in F. S. Regs., Part II. and the Staff Manual respectively. Title pages will be prepared in manuscript.

WAR DIARY of 11th BN DURHAM or ~~INTELLIGENCE SUMMARY.~~ LIGHT INFANTRY

(Erase heading not required.)

Place	Date	Hour	Summary of Events and Information	Remarks and references to Appendices
			[driven back]	
	24/3/18		towards CANIZY. 'B' Coy. also regained their trench. Capt Endean meanwhile reported	
	"		that the enemy were working round the right flank down the HAM-NESLE	
	"		road. A hostile aeroplane flew low over the cutting. Lt. Col. Moore decided to dig	
	"		in north of the cutting with 100 men of the K.R.R. who were in Reserve there.	
	"		Capt Endean started to form a defensive flank astride the HAM-NESLE Road.	
	"		Hostile machine gun fire then was directed on the cutting + on some troops	
	"		who were retiring in the open westwards in J.33.b from J.34.a. The	
	"		enemy also fired down the railway line + had apparently seized the	
	"		cutting at J.34.a.17. The troops on the right, some of the 36th Division +	
	"		mixed parties + some of the troops from the railway retired on the	
	"		right + formed a defensive flank on the line approximately CALVARY FARM -	
	"		Stone + the railway cutting in J.26.d. This mixed body of troops were	
	"		joined up with the 12 KRRC. + moved forward to about J.33.a.4.4 +	
	"		thence to railway. There was a partially dug strong point at CALVARY	
	"		FARM. This was also manned. Lt Col. Hayes with Lt Cooke + 2/Lt Ellwood went	
	"		out to the South on receipt of a message for Capt Endean that the enemy was	

D. D. & L., London, E.C. (A7883) Wt. W809/M1672 350,000 4/17 Sch. 52a Forms/C/2118/14

Instructions regarding War Diaries and Intelligence Summaries are contained in F. S. Regs., Part II, and the Staff Manual respectively. Title pages will be prepared in manuscript.

WAR DIARY for 11th Bn DURHAM LIGHT INFANTRY
or
~~INTELLIGENCE SUMMARY.~~
(Erase heading not required.)

Army Form C. 2118.

Place	Date	Hour	Summary of Events and Information	Remarks and references to Appendices
	24/3/18		[enemy was] working round the right flank. There a complete gap was found as far as ESMERY HALLON. The southern exits of ESMERY HALLON were being shelled + slight hostile machine gun + rifle fire was directed from this direction against a platoon of the Warwicks who were widely extended on this flank. The situation was now very obscure + Capt. Endean had already proceeded to find the nearest Bde. HQ to explain the local situation. Lt. Col Moore was still in the same position + the force east of CALVARY FARM was easily holding out. Several parties had retired previous to this through HOMBLEUX, some down the HAM – NESLE Road + one strong party from the direction of the cutting in T.26.c. Lt. Col. Moore + some of the K.R.R's + some of 'B' Coy under C.S.M. Craggs had remained there + held the enemy back. At this time there were the troops of 4 different divisions mixed up + control on a large scale was impossible. At about 2.30 pm approximately the platoon on the right flank were driven back and the enemy advanced on to the ridge dominating CALVARY FARM from the south + also the road to HOMBLEUX. The force then retired through HOMBLEUX to the Canal at BREUIL. The action of some Canadian motor machine guns	

D. D. & L., London, E.C.
(A7883) Wt. W803/M1672 350,000 4/17 Sch. 52a Forms/C/2118/14

Instructions regarding War Diaries and Intelligence Summaries are contained in F. S. Regs., Part II. and the Staff Manual respectively. Title pages will be prepared in manuscript.

WAR DIARY of 11th Bn. DURHAM LIGHT INFANTRY
or
~~INTELLIGENCE SUMMARY.~~
(Erase heading not required.)

Army Form C. 2118.

Place	Date	Hour	Summary of Events and Information	Remarks and references to Appendices
	24/3/18		[machine guns]	
			greatly assisted his somewhat disorderly retirement + undoubtedly prevented	
	"		circumstances which might have been infinitely more serious. The G.O.C.	
	"		60th Bde at BREUIL ordered the men of the 20th Division to man the western	
	"		edge of the canal from BUVERCHY to to BREUIL. One party of 30 men under	
	"		Capt Endean + Lieut Bushell dug in near the bridge at BREUIL and Lt. Cooke	
	"		collected another party + dug in with the K.S.L.I ~~near~~ BUVERCHY. HQ	
	"		then consisting of Lieut. Col Hayes, Lt. Cooke, 2/Lt Ellwood with Cpl Passey +	
	"		3 signallers and one runner occupied a small house about 100 yds in rear	
	"		of the Canal with Capt Endean's party. The night was quiet except for bursts	
	"		of rifle + machine gun fire chiefly from the French who were dug in	
	"		along the canal bank in sections. Orders were received stating sections	
	"		of the Canal to be held. Capt. Endean's party then came under the 12th KRR.	
	"		Sector + C.S.M. Rambert's party then came under the K.S.L.I. sector.	
	25/3/18		The remainder of Bn. HQ marched back at dawn 24th to gather together the	
			rest of the Battn. + ascertain the situation + to try + straighten matters out.	
			The transport was with the 59th Bde. Group + the majority of the men that were known	

D. D. & L., London, E.C.
(A7583) Wt. W809/M1672 350,000 4/17 Sch. 52a Forms/C/2118/14

Instructions regarding War Diaries and Intelligence Summaries are contained in F. S. Regs., Part II. and the Staff Manual respectively. Title pages will be prepared in manuscript.

WAR DIARY of 11th Bn DURHAM LIGHT INFANTRY
~~or~~
~~**INTELLIGENCE SUMMARY.**~~
(Erase heading not required.)

Army Form C. 2118.

Place	Date	Hour	Summary of Events and Information	Remarks and references to Appendices
	25/3/18		[were known]	
			were with the 60th Bde. The C.O. + Lt. Cooke, after seeing the Transport + arranging for	
	〃		Lewis Guns + ammunition returned + reported to G.O.C 60th Bde. No stragglers or	
	〃		parties were organised as orders had been issued for these to be collected at	
	〃		the transport lines. Lt. Col. Hayes + Lt. Cooke were sent down by the G.O.C. 60th Bde	
	〃		with Capt. Bell of the 60th Bde HQ to restore the situation during the day at	
	〃		LONGUEVOISIN. The line was turned back + advanced + the situation was restored	
	〃		without difficulty. In the evening owing to the flanks giving way, the two parties	
	〃		of the DLI then in the line fought a rearguard action through CRESSY then	
	〃		retired on ROYE where the Battn. was ordered to collect + reform. At ROYE on	
	〃		the night of the 25th Lt Col Hayes who had been slightly affected by odd gas shells	
	〃		during the day whilst in the French line collapsed temporarily + was taken away	
	〃		by No. 50 CCS at ROYE. He was sent down to ROUEN + returned a few days later	
	26/3/18		Capt Sear M.C. then took Command of the Battalion on the evening of the 26th	

(A7883) Wt. W803/M1672 350,000 4/17 **Sch. 52a** Forms/C/2118/14
D. D. & L., London, E.C.

Instructions regarding War Diaries and Intelligence Summaries are contained in F. S. Regs., Part II. and the Staff Manual respectively. Title pages will be prepared in manuscript.

WAR DIARY of 11th Bn. DURHAM LIGHT INFANTRY
~~or~~
~~**INTELLIGENCE SUMMARY.**~~
(Erase heading not required.)

Army Form C. 2118.

Place	Date	Hour	Summary of Events and Information	Remarks and references to Appendices
	26/3/18	1.30pm	At 1.30pm orders received to join 60th Bde. and dig defences at LE QUESNEL. Bn. Commdrs. with Brigadier Genl. reconnoitred line, At 7.30pm. Battn. was ordered to proceed to ARVILLERS. On arrival the night was spent digging in, and improving defences. During night valuable reconnaissance work was done by Capt. Jee as far as ERCHES + BOUCHOIR. The 36th Division was holding a line between ARKVILLERS + ERCHES	
	27/3/18	11am.	The 36th Div. retired. The K.R.R.C. were on our left, but touch could not be got with anybody on our right. Enemy did not come nearer than about 1200yds. Great movement observed towards the right in enemy lines all the rest of the day; of which the Bde. was constantly informed. Active patrols all night revealed no further approach of enemy. French commenced about 8 am, to make	
	28/3/18	8am.	arrangements for relief when the enemy attacked. Our advanced post, in a very strong position, was very heavily shelled + Lewis guns damaged + garrison driven in. Enemy came forward on our right flank massing in woods. A defensive flank was thrown back + an attempt made to drive the enemy out of the woods, but they were too strong. Orders were received from	

D. D. & L., London, E.C. (A7853) Wt. W803/M1672 350,000 4/17 Sch. 52a Forms/C/2118/14

Instructions regarding War Diaries and Intelligence Summaries are contained in F. S. Regs., Part II. and the Staff Manual respectively. Title pages will be prepared in manuscript.

WAR DIARY of 11th Bn. DURHAM LIGHT INFANTRY
~~or INTELLIGENCE SUMMARY.~~
(Erase heading not required.)

Army Form C. 2118.

Place	Date	Hour	Summary of Events and Information	Remarks and references to Appendices
	28/3/18		[received from] Brigade to retire on FRESNOY. Bn. complimented by Brigadier Gen. for this work. From FRESNOY Battn. immediately marched on to a wood behind MEZIÈRES, & stayed here all night in heavy rain. Capt. Pemberton rejoined here & assumed command of the Battn.	
	29/3/18		Enemy attacking MEZIÈRES. Bn. in reserve with 7th KSLI.	
		3.15pm	The Bn was ordered to attack MEZIÈRES from the north – Zero being 4 pm. The Battn proceeded to a wood on the left of MEZIÈRES which was the jumping off position. At 4pm. the Bn. 10 Officers + 130 OR strong attacked the village. In crossing a clearing about 300 yds from the village, the enemy dropped a T.M. barrage on the Battn. Some enemy M.G.s also infiladed our position inflicting very heavy casualties. Capt. Pemberton & a few men succeeded in reaching the village, working through to the western edge. Lt. King on the left also succeeded in entering the village, but all his party having become casualties, he was compelled to withdraw. Capt. Pemberton having only two men with him was also compelled to withdraw to the jumping off position, to which the remainder of the Battn.	

D. D. & L., London, E.C. (A7883) Wt. W809/M1672 350,000 4/17 Sch. 52a Forms/C/2118/14

Instructions regarding War Diaries and Intelligence Summaries are contained in F. S. Regs., Part II. and the Staff Manual respectively. Title pages will be prepared in manuscript.

WAR DIARY of 11th Bn DURHAM LIGHT INFANTRY

~~or INTELLIGENCE SUMMARY.~~

(Erase heading not required.)

Army Form C. 2118.

Place	Date	Hour	Summary of Events and Information	Remarks and references to Appendices
	29/3/18		[of the Battn.] had already withdrawn. The strength of the Battn. was then 4 officers, 34 men. The G.O.C. 60th Bde then ordered the Battn. to take up a line between THENNES + HOURGES. The night was spent quietly in this position.	
	30/3/18		The day was uneventful except that in the morning many men were observed withdrawing on the left + the French also had been driven out of their positions on the right. Our line was slightly altered to form a defensive flank facing right + later the situation was restored by the cavalry.	
	31/3/18		In the morning the enemy broke through on the right flank + many men were seen withdrawing on the left. The men of the Battn. with Capt Pemberton proceeded to the top of the hill S.E. of THENNES + joined the cavalry in forming a line about 600 yds from the wood which was occupied from the enemy.	
		4pm	The enemy tried to attack our position, but was driven back by rifle + M.G. fire leaving many dead. Capt. Endean was hit about this time. Beyond desultory shelling along all the front the enemy was inactive + a quiet night was passed.	
			Col. Hayes rejoined the Battalion in the morning + proceeded to the line. Capt Pemberton could not be found so he took command of a mixed party of the 20th Division + remained with them till relieved on the night 2nd/3rd April by troops of the 61st Division	

(A7883) Wt. W593/M1672 350,000 4/17 Sch. 52a Forms/C2118/14

Instructions regarding War Diaries and Intelligence Summaries are contained in F. S. Regs., Part II. and the Staff Manual respectively. Title pages will be prepared in manuscript.

WAR DIARY
or
~~INTELLIGENCE SUMMARY.~~ Continued.
(*Erase heading not required.*)

Army Form C. 2118.

Place	Date	Hour	Summary of Events and Information	Remarks and references to Appendices
			Casualties.	
	22/3/18		Missing 2/Lieut H G Craig R.R. GALLEY. H RUTHERFORD. W.T. ALEXANDER	
			W. BANKS.	
	23/3/18		Killed = 2/Lt VG DUCKETT. Wounded 2/Lt F NAYLOR - EW. ENGLISH.	
	24/3/18		Wounded = 2/Lt. N F GIBSON. Missing 2/Lt F ARNOTT.	
	25/3/18		" = 2/Lt J.H DODDS.	
	28/3/18		" = 2/Lt A.E. WILKINSON –	
	29/3/18		" = Captain W.G.L SEAR M.C. 2/Lt H.J.E. WHITFIELD.	
			" & Missing. Lt R. BUSHELL 2/Lts D.E. ELLWOOD – T.W. APPLEGARTH –	
			C.A. MORRIS	
	31/3/18		~~Captain~~ Wounded - Captain W.J. ENDEAN.	
	22/3/18 to 31/3/18		O.Rs Killed 16. D of Wounds 3 - Wounded 221. Missing - 215	
			Totals - K. D of W. W Missing & Wounded Missing	
			Officers 1 . . 8 3 7 = 19	
			O.Rs 16 3 . 221 . 215 - 455.	

D. D. & L., London, E.C. (A7883) Wt. W803/M1672 350,000 4/17 Sch. 52a Forms/C/2118/14

Army Form C. 2118.

Instructions regarding War Diaries and Intelligence Summaries are contained in F. S. Regs., Part II, and the Staff Manual respectively. Title pages will be prepared in manuscript.

WAR DIARY
or
INTELLIGENCE SUMMARY.
(Erase heading not required.) Continued.

Place	Date	Hour	Summary of Events and Information	Remarks and references to Appendices
			Strength	
			1st March 1918. Officers 48 O.R. 830	
			1st April 1918. ~~24~~ 24 " 505.	
			C. Hayes. Lieut-Col	
			Comdg 11th D. L. Infantry.	

D. D. & L., London, E.C.
(A7883) Wt. W809/M1672 350,000 4/17 Sch. 52a Forms/C/2118/14

'B' Coy

B Co

Instructions regarding War Diaries and Intelligence Summaries are contained in F. S. Regs., Part II, and the Staff Manual respectively. Title pages will be prepared in manuscript.

'B' Company WAR DIARY of 11th Bn. or ~~INTELLIGENCE SUMMARY.~~ DURHAM LIGHT INFANTRY.

(Erase heading not required.)

Army Form C. 2118.

Place	Date	Hour	Summary of Events and Information	Remarks and references to Appendices
	24/3/18		The XI DLI details ~~[illegible]~~ with details of 20th Div. were in position 1 mile N. of ROUY LE PETIT	
	"		The Germans attacked at dawn. At 9am the details were in the front line.	
	"		At 10am they gave supporting fire to an unsuccessful counter attack of 61st Division	
	"		from MESNIL ST. NICAISE towards BETHENCOURT. The enemy took ROUY LE PETIT at	
	"		2pm. behind the party. A line was then dug on the side of the hill	
	"		forming a defensive flank facing the village. Here, 2/Lt. Dodds was wounded.	
			At about 4pm a retirement was made to a line S.E. of MESNIL ST NICAISE. This	
			was done to conform with flanks. After several more retirements a position was	
			taken up defending NESLE North of the NESLE - HAM railway; Major	
			Storr being still in command.	

D. D. & L., London, E.C. (A7883) Wt. W803/M1672 350,000 4/17 Sch. 52a Forms/C/2118/14

Instructions regarding War Diaries and Intelligence Summaries are contained in F. S. Regs., Part II. and the Staff Manual respectively. Title pages will be prepared in manuscript.

WAR DIARY of 11th Bn. DURHAM LIGHT INFANTRY

or ~~INTELLIGENCE SUMMARY.~~

(Erase heading not required.)

Army Form C. 2118.

Place	Date	Hour	Summary of Events and Information	Remarks and references to Appendices
	25/3/18		The DLI party & 20th Div. details under Major Storr held the position north of the NESLE-HAM	
	"		railway under intense fire from 7.30 am until 10.30 am. The Royal Berks Regt. on the	
	"		left being driven back, Major Storr gave the order to retire to a line S.W. of	
	"		NESLE. In this retirement the DLI. party became detached and formed two	
	"		parties; the left party under Capt Jee, and the right under 2/Lt King. The NESLE-	
	"		ROYE main road divided the two parties. An outpost line was then held in	
	"		conjunction with the French who arrived at 11am. This line was 200yds S.W. of	
	"		HERLY-BILLANCOURT Road. At 5pm the enemy again attacked. The French withdrew	
	"		& the DLI covered their retirement & then fell back into their front line in front	
	"		of RETHONVILLERS.	

(A7092). Wt. W12839/M1293. 750,000. 1/17. D. D. & L., Ltd. Forms/C.2118/14.

Instructions regarding War Diaries and Intelligence Summaries are contained in F. S. Regs., Part II. and the Staff Manual respectively. Title pages will be prepared in manuscript.

WAR DIARY of 11th DURHAM LIGHT INFANTRY
~~or~~
~~INTELLIGENCE SUMMARY.~~

(Erase heading not required.)

Army Form C. 2118.

Place	Date	Hour	Summary of Events and Information	Remarks and references to Appendices
	26/3/18.		At 1a.m. the DLI. details under Capt Lee received orders that the 20th Division were assembling at ROYE. They went there & joined Capt. Endean's party with A + B Coys. They then marched with the 59th Bde. to LE QUESNEL	

(A7092). Wt. W12839/M1293. 750,000. 1/17. D. D. & L., Ltd. Forms/C.2118/14.

'D' Coy

D Coy

Instructions regarding War Diaries and Intelligence Summaries are contained in F. S. Regs., Part II. and the Staff Manual respectively. Title pages will be prepared in manuscript.

Army Form C. 2118.

"D" Company WAR DIARY of 11th Bn Durham or ~~INTELLIGENCE SUMMARY.~~

(Erase heading not required.)

Place	Date	Hour	Summary of Events and Information	Remarks and references to Appendices
	21/3/18	8.45pm	D Coy, marched to DURY to report to B.G. 61st Bde. OC Coy. proceeded to forward Bde HQ at ST. SIMON: he was there instructed to remain at DURY + await orders.	
	22/3/18	8am.	Orders received from Major Norman R.E. to report with all available tools to Lt. Col. Vince DSO. Cmdg. 12th Kings at TUGNY. OC Coy met Lt. Col. Vince on the road and with him the B.G. Comdg. 61st Bde. who instructed him, verbally, to take all orders from the C.O. 12th Kings, and in the event of an attack to place himself at the disposal of the OC. Kings. Small trenches were constructed on the hillside between DURY + TUGNY + on the high ground N.E. of TUGNY. At about 3pm the platoons were withdrawn from their work with the consent of Lt Col. Vince DSO. + took up a position in an old German trench at about L.19.b.5.0. (Sheet 66D NE.)	
		6pm	Warning order received from OC 12th Kings to be ready to move to L.31 central and to send an officer to reconnoitre the road.	
		6.30pm	Lt Col Hayes DSO, Capt Kemp and Capt Endean visited the position.	
		7.15pm	Coy received orders to move. They did so + reported to the adjutant 12th Kings + crossed the canal. After waiting an hour on the road between the canal and	

D. D. & L., London, E.C.
(A7883) Wt. W803/M1672 350,000 4/17 Sch. 52a Forms/C/2118/14

Instructions regarding War Diaries and Intelligence Summaries are contained in F. S. Regs., Part II. and the Staff Manual respectively. Title pages will be prepared in manuscript.

WAR DIARY 11th Bn. DURHAM LIGHT INFANTRY

~~or INTELLIGENCE SUMMARY.~~

(Erase heading not required.)

Army Form C. 2118.

Place	Date	Hour	Summary of Events and Information	Remarks and references to Appendices
	22/3/18		[Canal and] The SOMMETTE River. Orders were received to report to Bde. HQ at OLLEZY. OC Coy, was then instructed to bivouac on the road from OLLEZY to SOMMETTE-EAUCOURT in support of a coy of the 12th Kings who were posted on the Canal Bank.	
	23/3/18	6am.	OC. Coy got into touch with OC 12th Kings on the Railway Embankment south of OLLEZY. As there was no cover at all on the road on which they had spent the night, or in the fields adjacent, with the approval of the C.O. 12th Kings the Coy. was withdrawn to the Railway Embankment.	
		7.30am	Orders received from the B.G. Comdg. to place the Coy at the disposal of Major Norman R.E. for the purpose of digging Strong points. Information was then received that the enemy had crossed the Canal at OLLEZY on the Coy's right flank.	
		12noon	The Coy. manned strong points facing due east; 3 platoons in strong point $\frac{3}{4}$ mile west of ANNEUX and $\frac{1}{2}$ mile S. of broad guage railway; 1 platoon (with 2/Lt. Duckett + C.S.M. Robson) in strong point 1 mile due west of this. The three platoons (Lt. Cooper, 2/Lt. Banks, 2/Lt. Gibson) came into action in support of a coy. of the 12th Kings at about 2pm: but the enemy were not in force + the coy. of	

D. D. & L., London, E.C. (A7883) Wt. W803/M1672 350,000 4/17 Sch. 52a Forms/C/2118/14

Army Form C. 2118.

Instructions regarding War Diaries and Intelligence Summaries are contained in F. S. Regs., Part II. and the Staff Manual respectively. Title pages will be prepared in manuscript.

WAR DIARY of 11th Bn DURHAM LIGHT INFANTRY

~~or~~

~~INTELLIGENCE SUMMARY.~~

(Erase heading not required.)

Place	Date	Hour	Summary of Events and Information	Remarks and references to Appendices
	23/3/18		[Coy. of] the 12th Kings advanced again into ANNEUX Wood. On the right 2/Lt Duckett came up with No 13 platoon in support of another Coy. of the 12th Kings in front of CUGNY. This is the last time this officer and his platoon were seen by the Coy Commander.	
		6pm	The Coy. of 12th Kings fell back on a strong point, + about 20 OR Somersets. L. Infy. with 2 officers retired across the railway on the left of the Coy. They reported that there were no British troops on our left across the railway. A patrol was sent out to the left flank, but they were unable to find any one or obtain any information.	
		6.45 pm	Report received that troops on the right of the Coy. had retired on CUGNY. Coy then retired by sections in good order on CUGNY Railway Cutting, bringing with them two officers of the 12th Kings Regt. who were both wounded in the legs. The Railway Cutting was held by a Coy. of an Irish Regt. whose line we extended to the left. An officer of the Irish Regt reported that he was in touch with other troops on either flank + that the 12th Kings were in support in CUGNY. This information was incorrect. O.C. Coy was unable to find any post on the left. On the right 2 serjeants of the Irish reported	

D. D. & L., London, E.C.
(A7883) Wt. W503/M1672 350,000 4/17 Sch. 52a Forms/C/2118/14

Instructions regarding War Diaries and Intelligence Summaries are contained in F. S. Regs., Part II. and the Staff Manual respectively. Title pages will be prepared in manuscript.

WAR DIARY ~~or INTELLIGENCE SUMMARY.~~ of 11th BN DURHAM LIGHT INFANTRY

(Erase heading not required.)

Army Form C. 2118.

Place	Date	Hour	Summary of Events and Information	Remarks and references to Appendices
	23/3/18.		[Irish reported] that the enemy was already on the flank. On entering CUGNY the Coy Cmdr. found the village deserted. After consulting with his officers he decided to retire towards GUISCARD until he came into touch with our own forces. As the officer of the Irish was in a highly excited condition, OC Coy. detailed 2/Lt. Banks to assist him in getting his men out. OC Coy then led his men through the village, but as 2/Lt. Banks did not follow, 2/Lt. Gibson & the Coy. Cmdr. went back with a few men through the village, but were unable to find anyone else. Later the first organised body of troops was found digging in 3/4 mile N.E of VILLESELVE. OC Coy. reported to 61st Bde. HQ. and asked for rations & ammunition. No rations were available, but 3 boxes of ammunition were obtained; also sufficient biscuits & some preserved meat.	
	24/3/18	6am.	Coy moved forward from VILLESELVE in a thick mist but was unable to get into touch with any of the 61st Bde, so they dug in facing north on a road about 1 mile N.E. of VILLESELVE with a Coy. of Irish & a section of the MGC. on the left & a unit of the 14th. Div. facing East on the right	
		12noon	Mist cleared, and the Coy. came under shell fire from East & South, so changed	

D. D. & L., London, E.C. (A7883) Wt. W803/M1672 350,000 4/17 Sch. 52a Forms/C/2118/14

Instructions regarding War Diaries and Intelligence Summaries are contained in F. S. Regs., Part II. and the Staff Manual respectively. Title pages will be prepared in manuscript.

WAR DIARY of 11th BN. DURHAM LIGHT INFANTRY

~~or INTELLIGENCE SUMMARY.~~

(Erase heading not required.)

Army Form C. 2118.

Place	Date	Hour	Summary of Events and Information	Remarks and references to Appendices
	24/3/18.		[So changed] direction, facing east.	
		3pm.	Troops on left retired towards VILLESELVE. At 3.30pm Coy. retired on Sunken Rd. due East of + just outside VILLESELVE. The Coy. was joined by the 7th D.C.L.I. + came under	
		4pm.	orders of the C.O. that Bn. The Cavalry + French mitrailleurs in front retired through the Coy. The enemy was advancing slowly. The O.C. of D.C.L.I. would not allow any one to fire, except at an enemy aeroplane which flew low over the Coy, during the whole of the afternoon. Enemy machine gunners gradually advanced + swept the top of Sunken road. The enemy's field guns	
		6pm.	came into action at a range of about 1500yds. Black shrapnel	
		6.30	burst immediately over the position at a very effective height. Soon after this the line broke. The only line of retreat was through VILLESELVE along a road, the first 200yds. of which was swept by enemy machine guns.	
		7.45	Passing through GUISCARD the Coy were shelled by gas shells. Everyone was moving back, + the Coy. Cmdr. was unable to find any formed unit of the 61st Bde. or Bde. H.Q. In the dark he got separated from the main body + found himself at about 10pm. with 4 of his Coy. at MUIRANCOURT. Directed by an M.M.P. he proceeded	

D. D. & L., London, E.C. (A7883) Wt. W609/M1672 350,000 4/17 Sch. 52a Forms/C/2118/14

Instructions regarding War Diaries and Intelligence Summaries are contained in F. S. Regs., Part II. and the Staff Manual respectively. Title pages will be prepared in manuscript.

WAR DIARY of 11th Bn. DURHAM LIGHT INFANTRY
~~or INTELLIGENCE SUMMARY.~~
(Erase heading not required.)

Army Form C. 2118.

Place	Date	Hour	Summary of Events and Information	Remarks and references to Appendices
			[he proceeded]	
			to BUSSY where he found the M.O. of the DCLI. and one other officer of the same Bn.	
			& managed to collect about 25 stragglers of all units of the 61st Bde.	
	25/3/18	3am.	A squadron of Cavalry passed back through BUSSY. The Coy. Comdr. then learned from	
			the officer in command that there was no infantry in front of the Coy., but only	
			cavalry patrols + field artillery which were all retiring. O.C. Coy. then proceeded	
			to LIGNY which he reached at about 6am. O.C. Coy. received information from a	
			Signalling Officer that the 20th Division was at ROYE. He proceeded there, and arrived	
			at about 4pm, and reported to Major Norman R.E. who arranged billets for the	
			party; which had been increased by some more men under a Captain of the	
			D.C.L.I. at CONCHY-LES-POTS.	
	26/3/18		The Coy. marched from CONCHY-LES-POTS to LE QUESNEL + joined the Battalion.	

D. D. & L., London, E.C.
(A7883) Wt. W803/M1672 350,000 4/17 Sch. 52a Forms/C/2118/14

Instructions regarding War Diaries and Intelligence Summaries are contained in F. S. Regs., Part II. and the Staff Manual respectively. Title pages will be prepared in manuscript.

WAR DIARY of 11th (S) Bn. Durham L.I. (Prs)
or
~~INTELLIGENCE SUMMARY.~~
(*Erase heading not required.*)

Army Form C. 2118.

April 1918

Place	Date	Hour	Summary of Events and Information	Remarks and references to Appendices
	1/4/18		Battn. now in the line south of THENNES. About 7pm the Battn. was	
	— " —		relieved by a Battalion of the 14th Division and proceeded to the main	
	— " —		AMIENS road & there embussed for QUEVAUVILLERS.	
QUEVAUVILLERS	2/4/18		Battn. resting	
— " —	3/4/18		Inspections and cleaning of equipment.	
— " —	4/4/18		Drill under Coy. Commanders. 470 O.Ranks joined, Capt. P.V. Kemp rejoined	
— " —	5/4/18		Re-organisation of Coys, and drill under Coy Commanders	
— " —	6/4/18		Training under Coy Commanders continued. Lieuts A. Floyd and M. Cooper joined.	
LINCHEUX	7/4/18		Battn. proceeded from QUEVAUVILLERS to LINCHEUX by march route. Arrived 2pm.	
— " —	8/4/18		Coy. training 8·30am to 4·30pm.	
— " —	9/4/18		Coy. training	
— " —	10/4/18		Battn. paraded at 9·45am and proceeded by march route to HUPPY.	
			arriving about 7pm. 108 O.Ranks joined	
HUPPY	11/4/18		Battn. paraded at 9·30 am & proceeded by march route to RIEUX arriving at 3pm.	
RIEUX	12/4/18		Coy. training, musketry & training of specialists 8·30am to 4·30pm.	
— " —	13/4/18		Coy. training – musketry & training of specialists – 8·30am to 4·30pm.	

D. D. & L., London, E.C.
(A7883) Wt. W503/M1672 350,000 4/17 Sch. 52a Forms/C/2118/14

Instructions regarding War Diaries and Intelligence Summaries are contained in F. S. Regs., Part II. and the Staff Manual respectively. Title pages will be prepared in manuscript.

Army Form C. 2118.

WAR DIARY of 11th (S) Bn. DURHAM L.I. (Prs)
~~or INTELLIGENCE SUMMARY.~~

(Erase heading not required.)

Place	Date	Hour	Summary of Events and Information	Remarks and references to Appendices
RIEUX	14/4/18		Inspection of kits & equipment. 111 O.Ranks transferred to Base.	
— " —	15/4/18		Drill under Coy. Commanders – Musketry and Training of Specialists.	
— " —	16/4/18		Drill under Coy. Cmdrs – Musketry & Training of Specialists. 80 O.Ranks transferred to the Base	
— " —	"		The following Officers joined 2/Lts. W.A.Charnley, M.M. Harrington, A.D. Hanfield,	
— " —	"		J.R. Kneale, R.E.C. Smith, W. Hunt, J.H. Taylor, T.T. Firth, A.H. Ainsworth,	
— " —	"		J.S. Dodson, G. Cain, G.F. Wood, G.H. Ault, J.C. Ratcliffe.	
— " —	17/4/18		Training of Coys Continued. Lieut. Col. G. Hayes DSO. proceeded to Base sick.	
— " —	"		Lieut. Col. R.E. Boulton 1st K.O.Y.L.I. assumed command of the Battn. vice Lt. Col. G. Hayes	
— " —	18/4/18		The Battn. proceeded by motor-bus to SAVY and arrived at 8pm, and then	
— " —	— " —		proceeded to FREVILLERS arriving at 9.30 pm.	
FREVILLERS	19/4/18		Coys. training under Coy. Commanders	
— " —	20/4/18		8.30 to 4.30 pm Coy. Training – Musketry, Lectures	
— " —	21/4/18		Church Parades	
— " —	22/4/18		Drill – Musketry, Trench digging, & training of Specialists.	
— " —	23/4/18		Training of Coys. Continued. Lectures in the evening.	
— " —	24/4/18		Coy Training under Coy. Commanders. One Coy. on the rifle range.	

D. D. & L., London, E.C. (A7883) Wt. W809/M1672 350,000 4/17 Sch. 52a Forms/C/2118/14

Instructions regarding War Diaries and Intelligence Summaries are contained in F. S. Regs., Part II, and the Staff Manual respectively. Title pages will be prepared in manuscript.

WAR DIARY of 11th (S) Bn. Durham L. I. (Pioneers)
or
~~INTELLIGENCE SUMMARY.~~
(*Erase heading not required.*)

Army Form C. 2118.

Place	Date	Hour	Summary of Events and Information	Remarks and references to Appendices
FREVILLERS	25/4/18		8·30am to 12·45pm Coy. training & musketry 2 to 4·30pm. Instruction in Pioneer	
— " —	— " —		work. Attack practice in the wood. Lectures.	
— " —	26/4/18		Two Coys. on drill & musketry. One Coy on route march. Capt. R.L.S. Pemberton M.C.	
— " —	— " —		proceeded to XVIIIth Corps for duty as Educational Officer. Capt. A.F. Long M.C. 4th Bn.	
— " —	— " —		Suffolk Regt. joined, and assumed duty as 2nd in Command vice Capt. Pemberton.	
— " —	27/4/18		One Coy on Rifle Range, two Coys. on route march	
— " —	28/4/18		Church Parades & presentation of medal ribbons.	
— " —	29/4/18		"A" Coy. inspected by the Commanding Officer. "A" Coy on rifle range; B & D Coys	
			Company drill. Lewis Gunners on rifle range. Transport inspected by OC 20th Divl. Train.	
			25 o.Ranks joined	
	30/4/18		Inspection of "B" Coy. by the C.O. Inspection of arms by the Divisional Armourers. Three Coys.	
			at work under Coy. Commanders	

	Officers	o.Ranks.
STRENGTH 1st April	24	505
Joined during April	17	301
STRENGTH 1st May.	41	806

R.V. Boulton Lieut. Colonel
Comdg. XI (S) Bn. Durham L. I. (P'rs)

D. D. & L., London, E.C.
(A7883) Wt. W803/M1672 350,000 4/17 Sch. 52a Forms/C/2118/14

Instructions regarding War Diaries and Intelligence Summaries are contained in F. S. Regs., Part II. and the Staff Manual respectively. Title pages will be prepared in manuscript.

WAR DIARY or ~~INTELLIGENCE SUMMARY.~~

(Erase heading not required.)

of 11th (S) Bn. Durham L. I. (Pioneers). for month of MAY 1918.

Army Form C. 2118.

Vol 34

Place	Date	Hour	Summary of Events and Information	Remarks and references to Appendices
FREVILLERS.	1/5/18		Company and Platoon Training. 'D' Coy on the Rifle Range. By night practising setting men out on work, and marching with Box Respirators adjusted.	
— " —	2/5/18	9.30am	Battn with Transport paraded in Marching Order & proceeded to CANADA Camp Chateau de la HAIE	
CHATEAU de la HAIE	3/5/18		Cleaning camp & repairing roads in the vicinity of the camp.	
— " —	4/5/18		A & B Coys paraded in Marching Order and proceeded to billets at LIÈVIN. HQ. with D Coy and Bn. Transport paraded at 2.15 pm & proceeded to RATATA Camp CARENCY.	
RATATA Camp CARENCY	5/5/18		A & B Coys repairing & improving CYRIL & CLUCAS C.T.s. 'D' Coy at work on BROWN LINE	
— " —	6/5/18		Work continued as for the 5th. 19 O Ranks joined.	
— " —	7/5/18		Work on trenches continued. 5 O Ranks joined.	
— " —	8/5/18		Work continued as for 7th. 4 O Ranks joined.	
— " —	9/5/18		A & B Coys working on C.T.s. 'D' Coy working on ROLLENCOURT SWITCH.	
— " —	10/5/18		'A' Coy working on CYRIL C.T. 'B' Coy making de la PLANE SWITCH. 'D' Coy working on BROWN LINE. 11 O Ranks joined.	
— " —	11/5/18		Work continued as for 10th.	
— " —	12/5/18		'A' Coy working on BROWN LINE; 'B' Coy on de la PLANE SWITCH; D Coy wiring. 6 O Ranks joined. 3 O Ranks wounded.	

D. D. & L., London, E.C. (A7883) Wt. W803/M1672 350,000 4/17 Sch. 52a Forms/C/2118/14

Army Form C. 2118.

WAR DIARY
or
INTELLIGENCE SUMMARY.
(Erase heading not required.)

Instructions regarding War Diaries and Intelligence Summaries are contained in F. S. Regs., Part II. and the Staff Manual respectively. Title pages will be prepared in manuscript.

Place	Date	Hour	Summary of Events and Information	Remarks and references to Appendices
CARENCY	13/5/18		'A' Coy at work on POSTS 'B' Coy working on de la PLANE Switch 'D' Coy at work on the BROWN LINE. 2 O.Ranks wounded.	
— " —	14/5/18		Work continued as for the 13th. 8 O.Ranks joined.	
— " —	15/5/18		Work on POSTS continued by 'A' Coy. B + D Coys making Fire Steps and revetting. 2/Lt. W.J.E. Whitfield and 10 O.R. joined.	
— " —	16/5/18		Work on POSTS and trenches continued as for 15th.	
— " —	17/5/18		'A' Coy at work on POSTS, 'B' Coy working on la PLANE Switch; 'D' Coy wiring the South side of CYRIL C.T. 6 O.Ranks wounded.	
— " —	18/5/18		Work continued as for the 17th. 10 O.Ranks joined.	
— " —	19/5/18		'A' Coy at work on POSTS + BROWN LINE. 'B' Coy working on RED LINE. 'D' Coy wiring CYRIL C.T. 9 O.Ranks joined.	
— " —	20/5/18		'A' Coy continued work on POSTS + BROWN LINE. 'B' Coy at work on CRONEY & CRAZY Posts. 'D' Coy wiring CYRIL C.T. 5 O.Ranks joined.	
— " —	21/5/18		'A' Coy continued work on POSTS. 'B' Coy digging + revetting Fire Steps in RED LINE. 'D' Coy commenced work on new defences in L'HIRONDELLE WOOD.	

D. D. & L., London, E.C.
(A7883) Wt. W803/M1672 350,000 4/17 Sch. 52a Forms/C/2118/14

Instructions regarding War Diaries and Intelligence Summaries are contained in F. S. Regs., Part II. and the Staff Manual respectively. Title pages will be prepared in manuscript.

WAR DIARY of 11th (S) Bn. Durham L.I. (Pioneers)
or
~~INTELLIGENCE SUMMARY.~~
(Erase heading not required.)

Army Form C. 2118.

Place	Date	Hour	Summary of Events and Information	Remarks and references to Appendices
RATATA Camp CARENCY.	22/5/18		A Coy. digging new trench – BRICKSTACK to CEMETERY Post: B Coy. at work on the RED LINE and wiring la PLANE Switch: D Coy continued work in the L'HIRONDELLE WOOD.	
— " —	23/5/18		Three Coys. employed working under the orders of R.E. Special Coys. pushing trucks with Gas Cylinders to the Front Line. 3 O Ranks joined.	
— " —	24/5/18		Coys not working owing to heavy work the night previous. 1 OR wd-gas	
— " —	25/5/18		D Coy relieved A Coy at LIÈVIN. A+D Coys working on strong points in the L'HIRONDELLE WOOD. B Coy working in the RED LINE making Fire Steps etc. Capt. J. LIDDELL + Lieut A.S. PARKIN & 7 O Ranks joined. 2 OR. wounded.	
— " —	26/5/18		Work continued as for the 25th. 2 OR. joined	
— " —	27/5/18		A+B Coys. working on defences: D Coy not working on account of enemy gas shelling. 4 O Ranks joined. Capts P.V. Kemp, A. Philip; 2/Lts. T.A. Atlay, R. Conacher, P.F. Wood, E.R. Harbron, G. Cain, G.H. Ault, J.C. Ratcliffe, and 122 O Ranks wounded gas	
— " —	28/5/18		A Coy + 50 OR. D Coy, working in L'HIRONDELLE Wood: B Coy at work in RED LINE and C LUCAS C.T. 4 OR joined.	
— " —	29/5/18		Coys. at work as for 28th. Lieut D.E. Cooke proceeded to England on Signal Course. 4 OR. joined	

Instructions regarding War Diaries and Intelligence Summaries are contained in F. S. Regs., Part II. and the Staff Manual respectively. Title pages will be prepared in manuscript.

WAR DIARY of 11th (S) Bn. Durham L. I. (Pioneers)
or
~~INTELLIGENCE SUMMARY.~~
(Erase heading not required.)

Army Form C. 2118.

MAY. 1918

Place	Date	Hour	Summary of Events and Information	Remarks and references to Appendices
CARENCY RATATA Camp	30/5/18		A+D Coys at work on L'HIRONDELLE Wood; B Coy at work on RED LINE	
— " —	31/5/18		Work continued as for 30th. 4 O Ranks joined.	

	Officers	O Ranks		Officers	OR
Strength 1st May	41	806	INCREASE during May	3	162
DECREASE	7	55	DECREASE " "	10	217
Strength 1st JUNE	34	751	Total DECREASE "	7	55

R H Poulton Lieut. Colonel
Comdg. 11th (S) Bn Durham L. I.

D. D. & L., London, E.C. (A7883) Wt. W809/M1672 350,000 4/17 Sch. 52a Forms/C/2118/14

Instructions regarding War Diaries and Intelligence Summaries are contained in F. S. Regs., Part II, and the Staff Manual respectively. Title pages will be prepared in manuscript.

Army Form C. 2118.

WAR DIARY of 11th (S) Bn. ~~or INTELLIGENCE SUMMARY.~~ Durham L. I. (Pioneers). JUNE 1918

(Erase heading not required.)

VOL 35

Place	Date	Hour	Summary of Events and Information	Remarks and references to Appendices
CARENCY	1/6/18		A + B Coys at work on the BOIS de L'HIRONDELLE defences. D Coy working on	
			RED Line and CRAB Post. Capt. S. V. Kemp died from gas poisoning.	
"	2/6/18		Coys. at work as for 1st June. "A" Coy church parade + inspection by C.O.	
"	3/6/18		Work carried out as on 2nd June. "D" Coy moved from ASPIRE Post to CARENCY.	
"	4/6/18		Work as for 3rd June. B Coy moved from LIÉVIN to JENKS Siding, SOUCHEZ.	
"	5/6/18		B Coy resting. "A + D" Coys. at work in the forward area. 3.30am "TEST	
			MAN BATTLE STATIONS" was ordered. Coys marched to their Posts, and were all	
			in position by 6am. Commanding Officer inspected all Posts. 6 ORs joined.	
"	6/6/18		"A" Coy at work on BROWN LINE, "B" Coy working in the RED LINE, "D" Coy	
			working on defences in the BOIS de L'HIRONDELLE. 2 O.R.s wounded.	
"	7/6/18		Coys working as for the 6th. 5 ORs. joined.	
"	8/6/18		Work continued as for the 7th.	
"	9/6/18		Work continued in the Forward Area. Church Parade + Inspection.	
"	10/6/18		"A" Coy working on BROWN LINE. "B" Coy at work on the RED LINE. "D" Coy	
			Commenced work on the RIAUMONT Defences.	
"	11/6/18		Work continued as for 10th.	

D. D. & L., London, E.C.
(A7883) Wt. W809/M1672 350,000 4/17 Sch. 52a Forms/C/2118/14

Instructions regarding War Diaries and Intelligence Summaries are contained in F. S. Regs., Part II. and the Staff Manual respectively. Title pages will be prepared in manuscript.

WAR DIARY ~~or~~ ~~INTELLIGENCE~~ SUMMARY.

(Erase heading not required.)

of 11th (S) Bn. Durham L. I. (Pioneers) JUNE 1918

Army Form C. 2118.

Place	Date	Hour	Summary of Events and Information	Remarks and references to Appendices
CARENCY	12/6/18		A + B Coys working on the BROWN LINE; D Coy at work on the RIAUMONT Defences.	
— " —	13/6/18		Work continued as for 12th June 22 ORs joined.	
— " —	14/6/18		Work in Forward Area continued 2/Lt. R.A. King M.C. to hospital sick. 46 OR joined.	
— " —	15/6/18		Work continued on defences and C.T.s	
— " —	16/6/18		A + B Coys. working on C.T.s D Coy at work on RIAUMONT Defences.	
— " —	17/6/18		A Coy. working on BROWN LINE and CASKET C.T. B Coy commenced work on CAVALRY TRENCH. D Coy continued work on RIAUMONT Defences.	
— " —	18/6/18		Work continued as for 17th.	
— " —	19/6/18		Work continued as for 18th. 9 OR joined, 2 OR wounded.	
— " —	20/6/18		Work in the Forward Area continued, day + night work.	
— " —	21/6/18		Day + night work in the Forward Area.	
— " —	22/6/18		Work in Forward Area continued 2/Lt R.A. King M.C. rejoined from hospital.	
— " —	23/6/18		A Coy at work in L'HIRONDELLE Wood + BROWN LINE. B Coy erecting wire in front of CAVALRY TRENCH; D Coy working on the RIAUMONT Defences. 10 OR joined.	
— " —	24/6/18		Work continued as for 23rd. 2 OR wounded.	
— " —	25/6/18			

D. D. & L., London, E.C. (A7883) Wt. W809/M1672 350,000 4/17 Sch. 52a Forms/C/2118/14

Instructions regarding War Diaries and Intelligence Summaries are contained in F. S. Regs., Part II. and the Staff Manual respectively. Title pages will be prepared in manuscript.

Army Form C. 2118.

WAR DIARY of 11th (S) Bn. Durham L. I. (Pioneers)

or

INTELLIGENCE SUMMARY.

(Erase heading not required.)

JUNE 1918.

Place	Date	Hour	Summary of Events and Information	Remarks and references to Appendices
CARENCY	25/6/18		Work on Defences + C.T.s in Forward Area continued. 20 ORs detached for duty with Divisional Trench Mortar Officer. 2/Lt G.F. Martin to hospital sick. 2/Lt R Waite attached to the Bn from the R.E. 1 OR wounded.	
— " —	26/6/18		Work continued in the Forward Area by the 3 Coys. 2 OR joined.	
— " —	27/6/18		'A' Coy. resting; 'B' + 'D' Coys. working on Defences + C.T.s.	
— " —	28/6/18		Work continued as for the 26th June. 'A' Coy. relieved 'B' Coy. at JENKS Siding. 'B' Coy. now at CARENCY.	
— " —	29/6/18		'D' Coy resting. A+B Coys. working on Defences + C.T.s.	
— " —	30/6/18		'A' Coy. working on the BROWN Line at LIÉVIN. 'B' Coy. resting; 'D' Coy. continued work on the RIAUMONT Defences.	

	Officers	O Ranks
Strength - 1st June	34	751
Total Decrease	—	—
" Increase	2	106
Strength 1st July	36	857

R.E. Boulton Lieut. Colonel
Comdg 11th Durham L.I.

D. D. & L., London, E.C. (A7883) Wt. W803/M1672 350,000 4/17 Sch. 52a Forms/C/2118/14

Instructions regarding War Diaries and Intelligence Summaries are contained in F. S. Regs., Part II. and the Staff Manual respectively. Title pages will be prepared in manuscript.

Army Form C. 2118.

WAR DIARY or INTELLIGENCE SUMMARY.

(Erase heading not required.)

of 11th (S) Bn Durham L.I. (Pioneers)

JULY 1918

VR 36

Place	Date	Hour	Summary of Events and Information	Remarks and references to Appendices
CARENCY	JULY 1		A, B, D Coys working on defences in Forward Area	
— " —	2		A Coy working on BROWN LINE. B Coy working on CAVALRY C.T. D Coy working on RIAUMONT Defences. 2/Lt H.E. Whitfield proceeded to England for R.A.F.	
	3		Work continued as for 2nd. 19 ORs wounded (gassed)	
	4		Work continued on defences. 3 OR joined; 1 OR wounded	
	5		Three Coys working on defences in Forward Area	
	6		Work continued as for 5th. Capt R. Joe + 2 NCOs proceeded to ROUEN Pioneer Course	
	7		A+D Coys working on defences; B Coy resting. Capt W.F.E. Badcock and Lieut. G.R. Burnett joined.	
	8		A Coy resting; B+D working on defences.	
	9		A+B Coys at work in the Forward Area; D Coy resting	
	10		A Coy working on BROWN LINE and CASKET C.T. B+D Coys working on defences. 6 OR wounded	
	11		A Coy working on BROWN LINE. B Coy working on CAVALRY TRENCH. D Coy working on RIAUMONT DEFENCES. 13 OR joined	
	12		Work continued as for the 11th. Capt J.G. Taylor M.C. joined	

D. D. & L., London, E.C. (A7884) Wt. W809/M1672 350,000 4/17 Sch. 52a Forms/C/2118/14

Instructions regarding War Diaries and Intelligence Summaries are contained in F. S. Regs., Part II. and the Staff Manual respectively. Title pages will be prepared in manuscript.

WAR DIARY of 11th (S) Bn Durham L.I. (Pioneers)

~~or~~

~~INTELLIGENCE~~ SUMMARY.

(Erase heading not required.)

Army Form C. 2118.

JULY 1918

Place	Date	Hour	Summary of Events and Information	Remarks and references to Appendices
	JULY			
CARENCY	13		Three Coys working at night pushing trucks for "Gas Beam" Attack.	
	14.		A Coy resting; B + D Coys working on defences: 4 OR joined, 2 OR wounded.	
	15		D Coy resting: A + B Coys working on defences.	
	16.		B Coy resting A + D Coys working on defences: 3 OR joined.	
	17		Work in forward Area continued as for 16th	
	18.		A Coy working in CASKET CT. B Coy in CAVALRY TRENCH. D Coy working on	
			RIAUMONT Defences. 3 OR joined	
	19		Work continued as for the 18th 4 OR joined	
	20		Work continued as for 19th 1 OR joined	
	21.		A Coy working on CASKET CT. B Coy working on defences in BROWN LINE.	
			D Coy resting. 3 Officers, 6 N.C.O.s proceeded to Corps Pioneer School	
	22.		Three Coys working on defences: 7 OR joined	
	23		A + D Coys working on defences. B Coy resting. 2 OR joined	
	24		A Coy at work on new trench leading from CAVALRY Trench. B Coy	
			working on CAVALRY trench + defences in BROWN Line. D Coy working	
			on RIAUMONT Defences and IRISH Trench.	

D. D. & L., London, E.C.
(A7883) Wt. W803/M1672 350,000 4/17 Sch. 52a Forms/C/2118/14

Instructions regarding War Diaries and Intelligence Summaries are contained in F. S. Regs., Part II, and the Staff Manual respectively. Title pages will be prepared in manuscript.

WAR DIARY of 11th (S) Bn. Durham L.I. (Pioneers) or ~~INTELLIGENCE SUMMARY.~~

(*Erase heading not required.*)

Army Form C. 2118.

JULY 1918

Place	Date	Hour	Summary of Events and Information	Remarks and references to Appendices
CARENCY.	JULY 25		Work continued as for 24th.	
	26		Work continued as for 25th.	
	27		Work on defences and C.T.s. continued 2 OR joined	
	28		A Coy resting. B+D Coys at work on defences and C.T.s. 2 OR proceeded to England for the purpose of taking Commissions.	
	29.		Three Coys. at work on defences and C.T.s Capt. W. F. E. Badcock proceeded on transfer to join 6th Bn. D.L.I.	
	30.		D Coy resting. A+B Coys at work as for 29th	
	31.		A+D Coys. at work on defences. B Coy resting. Battn. Transport Horse Show held in the afternoon.	
			Officers — Ranks.	
		STRENGTH	1st JULY — 36 — 857	
		Total	Increase — 6 — 55	
		"	DECREASE — 6 — 73	
STRENGTH	1st		AUGUST — 36 — 839	

R. E. Boulton Lieut. Col.
Comdg. 11th Durham L.I. (Pnrs)

D. D. & L., London, E.C. (A5834) Wt W809/M1672 350,000 1/17 Sch. 52a Forms/C/2118/14

Instructions regarding War Diaries and Intelligence Summaries are contained in F. S. Regs., Part II, and the Staff Manual respectively. Title pages will be prepared in manuscript.

WAR DIARY of 11th (S) Bn. DURHAM L. I (Pioneers) ~~or INTELLIGENCE SUMMARY~~.

Army Form C. 2118.

(Erase heading not required.)

AUGUST 1918

VOL 37

Place	Date	Hour	Summary of Events and Information	Remarks and references to Appendices
CARENCY (Ratata Camp) X.16.d.1.4.	August 1		Three Coys working on defences and communication trenches in the Forward Area	
	2.		Work continued as for 1st Capt G.H. Houston R.A.M.C. assumed Medical Charge of Battn.	
	3.		Work on defences continued. "Test Man Battle Stations" received at 8.45pm All posts were manned, and Companies in position by 11pm.	
	4.		Three Coys resting. 2/Lts. T.T. Firth, H. Padley, + J.S. Dodds proceeded to Corps Pioneer School	
	5.		"A" Coy. working on Posts; B+D Coys at work on defences. Capt J. Liddell and 2 O.Ranks proceeded to R.E. Depot ROUEN for Course of Instruction.	
	6.		Three Coys. working as for 5th.	
	7.		Work continued as for 6th. 2/Lt. J. Taylor and 11 O.Ranks proceeded to 1st Army Rifle meeting.	
	8.		Work on Defences Continued.	
	9.		Three Coys at work on defences and C.T.s. 13 O.Ranks joined.	
	10.		Work continued as for 9th.	
	11.		"B" Coy. resting. A+D Coys. working on defences. 2/Lt. O.G. Day proceeded on Gas Course	

D. D. & L., London, E.C. (A7883) Wt W809/M1672 350,000 4/17 Sch 52a Forms/C/2118/14

Instructions regarding War Diaries and Intelligence Summaries are contained in F. S. Regs., Part II, and the Staff Manual respectively. Title pages will be prepared in manuscript.

WAR DIARY

or

~~INTELLIGENCE SUMMARY.~~

(Erase heading not required.)

Army Form C. 2118.

Place	Date	Hour	Summary of Events and Information	Remarks and references to Appendices
CARENCY X.16.d.1.4	August 12		A Coy resting: B Coy. working on ARTHURS SEAT Defences: D Coy. working on RIAUMONT and L'HIRONDELLE Defences. Lieut H.S. Parkin to hospital sick; 4 OR joined.	
	13.		A+B Coy. at work on defences; D Coy. resting: 6 ORanks joined.	
	14.		A, B, + D Coys working on defences: 6 ORanks joined. Lieut. Col. T.H. Carlisle D.S.O., M.C., R.E. assumed command of Battn. vice Lieut. Col. R.E. Boulton transferred	
	15.		Three Coys. at work on defences + C.T.s.	
	16.		Work continued as for the 15th.	
	17.		Work Continued as for 14th + 15th. 2/Lt. O.G. Day returned from Corps Gas School	
	18.		Work on defences and C.T.s continued. 1 ORank killed.	
	19.		A+D Coys. working on defences: B Coy. resting.	
	20.		Three Coys. at work digging a new fire trench; 1st task completed. 4 OR joined.	
	21		Work on new C.T. continued; second task completed	
	22		Work on defences and C.T.s continued.	
	23.		A Coy working on C.T.s. B Coy. working on new trench; D Coy. on defences.	
	24.		Coys. resting.	
	25.		Work on defences and C.T.s continued. 2/Lts. T.T. Firth, H. Sadler, J.S. Dodds returned from Corps Pioneer School.	

(A7883) Wt W809/M1072 350,000 4/17 D. D. & L. London, E.C. Sch. 52a Forms/C2118/14

Instructions regarding War Diaries and Intelligence Summaries are contained in F. S. Regs., Part II. and the Staff Manual respectively. Title pages will be prepared in manuscript.

WAR DIARY of 11th Bn. Durham L. I. (Pioneers)

~~or~~ ~~INTELLIGENCE SUMMARY.~~

(Erase heading not required.)

Army Form C. 2118.

AUGUST 1918.

Place	Date	Hour	Summary of Events and Information	Remarks and references to Appendices
CARENCY	August			
X.16.d.1.4.	26		Work on C.T.s and defences in Forward Area continued. 5 ORanks joined.	
	27		A Coy repairing C.T.s. B Coy. working on new trench. D Coy. working on RIAUMONT Defences. 2/Lts C.A. Bonson, M.M. Harrington, and F.G. McGeechin proceeded to Corps Pioneers School for course of Instruction.	
	28.		Work on defences + C.T.s continued. 2/Lt. W.H. Charnley and 40 ORanks attached to 185 Tunnelling Coy. R.E. 6 ORanks joined.	
	29.		Work on defences continued	
	30.		As for 29th 2 ORanks joined.	
	31.		A + B Coys. cutting a new trench through BOIS de L'HIRONDELLE. D Coy. move from Camp at JENKS Siding to CELLARS Camp NEUVILLE ST. VAAST.	

	Officers	ORanks.	
STRENGTH 1st AUGUST	36	839	From 23rd to 31st:– Intensive training of 3 platoons daily.
Total Increase	1	93	
" Decrease	3	41	
STRENGTH 1st SEPTEMBER	34	891	

? Carlisle Lieut. Col. R.E.
Comdg. 11th Durham L. I.

D. D. & L., London, E.C. (A7883) Wt. W809/M1672 350,000 4/17 Sch. 52a Forms/C/2118/14

Instructions regarding War Diaries and Intelligence Summaries are contained in F. S. Regs., Part II. and the Staff Manual respectively. Title pages will be prepared in manuscript.

WAR DIARY of 11th (S) Bn. DURHAM LIGHT INFANTRY (Pioneers)
or
~~INTELLIGENCE SUMMARY.~~
(Erase heading not required.)

Army Form C. 2118.

SEPTEMBER 1918

VR 38

Place	Date	Hour	Summary of Events and Information	Remarks and references to Appendices
CARENCY X.16.d.1.4	Sept. 1		Companies resting; 2 O.R. joined.	
	2		Three companies at work on communication trenches in the forward area.	
	3.		Work continued on C.T.s as for 2nd, 4 other ranks joined.	
	4.		Three companies at work on communication trenches.	
	5.		Work continued as for 4th. 2 other ranks joined.	
	6.		Three companies at work on communication trenches.	
	7.		Work continued as for the 6th 44 O.R. working with 185 Tunnelling Coy.	
			Intensive training of 3 platoons carried on daily throughout the week	
	8.		'A' & 'B' Coys. working on trenches in forward area. 'D' Coy resting.	
	9.		'A' Coy at work repairing KINGSTON Road: 'B' Coy working on RED Trench.	
			'D' Coy training. 5 O.R. joined.	
	10.		'A' Coy working on KINGSTON Road - also 'D' Coy. 'B' Coy at work on RED Trench	
	11.		'A' & 'B' Coys. at work repairing KINGSTON Road. 'D' Coy repairing LA COULOTTE Road.	
	12.		Work continued as for 11th 2/Lt T.E. UPTON and 2 O.R. joined.	
	13.		Three Companies at work on roads as for 12th	

D. D. & L., London, E.C.
(A7883) Wt W809/M1672 50,000 4/17 Sch 52a Forms/C/2118/14

Instructions regarding War Diaries and Intelligence Summaries are contained in F. S. Regs., Part II, and the Staff Manual respectively. Title pages will be prepared in manuscript.

Army Form C. 2118.

WAR DIARY of 11th (S) Bn. DURHAM LIGHT INFANTRY (Pioneers)
~~or~~
~~INTELLIGENCE SUMMARY~~
(Erase heading not required.)

SEPTEMBER 1918.

Place	Date	Hour	Summary of Events and Information	Remarks and references to Appendices
CARENCY. X.16.d.1.4.	SEPT. 14		'A' & 'B' Companies at work on KINGSTON Road; 'D' Coy working on LA COULOTTE Rd and KINGSWAY C.T.	
	15.		'A' Coy working on KINGSTON Rd. 'B' Coy. on HIRONDELLE Spur. 'D' Coy working on LA COULOTTE Road and KINGSWAY C.T. Intensive training of 3 platoons daily throughout the week: 2 O.R. joined.	
	16.		'A' Coy working on KINGSTON Road; B & D Coy. working on C.T.s.	
	17		'A' & 'B' Coys. working on KINGSTON Rd, 'D' Coy on LA COULOTTE Road.	
	18.		'A' & 'B' Coys working as for 17th.	
	19.		'A' Coy. working on KINGSTON Rd. 'B' Coy. working on HIRONDELLE C.T. 'D' Coy. working on KINGSWAY C.T. and NEW Trench. 1 O.R. killed 2 O.R. joined.	
	20.		'A' & 'B' Coy. working as for the 19th. 'D' Coy. working on C.T.s.	
	21.		Work continued as for the 20th.	
	22.		Work in forward area continued by 3 Coys. Intensive training of 3 platoons daily throughout the week. 72 O.R. trained in the use of the Lewis Gun throughout the week. Capt. G. S. Baines & 2/Lt. Phillips joined. Major R. L. S. Pemberton M.C. rejoined Battn. from VIII Corps.	

D. D. & L., London, E.C. (A7883) Wt W8c9/M1672 750,000 4/17 Sch. 52a Forms/C/2118/14

Instructions regarding War Diaries and Intelligence Summaries are contained in F. S. Regs., Part II. and the Staff Manual respectively. Title pages will be prepared in manuscript.

WAR DIARY ~~or INTELLIGENCE SUMMARY.~~ of 11th (S) Bn Durham Light Infantry (Pioneers)

(Erase heading not required.)

Army Form C. 2118.

SEPTEMBER 1918

Place	Date	Hour	Summary of Events and Information	Remarks and references to Appendices
CARENCY X.16.d.1.4	Sept. 23.		Three Coys. at work on roads and trenches in the forward area	
			2/Lieuts. W. Lazenby and S. H. Davis, and 3 OR. joined.	
	24		Work continued as for 23rd	
	25		'A' Coy working on KINGSTON Rd. 'B' Coy. on HIRONDELLE C.T. & RED Trench;	
			'D' Coy. working on LA COULOTTE Road and trenches in the forward area.	
	26.		Work continued as for 25th. 4 O.R. joined.	
	27.		'A' & 'D' Coys. working as for 26th. 'B' Coy. training and inspections.	
			2/Lieuts A. Padley and F. J. McGreehin proceeded to England for R.A.F. 2 OR joined	
	28.		Three Coys. at work on roads and C.T.s. in forward area.	
	29.		Work continued in the forward area by three companies. Intensive training	
			of three platoons daily throughout the week. 72 O.Ranks trained in	
			use of the Lewis Gun throughout the week. 1 OR. joined	
	30.		Three companies working on roads and trenches in the forward area.	

D. D. & L., London, E.C. (A7883) Wt W859/M1672 350,000 4/17 Sch 52a Forms/C/2118/14

Instructions regarding War Diaries and Intelligence Summaries are contained in F. S. Regs., Part II. and the Staff Manual respectively. Title pages will be prepared in manuscript.

WAR DIARY of 11th (S) Bn. DURHAM LIGHT INFANTRY (Pioneers)

or

~~INTELLIGENCE SUMMARY.~~

(*Erase heading not required.*)

SEPTEMBER 1918.

Army Form C. 2118.

Place	Date	Hour	Summary of Events and Information			Remarks and references to Appendices
				Officers	O. Ranks	
			STRENGTH SEPTEMBER 1st 1918	34	891	
			INCREASE during September	6	73	
			DECREASE " "	4	87	
			STRENGTH OCTOBER 1st	36	877.	

11th SERVICE BATTALION 1.10.18 DURHAM L. I. (PION.)

J. G. Carlisle
Lieut.Col. R.E.
Comdg. 11th (S) Bn D.L.I. (Prs)

D. D. & L., London, E.C.
(A7883) Wt W809/M1672 250,000 4/17 Sch 52a Forms/C/2118/14

Instructions regarding War Diaries and Intelligence Summaries are contained in F. S. Regs., Part II. and the Staff Manual respectively. Title pages will be prepared in manuscript.

Army Form C. 2118.

WAR DIARY of 11th (S) Bn. Durham Light Infantry (Pioneers)
or
~~INTELLIGENCE SUMMARY.~~
(Erase heading not required.)

for OCTOBER 1918.

Place	Date	Hour	Summary of Events and Information	Remarks and references to Appendices
CARENCY Ratata Camp X.16.d.1.4.	October 1		'A' Coy working on KINGSTON Road: 'B' Coy working in New Red Trench, HIRONDELLE & IRISH C.Ts; cutting and revetting firesteps: 'B' Coy also repairing KINGSTON Rd. 'D' Coy working on LA COULOTTE Rd. Reorganisation of firebays and cleaning done in BROWN LINE (Right Bde Area) & MERSEY C.T.	37
——	2		'A' Coy. continued repairs on KINGSTON Rd; 'B' Coy at work on HIRONDELLE, PHELAN, & IRISH C.T.s cleaning trenches & relaying trenchboards. 'D' Coy at work on LA COULOTTE Rd., BROWN LINE and BLIGHTY C.T.	
	3		Three Coys. on work as for the 2nd. 2/Lts G.F. Martin and W. Hunt proceeded on Pioneer Course, FRESSIN. Capt. J.G. Taylor M.C. rejoined from Pioneer Course ROUEN. Enemy withdrew on Divisional front. 'D' Coy marched to billets in RED LINE at 17.30; 'B' Coy to JENKS SIDING.	
	4.		'A', 'B', 'D' Coys. at work on KINGSTON & QUEBEC Rds. 'A' Coy also working on track through AVION. 2/Lts. B.C. Barrans & O.G. Day proceeded on Platoon Commanders' Course.	
	5.		Coys. on work as for 4th. Capt G.P. Barnes MC proceeded to Pioneer Course at ROUEN.	
			Intensive training of three platoons daily throughout the week.	

D. D. & L., London, E.C. (A7883) Wt W8o/M1672 350,000 4/17 Sch 52a Forms/C2118/14

Instructions regarding War Diaries and Intelligence Summaries are contained in F. S. Regs., Part II. and the Staff Manual respectively. Title pages will be prepared in manuscript.

WAR DIARY ~~or INTELLIGENCE SUMMARY.~~ of 11th Bn. Durham Light Infantry (Pioneers)

(Erase heading not required.)

Army Form C. 2118.

OCTOBER 1918

Place	Date	Hour	Summary of Events and Information	Remarks and references to Appendices
ESTREE CAUCHIE	October 6		Battn. with Transport moved by route march to ESTREE CAUCHIE. Left Ratata Camp CARENCY at 1400; arrived at ESTREE CAUCHIE 15.20. 4 O.R. joined.	
— " —	7		Inspection of clothing & equipment by Platoon Commanders. O.C. Coys. inspected by tools. Major R.L.S. Pemberton rejoined from Course on catering. 2 O.R. joined.	
— " —	8.		Three Coys. training under Coy Commanders; Lewis Gunners under L.G.O., Signallers under Signal Sergeant. 2/Lt. R.B. Marsham joined Battn.	
— " —	9		Three Coys. training as on 8th. Stretcher Bearers training under M.O. 1 OR joined	
— " —	10		Battn. training as for 9th. 6 OR joined.	
— " —	11		A, B, D Coys. training. 'A' + 'B' Coys. attacking strong points. 2 OR joined	
— " —	12		Coys. training under O.C. 'D' Coy. practising the attack. Lieut. C.C. Page joined Battn.	
— " —	13		Companies resting. Church Parade at 11.30 am	
— " —	14		Coys. training under Coy. Commanders. Arms inspected by Divl. Armourer Sergts. Sigs. training under Signalling Sergt; Stretcher Bearers under M.O. 2 OR joined.	
— " —	15		Battn. inspected by the Commanding Officer. After the inspection Battn. proceeded on a route march.	
— " —	16		Coys. training under Coy Commanders. 2 OR joined Battn.	

D. D. & L. London, E.C. (A7883) Wt W809/M1672 350,000 4/17 Sch. 52a Forms/C/2118/14

Instructions regarding War Diaries and Intelligence Summaries are contained in F. S. Regs., Part II, and the Staff Manual respectively. Title pages will be prepared in manuscript.

WAR DIARY of 11th (S) Bn. Durham Light Infantry (Pioneers)

~~or~~ ~~**INTELLIGENCE SUMMARY.**~~

(Erase heading not required.)

OCTOBER 1918

Army Form C. 2118.

Place	Date	Hour	Summary of Events and Information	Remarks and references to Appendices
ESTREE CAUCHIE	October 17		Coys. training under O.C. Coys. Signallers under Signalling Sergt; Lewis Gunners under L.G.O.	
			Stretcher Bearers under M.O. S.B.R. inspected by Divl. Gas N.C.O.s.	
—"—	18		Coy. training as for 17th. Half of 1st line transport practising crossing a pontoon bridge.	
—"—	19		Training as for 17th. 2/Lts R.E. Foster & R.C. Robinson joined Battn.	
—"—	20		No Parades; Voluntary Church services.	
—"—	21		Training as on 19th. 3 O.R. joined.	
—"—	22		Coy. Signallers, Lewis Gunners, Stretcher Bearers training	
—"—	23		Training continued as for 22nd.	
—"—	24		Company training continued. 5 O.R. joined.	
—"—	25		Training as for 24th. 2/Lt. G.F. Martin rejoined from Corps Pioneer Course	
—"—	26		Coy. training as on 25th. Transport inspected by O.C. Divl. Train.	
—"—	27		No Parades: Voluntary Church Services: 1 O.R. joined.	
—"—	28		Coy. training under O.C. arrangements. Lewis Gunners under L.G.O.,	
			Signallers under Signalling Sergt. S.B.'s under M.O. 2. O.R. joined.	
—"—	29		Companies training as on 28th	
—"—	30		Battn. with Transport left billets at ESTREE CAUCHIE at 11.40; marched to TINCQUES and bivouaced for the night.	

D. D. & L., London, E.C. (A7853) Wt W809/M1672 350000 4/17 Sch 52a Forms/C/2118/14

Instructions regarding War Diaries and Intelligence Summaries are contained in F. S. Regs., Part II. and the Staff Manual respectively. Title pages will be prepared in manuscript.

Army Form C. 2118.

WAR DIARY of 11th (S) Bn. Durham L. I. (Pioneers)

~~INTELLIGENCE SUMMARY~~.

(Erase heading not required.)

OCTOBER 1918.

Place	Date	Hour	Summary of Events and Information	Remarks and references to Appendices
TINCQUES	October 31		Battn. with Transport entrained at TINCQUES Station at 07.00 hours and arrived at detraining station FREMICOURT at 13.00 hours. HQ + Companies embussed at 13.45 hours and proceeded to CAMBRAI arriving there at 16.15 hours. Transport proceeded by road and arrived at 21.50 hours.	

	Officers	OR.
STRENGTH OCTOBER 1st 1918	36	877.
Increase during "	4	53.
Decrease " "	–	20.
STRENGTH NOVEMBER 1st 1918.	40	910
RATION STRENGTH Nov. 1st 1918.	29	836.

G. E. Carlisle Lieut Col. R.E.
Comdg. 11th Durham L. I. (Pioneers)

Instructions regarding War Diaries and Intelligence Summaries are contained in F. S. Regs., Part II, and the Staff Manual respectively. Title pages will be prepared in manuscript.

WAR DIARY of 11th (S) Bn. Durham L.I. (Pioneers)

or

~~INTELLIGENCE SUMMARY.~~

(*Erase heading not required.*)

Army Form C. 2118.

NOVEMBER 1918.

V8640

Place	Date	Hour	Summary of Events and Information	Remarks and references to Appendices
	NOVEMBER			
CAMBRAI	1		Battn. resting. Arms inspected under Company arrangements. Battn. with	
	2.		Transport moved from Barrack 27 to RENEL Barracks in the afternoon. Capt. G.P. Barnes M.C.	
			rejoined from Pioneer Course, ROUEN.	
RIEUX	3		Whole Battn. moved by route march to billets at RIEUX — marched off	
			at 10.30 hrs and arrived at RIEUX at 13.20 hrs.	
MONTRECOURT	4	10.30	Battn. with Transport proceeded by route march to MONTRECOURT arriving there at	
			14.07 hrs. Capt + Adjt. G.H. Tollit rejoined from leave.	
MONTRECOURT	5		Companies resting. Inspection of feet by Platoon Commanders.	
	6.		Companies resting. Parties working on repairs to billets.	
	7.		Battn. marched to SEPMERIES arriving at 17.00 hours.	
SEPMERIES	8.		Left SEPMERIES at 11.15 hrs and marched to JENLAIN arriving at 13.15 hrs	
	9.		Battn. marched to ST. WAAST. Major H.F. Ling M.C. proceeded to join 197th Inf. Bde.	
ST. WAAST-LA-VALLEE	10		Inspection of clothing & equipment. 'D' Coy at work on road.	
	11		Battn. marched to FEIGNIES arriving at 1700 hrs. Lt Cooper rejoined from Course.	
			At 8 am. wire received ordering cessation of hostilities, and troops to	
			stand fast on line reached at 1100 hrs.	

D. D. & L., London, E.C. (A7883) Wt W809/M1672 350,000 4/17 Sch 52a Forms/C/2118/14

Instructions regarding War Diaries and Intelligence Summaries are contained in F. S. Regs., Part II. and the Staff Manual respectively. Title pages will be prepared in manuscript.

WAR DIARY of 11th (S) Bn. Durham L.I. (Pioneers) Army Form C. 2118.

~~**INTELLIGENCE**~~ **SUMMARY.**

(*Erase heading not required.*)

NOVEMBER 1918

Place	Date	Hour	Summary of Events and Information	Remarks and references to Appendices
FEIGNIES	12th		'A' Coy moved to BERSILLIES for work on roads. 'B' Coy moved to GOEGNIES for work on roads. One platoon of 'D' Coy moved to OUVERAGE to repair road craters.	
— " —	13th		HQ + D Coy at FEIGNIES. 'D' Coy at work on road repairs and making facines. 'A' Coy at BERSILLIES repairing roads + filling in craters. 'B' Coy at GOEGNIES filling in craters.	
— " —	14th		Coys working as for 13th.	
— " —	15th		9 Platoons repairing roads; 3 Platoons making facines. Inspection of Equipment.	
— " —	16th		9 Platoons repairing roads etc. 3 Platoons salving stores.	
— " —	17th		Kit Inspection. 'A' Coy returned to FEIGNIES at 11.00 hrs. HQ Transport + 2 Coys at FEIGNIES. 'B' Coy at GOEGNIES – CHAUSSE.	
— " —	18th		'B' Coy returned to FEIGNIES. Lieut G. S. Dennis rejoined from 6 mths Tour of Duty in England	
— " —	19th		Coys working under Coy Commdrs. 1 Platoon 'A' Coy erecting shelter for refugees.	
— " —	20th		Coys on improvement of billets.	
— " —	21st		3 Coys. working on railway removing torn lines and filling craters.	
	22nd		1 Platoon at work on railway. 1 Platoon working under CRE. 10 Platoons under Coy Commdrs.	

Instructions regarding War Diaries and Intelligence Summaries are contained in F. S. Regs., Part II. and the Staff Manual respectively. Title pages will be prepared in manuscript.

WAR DIARY of 11th Durham L. I. (Pioneers)

~~or INTELLIGENCE SUMMARY.~~

(Erase heading not required.)

Army Form C. 2118.

NOVEMBER 1918

Place	Date	Hour	Summary of Events and Information	Remarks and references to Appendices
FEIGNIES	23rd		The Battn. paraded at 11.50 in marching order and proceeded to LE PISSOTIAU arriving at 13.30. HQ at chateau RAMETZ.	
LE PISSOTIAU	24th		Battn. left for MARESCHES at 10.40, arriving there at 14.00.	
MARESCHES	25th		Marched to ST. AUBERT arriving at 14.15	
ST. AUBERT	26th		Battn. stayed one day at ST. AUBERT. Details from Reception Camp arrived at 1700	
— "	27th		Marched to CAMBRAI arriving at 14.00 Lieut F. G. Andrew, 2/Lt. E R Harbron and 2/Lt. M. A. Latham joined from England.	
CAMBRAI	28th		Battn. resting at CAMBRAI. Capt. W.A. Brodie RAMC proceeded to England on transfer. Capt. J. Kirton RAMC joined.	
— " —	29th		Coys. cleaning equipment.	
— "	30th		Orders received for 200 miners to proceed for examination as to fitness for work in mines. Medical Inspection of 182 miners for discharge. Lieut. J.A. Anderson joined Battn. 2/Lt. R.A. King M.C rejoined from England. Battn. Transport left CAMBRAI for BEUGNATRE travelling by road.	

D. D. & L., London, E.C. (A7883) Wt. W809/M1672 350,000 1/17 Sch. 52a Forms/C/2118/14

Army Form C. 2118.

Instructions regarding War Diaries and Intelligence Summaries are contained in F. S. Regs., Part II. and the Staff Manual respectively. Title pages will be prepared in manuscript.

WAR DIARY ~~or~~ ~~INTELLIGENCE SUMMARY~~. of 11th DURHAM L.I. (Pioneers)

(Erase heading not required.)

NOVEMBER 1918

Place	Date	Hour	Summary of Events and Information			Remarks and references to Appendices
				Officers	OR.	
			STRENGTH NOV. 1st 1918	40	910	
			Total increase during Novr.	–	30	
			STRENGTH DECR. 1st 1918	40	940	
			RATION STRENGTH DEC. 1st 1918	31	840.	

Service Battalion [illegible] Durham [illegible] 1.12.18

[illegible] Lieut Col RE
Cmndg 11th Durh. L.I.

D. D. & L., London, E.C.
(A7883) W1 W809/M1672 350,000 4/17 Sch 52a Forms/C/2118/14

Instructions regarding War Diaries and Intelligence Summaries are contained in F. S. Regs., Part II. and the Staff Manual respectively. Title pages will be prepared in manuscript.

WAR DIARY of 11th Bn Durham L.I. (Pioneers)
or
~~INTELLIGENCE SUMMARY.~~
(Erase heading not required.)

Army Form C. 2118.

DECEMBER 1918

V 41

Place	Date	Hour	Summary of Events and Information	Remarks and references to Appendices
	December			
CAMBRAI	1st		Companies under Coy Commanders. 182 other ranks (miners) to England.	
—"—	2nd		Three companies and Battn HQrs proceed by motor bus and lorry to THIÉVRES, arriving at 16.30	
THIÉVRES	3rd		Inspection of billets by Commanding Officer. Companies under Coy Commanders.	
—"—	4th		"B" Company, 5 officers and 179 other ranks strong, proceeded on detachment to PAS. Companies under Coy Commanders.	
—"—	5th		Improving billets. 2nd Lieut A.H. Lewis and 2 O.R. joined.	
—"—	6th		"D" Company, 7 officers and 181 O.R., proceed to new billets at HALLOY.	
—"—	7th		"A" Company under O.C. company: drill, etc. "B" Company on route march. "D" Company repairing billets at GRENAS.	
—"—	8th		Sunday: "D" Company improving billets at GRENAS	
GRENAS	9th		"A" Company and Battn HQrs move to new billets at GRENAS. "B" Company working at PAS. "D" Company improving billets at GRENAS.	
—"—	10th		General improvement of billets: erecting huts, etc.	
—"—	11th		Same.	
—"—	12th		"B" Company moved into billets at GRENAS. "A" and "D" Coys working on billets. Major H.C. Boxer joined.	

D. D. & L., London, E.C. (A7883) Wt. W609/M1672 350,000 4/17 Sch. 52a Forms/C/2118/14

Instructions regarding War Diaries and Intelligence Summaries are contained in F. S. Regs., Part II. and the Staff Manual respectively. Title pages will be prepared in manuscript.

WAR DIARY of 11th Bn Durham L.I. (Pioneers)
or
~~INTELLIGENCE SUMMARY.~~
(Erase heading not required.)

Army Form C. 2118.

DECEMBER 1918

Place	Date	Hour	Summary of Events and Information	Remarks and references to Appendices
	December			
GRENAS	13th		Companies under Coy Commanders: drill and improvement of billets.	
—"—	14th		One platoon "D" Company proceeded to PAS for work at Divisional H.Qrs.	
			"A" and "B" Companies and three platoons of "D" Company working on billets.	
—"—	15th		Sunday: Lieut C.C. Page proceeded to Lille (Chemistry Course).	
—"—	16th		Three platoons "D" Company came into billets at GRENAS.	
			"A" and "B" Companies under Coy Commanders	
—"—	17th		Inspection of arms and equipment; drill under Coy Commanders.	
—"—	18th		Erecting huts and improving Horse Standings.	
—"—	19th		Work continued as for 18th	
—"—	20th		50 miners proceeded to England. 100 men at work on Divisional Recreation Ground. Work on hutments and horse standings continued.	
—"—	21st		"D" Company bathing. "A" and "B" Companies working on billets and improving transport lines. 50 other ranks working on Divisional Recreation Ground.	
—"—	22nd		Improvement of billets continued: "D" Company making tables and forms.	
—"—	23rd		One platoon rejoined battalion from PAS. Companies under O.C. Coys.	
—"—	24th		Men bathing and working on billets. 25 miners proceeded to England.	

D. D. & L., London, E.C.
(A7883) Wt. W809/M1672 350,000 4/17 Sch. 52a Forms/C/2118/14

Instructions regarding War Diaries and Intelligence Summaries are contained in F. S. Regs., Part II, and the Staff Manual respectively. Title pages will be prepared in manuscript.

WAR DIARY of 11th Bn Durham L.I. (Pioneers)
or
~~INTELLIGENCE SUMMARY.~~
(Erase heading not required.)

Army Form C. 2118.

DECEMBER 1918

Place	Date	Hour	Summary of Events and Information	Remarks and references to Appendices
GRENAS	December 25th		Xmas Day: Church Parades for C. of E. and R.C.'s	
—"—	26th		Companies under Coy Commanders.	
—"—	27th		Bad weather prohibited any work being done.	
—"—	28th		One platoon "D" Company proceeded to PAS on detachment; one platoon "B" Coy proceeded to HUMBERCAMPS for work on Horse Lines. Bad weather prevented any work being done outside of billets.	
—"—	29th		Church Parades and inspection of arms.	
—"—	30th		Two platoons working at HURTEBISE FARM. Eight platoons training	
—"—	31st		Three miners proceeded to England. Lieut E. Fleming joined. Bad weather prevented any work being done outside of billets.	
			STRENGTH December 1st 1918 — 40 officers — 940 other ranks	
			Increase during December — 4 " — 35 " "	
			Decrease " " — 1 " — 296 " "	
			STRENGTH January 1st 1919 — 43 " — 679 " "	
			Ration Strength January 1st 1919 — 34 offs — 533 O.R.s	
1/1/19				

for Lt. Col. [illegible]
Lieut-Col. R.E.
Cmdg 11th D.L.I. (P.)

Instructions regarding War Diaries and Intelligence Summaries are contained in F. S. Regs., Part II. and the Staff Manual respectively. Title pages will be prepared in manuscript.

WAR DIARY of 11th (S) Bn DURHAM L.I. (Prs) ~~or INTELLIGENCE SUMMARY~~.
(Erase heading not required.)

Army Form C. 2118.

JANUARY 1919

20 ~~W~~

V 8 42

Place	Date	Hour	Summary of Events and Information	Remarks and references to Appendices
GRENAS	JANUARY 1st		Commanding Officer's inspection. Two platoons on detachment making stables etc. One platoon working at HURTEBISE Farm under R.E's	
—"—	2nd		Battalion Route March. Two platoons on detachment	
—"—	3rd		Company training. Two platoons working at HURTEBISE Farm. Two platoons on detachment	
—"—	4th		Parades etc as for 3rd	
—"—	5th		Church services. Major J.G. Taylor M.C. and 4 other ranks proceed to Demobilisation Centre.	
—"—	6th		Company Training. Two platoons on detachment.	
—"—	7th		Parades etc as for 6th. Instruction in Shorthand given by Education Officer.	
—"—	8th		Company Training. Instruction in Book-keeping given by Education Officer.	
—"—	9th		Company Training. Class of instruction in First Aid held.	
—"—	10th		Platoon and Company training. Shorthand Class held.	
—"—	11th		Platoon training and inspections	
—"—	12th		Church services. Capt A. Floyd, 2nd Lieut R.H. King M.C., and 23 other ranks proceed to Demobilisation Centre.	
—"—	13th		Inspection of equipment and ceremonial training	

(A9173) W: W2358/P360 600000 12/7 D. D. & L. Sch. 52a. Forms/C2118/15

Instructions regarding War Diaries and Intelligence Summaries are contained in F. S. Regs., Part II. and the Staff Manual respectively. Title pages will be prepared in manuscript.

WAR DIARY of 11th (S) Bn Durham L.I. (Pns) or ~~INTELLIGENCE SUMMARY~~.

(Erase heading not required.)

Army Form C. 2118.

JANUARY 1919

Place	Date	Hour	Summary of Events and Information	Remarks and references to Appendices
	JANUARY			
GRENAS	14th		Company Training. Shorthand Class held	
—"—	15th		Ceremonial Parades. Educational Classes held.	
—"—	16th		Company Training. Lecture by Medical Officer. Education classes held.	
—"—	17th		Company Training. Education classes held.	
—"—	18th		Company and Platoon training. Major R.L.S. Pemberton M.C., 2nd Lieut [illegible] and 25 other ranks proceed to Demobilization Centre.	
—"—	19th		Commanding Officer's inspection and Church services.	
—"—	20th		Company Training. Education classes held. 2nd Lieut A.H. Ainsworth and 26 Other Ranks proceed to Demobilisation Centre. Billets inspected by G.O.C. Division.	
—"—	21st		Platoon Training; educational training. 2nd Lieut R.E.C. Smith and 24 other ranks proceed to Candas Demobilisation Centre.	
—"—	22nd		Company Training. Divisional Wood Fatigue of 50 O.R. 2nd Lieut W Lazenby and 23 other ranks leave for Demobilisation Centre.	
—"—	23rd		Company Training. Wood Fatigue at Pas. Education classes held.	
—"—	24th		C.O.'s inspection of Transport. Hospital Nissen hut for recreation purposes erected.	
—"—	25th		Training under Company Commanders. Divisional Wood Fatigue	

(A9189) Wt W3335/P560 800,000 12/17 D. D. & L. Sch. 52a. Forms/C2118/15

Instructions regarding War Diaries and Intelligence Summaries are contained in F. S. Regs., Part II. and the Staff Manual respectively. Title pages will be prepared in manuscript.

Army Form C. 2118.

WAR DIARY of 11th (S) Bn DURHAM L.I. (Pioneers)
~~INTELLIGENCE SUMMARY.~~
(Erase heading not required.)

JANUARY 1919

Place	Date	Hour	Summary of Events and Information	Remarks and references to Appendices
GRENAS	January 26th		Battalion inspected by C.O. Voluntary Church Services, C of E and R.C. 2nd Lieut J. Martin and 26 other ranks leave for demobilisation centre	
—"—	27th		Company Training. 2nd Lieut S. H. Davis and 40 O.R. proceed to Candas for demobilisation.	
—"—	28th		Platoon drill. Lieut B. H. Wood and 24 O.R. leave for Demobilisation Centre.	
—"—	29th		Training by companies. Wood Fatigue at Pas.	
—"—	30th		Ceremonial Drill Training: each company under the Company Commander. Wood Fatigue	
—"—	31st		Battalion Ceremonial Parade. Education classes held	

	Officers	Other Ranks
STRENGTH January 1st 1919	43	679
Increase during January	–	23
Decrease "	13	278
STRENGTH February 1st 1919	30	424

Ration Strength: February 1st 1919: 25 officers 294 other ranks.

11th Service Battalion ... 1/2/19

[illegible] Carlisle
Lieut-Col, R.E.
Cmdg 11th Durham L.I. (P.)

(A9175) Wt W2358/P360 600,000 12/17 D. D. & L. Sch. 52a. Forms/C2118/15

H.Q. 20th Division

Herewith original copy of War Diary for month of February 1919

[signature]
Captain,
A/O.C. 11th Durham L.I.

Instructions regarding War Diaries and Intelligence Summaries are contained in F. S. Regs., Part II. and the Staff Manual respectively. Title pages will be prepared in manuscript.

WAR DIARY of 11th (S) Bn DURHAM L.I.
or
~~INTELLIGENCE SUMMARY~~
(Erase heading not required.)
for FEBRUARY 1919

Army Form C. 2118.

P/2080W

43

Place	Date	Hour	Summary of Events and Information	Remarks and references to Appendices
	February			
GRENAS	1st		Inspection by C.O. and Ceremonial Parade. 15 other ranks to Demobilisation Centre	
—"—	2nd		Ceremonial Parade	
—"—	3rd		Presentation of the King's Colours to the Battalion by Maj-Gen Douglas Smith, C.B.	
—"—	4th		Company Training. Lecture by Major H.C. Boxer.	
—"—	5th		Company Training. Education Classes held.	
—"—	6th		Lecture by Major H.C. Boxer. Education Classes held. Lieut. C.C. Page and 19 other ranks to Demob. Centre.	
—"—	7th		Company Training and Kit Inspections.	
—"—	8th		Company Training. Education Classes held. Capt R. Jee and Lieut D.J. Rees to England	
—"—	9th		Voluntary Church Service.	
—"—	10th		Filling trenches at Mondicourt. 6 other ranks attested for Regular Army.	
—"—	11th		——"—— Major H.C. Boxer to England.	
—"—	12th		——"——	
—"—	13th		Work as for 12th. Lieut A.H. Lewis and 5 other ranks to Demobilisation Centre	
—"—	14th		Clearing up dis-used camps at Mondicourt. Lieut M. Cooper to England	
—"—	15th		40 other ranks erecting huts at Mondicourt; remainder filling trenches.	

-2-

Instructions regarding War Diaries and Intelligence Summaries are contained in F. S. Regs., Part II. and the Staff Manual respectively. Title pages will be prepared in manuscript.

Army Form C. 2118.

WAR DIARY of 11th (S) Bn DURHAM L.I. (Prs)
or
~~INTELLIGENCE SUMMARY~~. for FEBRUARY 1919

(Erase heading not required.)

Place	Date	Hour	Summary of Events and Information	Remarks and references to Appendices
GRENAS	February 16th		Church Parades	
— " —	17th		40 men erecting huts; remainder of battalion at drill.	
— " —	18th		2 companies working at Mondicourt; 1 company on salvage.	
— " —	19th		Work as for 18th 2 other ranks attested for Regular Army	
— " —	20th		3 companies working on salvage.	
— " —	21st		Work continued as for 20th 10 other ranks to Demobilisation Centre.	
— " —	22nd		2 companies at drill; 1 company on salvage work.	
— " —	23rd		Church Parades.	
— " —	24th		Working parties at Mondicourt; one company on salvage.	
— " —	25th		As for 24th	
— " —	26th		Kit inspections and selection of men for transfer.	
— " —	27th		Lieut E. Fleming, 2nd Lieuts O. G. Day, W.H. Charnley, F.E. Upton, E.R. Harbron, B.C. Barrans, J.H. Dodds, M.M. Harrington, R.E. Forster, M.A. Latham and 163 other ranks proceed to join 20th Battn D.L.I. in Army of Occupation.	
— " —	28th		31 other ranks proceed to Demob. Centre	

Instructions regarding War Diaries and Intelligence Summaries are contained in F. S. Regs., Part II, and the Staff Manual respectively. Title pages will be prepared in manuscript.

Army Form C. 2118.

WAR DIARY of 11th (S.) Bn Durham L.I. (Pns) ~~or INTELLIGENCE SUMMARY.~~ for FEBRUARY 1919

(Erase heading not required.)

Place	Date	Hour	Summary of Events and Information			Remarks and references to Appendices
GRENAS				Officers	Other Ranks	
			STRENGTH February 1st 1919	30	424	
			Increase during February	–	9	
			Decrease " "	15	231	
			STRENGTH March 1st 1919	15	202	
			Ration Strength : March 1st 1919	8 officers	127 other ranks	

11th SERVICE BATTALION No. ... Date 2/3/19 DURHAM L.I. (PIONEERS)

[signature] Captain,
a/O.C. 11th Durham L.I. (Pns)

(A9175) Wt. W2358/P360 600,000 12/17 D. D. & L. Sch. 52a. Forms/C2118/15.

Instructions regarding War Diaries and Intelligence Summaries are contained in F. S. Regs., Part II. and the Staff Manual respectively. Title pages will be prepared in manuscript.

Army Form C. 2118.

WAR DIARY of 11th DURHAM L. I. (Prs) ~~or INTELLIGENCE SUMMARY~~ for MARCH 1919

(Erase heading not required.)

B/2530W

VVl 44

Place	Date	Hour	Summary of Events and Information	Remarks and references to Appendices
	MARCH			
GRENAS	1		Adjusting billets and storing Government furniture	
—"—	2		Voluntary Church Services	
—"—	3		Checking Equipment	
—"—	4		C.O.'s Inspection	
—"—	5		Inspections and checking equipment.	
—"—	6		Inspections and fatigue duty.	
—"—	7		Fatigue duty. 9 other ranks to Demob. Centre	
—"—	8		Inspection of equipment	
—"—	9		Church Service	
—"—	10		Repairing Huts	
—"—	11		Inspection of billets and equipment	
—"—	12		Salvage duty	
—"—	13		Salvage duty	
—"—	14		12 other ranks proceed to Demob. Centre	
—"—	15		Salvage duty	
—"—	16		Church Service	

D. D. & L., London, E.C. (A7683) Wt W829/M1672 350,000 4/17 Sch 52a Forms/C/2118/14

Instructions regarding War Diaries and Intelligence Summaries are contained in F. S. Regs., Part II. and the Staff Manual respectively. Title pages will be prepared in manuscript.

WAR DIARY of 11th (S) Bn Durham L. I. (Ps)

~~INTELLIGENCE SUMMARY.~~

(Erase heading not required.) for MARCH 1919

Army Form C. 2118.

Place	Date	Hour	Summary of Events and Information	Remarks and references to Appendices
	March			
GRENAS	17		Inspections	
—"—	18		Salvage duty	
—"—	19		Inspections	
—"—	20		Moving into hutments	
—"—	21		Kit inspections	
—"—	22		Repairs and improvements to huts	
—"—	23		Church service	
—"—	24		Salvage duty	
—"—	25		Filling in trenches at Grenas	
—"—	26		Clearing up ground in vicinity of hutments	
—"—	27		Repairs to huts and packing wagons	
—"—	28		Inspections 6 other ranks to Demob Centre	
—"—	29		Fatigue duty and cleaning wagons	
—"—	30		1 man attested for Regular Army	
—"—	31		Working on wagons in wagon park	

D. D. & L., London, E.C. (A7883) Wt W8c9/M1672 750,000 4/17 Sch 52a Forms/C/2118/14

Instructions regarding War Diaries and Intelligence Summaries are contained in F. S. Regs., Part II, and the Staff Manual respectively. Title pages will be prepared in manuscript.

WAR DIARY of 11th Durham L. I. (Pio) or ~~INTELLIGENCE SUMMARY.~~ for MARCH 1919

(*Erase heading not required.*)

Army Form C. 2118.

Place	Date	Hour	Summary of Events and Information			Remarks and references to Appendices
GRENAS				Officers	Other Ranks	
			STRENGTH March 1st 1919	15	202	
			Increase during March	–	2	
			Decrease " "	2	76	
			STRENGTH April 1st 1919	13	128	
			Ration Strength : April 1st 1919	7 officers	84 other ranks	

11th SERVICE BATTALION No. Date 1·4·19 DURHAM L. I. (PION.)

J. W. [illegible]
Lieut-Col. R.E.
Cmdg 11th Durham L. I. (P)

D. D. & L., London, E.C. (A7883) Wt. W809/M1672 350,000 4/17 Sch. 52a Forms/C/2118/14

Instructions regarding War Diaries and Intelligence Summaries are contained in F. S. Regs., Part II. and the Staff Manual respectively. Title pages will be prepared in manuscript.

WAR DIARY of 11th DURHAM L.I. (Prs) ~~or INTELLIGENCE SUMMARY.~~ for APRIL 1919

(Erase heading not required.)

Army Form C. 2118.

8/20 [illegible]

WO 95/...45

Place	Date	Hour	Summary of Events and Information	Remarks and references to Appendices
	APRIL			
GRENAS	1		Inspection of arms and equipment.	
—"—	2		Rifle Exercises. Billets inspected.	
—"—	3		Salvage Duty.	
—"—	4		Work as on 3rd inst. Capt J. Liddell, Lieuts F.G. Andrew and A.C. Lynch, 2nd Lieuts C.H. Bonson and R.B. Masham and 1 O.R. proceed to Demob. Centre.	
—"—	5		Inspection of hutments. Camp clearing.	
—"—	6		Voluntary Church Services.	
—"—	7		Rifle exercises and physical drill.	
—"—	8		Taking up Light Railway track.	
—"—	9		As for 8th inst.	
—"—	10		Salving Light Railway material.	
—"—	11		Salvage Work on tramway area.	
—"—	12		Work programme cancelled owing to bad weather.	
—"—	13		Voluntary Church Service. Battalion Sports Meeting in fine weather.	
—"—	14		Salvage of Light Railway material.	
—"—	15		Battalion Cadre defeat 11th K.R.R. (59th Inf. Bde) in 1st round Division Tournament.	

D. D. & L., London, E.C.
(A7883) Wt W809/M1672 350,000 4/17 Sch. 52a Forms/C/2118/14

Army Form C. 2118.

Instructions regarding War Diaries and Intelligence Summaries are contained in F. S. Regs., Part II. and the Staff Manual respectively. Title pages will be prepared in manuscript.

WAR DIARY of 11th Durham L.I. (Ps)
~~INTELLIGENCE SUMMARY.~~
(Erase heading not required.) for APRIL 1919

Place	Date	Hour	Summary of Events and Information	Remarks and references to Appendices
	APRIL			
GRENAS	16		Morning salvage work. 2nd round Cadre Championship held — keen display results in victory for battalion (versus 6th K.S.L.I., 60th Inf. Bde)	
—"—	17		Salvage work and physical exercise.	
—"—	18		As for 17th. 3 other ranks leave for Candas Demob. Centre.	
—"—	19		Lieut J.H. Anderson and 41 O.R's proceed to No 63 P. of War Coy (Rouen). 9 men proceed to Ordnance Depot Calais for temporary transfer to R.A.O.C.	
—"—	20		Voluntary morning service for C. of E. Battalion wins contest against 12th King's.	
—"—	21		Rifle inspection. Clearing camp locality and boarding up vacant huts.	
—"—	22		Salvage Work.	
—"—	23		Final of Cadre Tournament and Divisional Sports held at PAS. Championship won by batt.	
—"—	24		Cleaning wagons.	
—"—	25 & 26		Inspection of billets. Rifle exercises.	
—"—	27		2 O.R's proceed to U.K. on re-engagement leave.	
—"—	28		Cleaning equipment.	
—"—	29		Clothing and Footwear inspection.	
—"—	30		Transport wagons overhauled.	

D. D. & L., London, E.C. (A7883) Wt W8:9/M1672 50,000 4/17 Sch 52a Forms/C/2118/14

Army Form C. 2118.

Instructions regarding War Diaries and Intelligence Summaries are contained in F. S. Regs., Part II. and the Staff Manual respectively. Title pages will be prepared in manuscript.

WAR DIARY of 11th DURHAM L.I. (Pes)
~~or INTELLIGENCE SUMMARY.~~
(Erase heading not required.)
for APRIL 1919

Place	Date	Hour	Summary of Events and Information	Remarks and references to Appendices
GRENAS			Officers — Other Ranks	
			STRENGTH APRIL 1st 1919 — 13 — 128	
			Increase during APRIL — - — 4	
			Decrease " " — 5 — 75	
			STRENGTH MAY 1st 1919 — 8 — 57	
			RATION STRENGTH ~~[illegible]~~ MAY 1st 1919 — 4 officers " 33 other ranks	

[illegible] Carlisle.
Lieut-Col., R.E.,
Cmdg 11th Durham L.I.

D. D. & L., London, E.C.
(A7883) Wt W809/M1672 150,000 4/17 Sch 52a Forms/C/2118/14

Instructions regarding War Diaries and Intelligence Summaries are contained in F. S. Regs., Part II. and the Staff Manual respectively. Title pages will be prepared in manuscript.

Army Form C. 2118.

WAR DIARY ~~INTELLIGENCE SUMMARY~~ of 11th DURHAM L.I. (Pns) for MAY 1919.

(Erase heading not required.)

P/20 Bn

WO 46

Place	Date	Hour	Summary of Events and Information	Remarks and references to Appendices
	MAY			
GRENAS	1		Checking of Unit Equipment.	
—"—	2		"Marching Order" inspection.	
—"—	3		Cleaning wagons.	
—"—	4		Sunday — nothing to report.	
—"—	5		5 "retainables" transferred to No 63 Prisoners of War Company.	
—"—	6		Rifle exercises preceded by inspection of arms.	
—"—	7		Cadre kit inspection	
—"—	8		Cleaning of personal equipment	
—"—	9		Capt G.P. Baines and 5 men left for Demob. Centre Candas. Cadre moved to PAS	
PAS EN ARTOIS	10		Improvement of billets — camp re-organisation.	
—"—	11		Sunday holiday.	
—"—	12		Filling in latrines at Grenas.	
—"—	13		Clearing up Grenas encampment — storing of R.E. material.	
—"—	14		Improving billets.	
—"—	15		Inspections.	
—"—	16		1 officer and 20 men proceeded to AMIENS for day's outing.	

D. D. & L., London, E.C. (A7883) Wt. W809/M1672 350,000 4/17 Sch. 52a Forms/C/2118/14

2

Army Form C. 2118.

Instructions regarding War Diaries and Intelligence Summaries are contained in F. S. Regs., Part II. and the Staff Manual respectively. Title pages will be prepared in manuscript.

WAR DIARY of 11th DURHAM L.I. (PRS)

~~INTELLIGENCE SUMMARY.~~

(Erase heading not required.)

MAY 1919

Place	Date	Hour	Summary of Events and Information	Remarks and references to Appendices
	MAY			
PAS EN ARTOIS	17		7 men sent to MONDICOURT for duty at 20th Divisional Wagon Park	
—"—	18		Sunday: Voluntary Church service for Divisional troops in Chateau grounds	
—"—	19		Unit equipment Overhauled	
—"—	20		As for 20th	
—"—	21		Completion of equipment clean-up.	
—"—	22		Nothing to report.	
—"—	23		Motor-lorry tour.	
—"—	24		Inspection of Cadre personnel.	
—"—	25		Physical & Recreational training.	
—"—	26		1 man proceeded to Rouen for duty with No 63 P.O.W. Coy.	
—"—	27		Nothing to report. Sunday rest.	
—"—	28		Overhauling of unit wagons in Mondicourt Wagon Park	
—"—	29		As for 28th	
—"—	30th		Organised games.	
—"—	31		Cleaning of personal equipment.	

D. D. & L., London, E.C.
(A7883) Wt. W809/M1672 350,000 4/17 Sch. 52a Forms/C/2118/14

Instructions regarding War Diaries and Intelligence Summaries are contained in F. S. Regs., Part II. and the Staff Manual respectively. Title pages will be prepared in manuscript.

WAR DIARY of 11th Durham L. I. (Prs)

~~INTELLIGENCE SUMMARY~~.

(*Erase heading not required.*)

Army Form C. 2118.

MAY 1919.

Place	Date	Hour	Summary of Events and Information	Remarks and references to Appendices
PAS EN ARTOIS			Officers — Other Ranks	
			STRENGTH ~~APRIL~~ MAY 1st 1919 — 8 — 57	
			Increase during month — – — 2	
			Decrease " " — 3 — 21	
			STRENGTH JUNE 1st 1919 — 5 — 38	
			RATION STRENGTH JUNE 1st 1919 = 2 officers and 20 other ranks	

11th SERVICE BATTALION No. Date 1.6.19 DURHAM L. I. (PIONEERS)

J. W. Carlisle.
Lieut-Col, R.E.,
Cmdg 11th Durham L.I. (Prs)

D. D. & L., London, E.C. (A7883) Wt W809/M1672 750,000 4/17 Sch 52a Forms/C/2118/14

D 457/[illegible]

HQ. 20th Division

Strength War Diary
for month of June 1918

30/6/18 R E Boulton Lieut Col
Comdg 11th Durham L I

Instructions regarding War Diaries and Intelligence Summaries are contained in F. S. Regs., Part II. and the Staff Manual respectively. Title pages will be prepared in manuscript.

20

Army Form C. 2118.

WAR DIARY
or
~~INTELLIGENCE SUMMARY.~~
(Erase heading not required.)

of 11th Durham L.I. (Pnrs)

JUNE 1919

Vol. 47

Ceased

Place	Date	Hour	Summary of Events and Information	Remarks and references to Appendices
	JUNE			
PAS EN ARTOIS	1		Sunday.	
—"—	2		Cleaning Mobilization Stores.	
—"—	3		Birthday of H.M. King George V : observed as a holiday	
—"—	4		Cleaning Mobilization Stores.	
—"—	5		As for 4th inst.	
—"—	6		Cleaning Wagons	
—"—	7		—ditto—	
—"—	8		Sunday	
—"—	9		Whit-Monday holiday. 2nd Lieut G. Phillips and "75% Cadre" with Battalion Colours proceed to Candas en route for U.K. (1 officer 25 other ranks)	
—"—	10		Remainder i.e. Unit Equipment Guard, remove to hutments at Mondicourt	
—"—	11		Repacking equipment in accordance with new regulations	
—"—	12		Work continued, as for 11th	
—"—	13		Complete repacking and checking of equipment.	
—"—	14		Wagons marked "AINTREE N.C.", "11th D.L.I." and numbered.	
—"—	15		Sunday	

D. D. & L., London, E.C. (A7853) Wt. W8o9/M1672 750,000 4/17 Sch 52a Forms/C/2118/14

Instructions regarding War Diaries and Intelligence Summaries are contained in F. S. Regs., Part II. and the Staff Manual respectively. Title pages will be prepared in manuscript.

~~WAR DIARY~~ of 11th Durham L.I. (Pio)

~~INTELLIGENCE SUMMARY.~~

(Erase heading not required.)

Army Form C. 2118.

JUNE 1919

No 2.

Place	Date	Hour	Summary of Events and Information	Remarks and references to Appendices
	~~April~~			
MONDICOURT	16		Preparing for entrainment on 17th	
—"—	17		Entrainment delayed by derailment at MONDICOURT Station of engine.	
—"—	18		Equipment Guard and Equipment entrained: strength 2 officers; 10 other ranks;	
			10 G.S. Wagons; 7 G.S. Limbers; 3 Cookers; 2 Water Carts; 1 Mess Cart	
			and 1 Maltese Cart	
HAVRE	19		Detrained Havre; equipment on wagons to embarking wharves and a guard;	
			remainder of Equipment at Harfleur	
HARFLEUR	20–22		Awaiting embarkation orders.	
HAVRE	23		Embarked for England (at HAVRE)	
SOUTHAMPTON	24		Disembarked Southampton 24.6.19 — Battalion Equipment handed over to Railway Carriers.	

J.R. Carlisle

Lieut-Col. R.E.

Cmdg 11th Durham L.I. (Pio)

www.ingramcontent.com/pod-product-compliance
Lightning Source LLC
Chambersburg PA
CBHW080853010526
44117CB00014B/2243